HEALTH AND WELLNESS
IN COLONIAL AMERICA

HEALTH AND WELLNESS
IN COLONIAL AMERICA

REBECCA TANNENBAUM

Health and Wellness in Daily Life
Joseph P. Byrne, Series Editor

 GREENWOOD

AN IMPRINT OF ABC-CLIO, LLC
Santa Barbara, California • Denver, Colorado • Oxford, England

Copyright 2012 by ABC-CLIO, LLC

Library of Congress Cataloging-in-Publication Data

Tannenbaum, Rebecca J. (Rebecca Jo)
   Health and wellness in colonial America / Rebecca Tannenbaum.
      p. cm. — (Health and wellness in daily life)
   Includes bibliographical references and index.
   ISBN 978–0–313–38490–5 (cloth : alk. paper) — ISBN 978–0–313–38491–2 (ebook) 1. Diseases and history—United States. 2. Public health—United States—History. 3. Medicine—United States–History. 4. Indians of North America—History. 5. Indians of North America—Health and hygiene.
I. Title.
R702.T36   2012
362.10973—dc23   2012022212

ISBN: 978–0–313–38490–5
EISBN: 978–0–313–38491–2

16 15 14 13 12   1 2 3 4 5

This book is also available on the World Wide Web as an eBook.
Visit www.abc-clio.com for details.

Greenwood
An Imprint of ABC-CLIO, LLC

ABC-CLIO, LLC
130 Cremona Drive, P.O. Box 1911
Santa Barbara, California 93116-1911

This book is printed on acid-free paper ∞

Manufactured in the United States of America

For my students,
Past, present, and future

Contents

Series Foreword

Communities have few concerns that are as fundamental as the health of their members. America's current concern for societal provision of health care is as much as political, ethical, economic, and social matter as it is a technical or "medical" one. Reflection on the history of health and medicine may help us to place our contemporary concerns in context, but it also shows how far humanity has come in being able and willing to provide for the highest levels of health and health care possible. It is a reminder, too, of the possibilities the future presents. Our culture believes in progress, but it is also aware that unforeseen challenges will continue to appear. Health and medicine are cultural as well as biological constructs, and we live each day with the constraints and opportunities that follow.

This series of seven monographs explores the courses that human health and medicine have taken from antiquity to the present day. Though far from being complete in their coverage, these volumes map out continuities and changes over time in a set of health and medical fields. Each author has taken on the same outline in order to allow the student of health, medicine and history to discover conditions, beliefs, practices, and changes within a given period, but also to trace the same concerns across time and place. With this in mind, each volume contains chapters on, for example, healers, children's health and healing, occupational and environmental threats, and epidemic disease. To the extent possible, we authors have attempted to emphasize the ways in which these topics have affected people in their daily lives, rather than viewing them through the lenses of the healers or their profession. Our hope is that these volumes constitute a small and very useful library of the history of health and medicine.

As editor, I have endeavored to bring on board authors who are medical historians as well as fine teachers who have the ability to transmit their knowledge in writing with the same enthusiasm they bring into the classroom. As an author, I am sharing the discoveries, the joys, and not least the challenges and frustrations that all of us encounter in producing this series.

Joseph P. Byrne
Honors Program
Belmont University

CHAPTER 1

Factors in Health and Wellness

Before 1492, North America was biologically isolated from Europe and Africa. Columbus's voyages and the subsequent migration of Europeans and Africans to America changed the health and disease environment of all three continents forever. Indigenous Americans faced diseases they had never experienced before; Europeans encountered new medicinal plants and life in a new environment; and millions of Africans experienced the forced migration of the slave trade and its devastating health consequences. All of these factors combined to create a unique environment for human health and wellness.

A cultural exchange accompanied the biological one. Each people had their own concepts of the body, disease, and healing, some of which they shared with each other to create a new, synthesized medical culture. Europeans sought out Native American medicines to export to their home countries; Native Americans hoped the newcomers had brought new cures along with their new diseases; and Africans strove to preserve their own traditions in the new world they inhabited.

Post-Columbian America also developed its own diet, sanitary issues, and living conditions. Each ethnic group saw variations in life expectancy and health according to where they lived, what they ate, and the kind of work they did. What follows outlines both the physical and cultural factors that shaped health and wellness in colonial America.

THE DISEASE ENVIRONMENT

Before contact with Europeans and Africans, the indigenous peoples of North America lived in an isolated disease environment. This is not to say that their world was free from disease. Archeological evidence demonstrates that illness and injury were part of life on the North American continent since human beings first lived there. Pre-Columbian peoples suffered from intestinal parasites, lung infections, malnutrition, infections of the bone, and possibly chicken pox and other herpes infections. In addition, snakebites, broken bones, wounds acquired in warfare, and other injuries could lead to debility and death.[1] However, the epidemics of plague, smallpox, and other diseases that devastated Europe and Asia had never reached the Americas. While estimates vary considerably, and are the subject of controversy, somewhere between 3 and 10 million people lived north of Mexico in 1492, with 700,000 of those living on the eastern seaboard.[2]

Another factor shaping the disease environment in North America was the lack of animal species that can serve as reservoirs for human disease. The black rat, which carried plague-infested fleas from Asia to Europe, did not exist on the continent. Nor had Native Americans domesticated livestock such as cattle and pigs, both of which can harbor germs that also affect human beings.[3]

The arrival of European settlers changed this environment profoundly. The most immediate change was the introduction of Old World disease germs to North America. Almost every account of European encounters with Indigenous Americans describes the ravages of epidemic disease. Writers as far apart geographically and culturally as the Spanish chronicler Bartolome de las Casas to William Bradford of Plymouth Plantation wrote of the devastating effects of disease.[4] In some cases, European explorers had brought the diseases with them before settlers arrived, devastating the locals and giving some later colonists the impression of an "empty" continent. When the English settlers arrived in Massachusetts in 1620, the area had already been ravaged by an epidemic in 1616, brought by English fishermen who had stopped to resupply on the coast. Wampanoag villages stood empty and abandoned. One writer noted that even five years later, "the bones and skulls upon the ... places of their habitations made ... a spectacle."[5]

When an entire population is vulnerable to a disease, it creates a social environment that exacerbates the biological effects of the pathogen. If every one of every age group falls ill at once, there is no one to nurse the sick. A person might survive a serious illness with adequate fluids, warmth, shelter, and other support, but if no one is available to provide these things, the victim is more likely to succumb. Furthermore, if everyone is ill, no one is available to tend crops, repair houses, or perform other crucial functions. The weakened survivors suffer from malnutrition and exposure, making them more vulnerable to the next epidemic. Finally, as more newcomers arrived, so did more germs. The successive waves of epidemics meant that there was little time for a population to recover before the next epidemic struck. More epidemics meant more social disruption; more social disruption created conditions in which epidemics spread more easily and were more deadly. Colonization created a new, catastrophic disease environment. By some estimates, 95 percent of the Native American population died by the end of the seventeenth century.[6]

While the biggest impact of this new environment was on the Native American population, European colonists and enslaved Africans did not entirely escape its effects. In the early seventeenth century, for instance, the English had established a colony in Virginia but "the rich lands of the tidewater were empty not simply for lack of immigrants but because the men who did come to settle on them died so fast." Virginia was a "death trap" for English immigrants.[7] Almost every settler who arrived in Virginia became ill. Colonists called this period of almost inevitable illness "seasoning," an experience that applied equally to English and African newcomers. While some survived their seasoning, many did not. It is not entirely clear what the diseases that killed the settlers were. It is likely, however, that some were especially deadly to newcomers in the same way that measles and influenza were especially deadly to Native Americans. One strong possibility is that new immigrants developed malaria, a disease brought to America from Europe and Africa.

Cultures of Health, Disease, and Healing

How the cultures of Colonial America dealt with the new diseases they encountered was shaped by many factors. One of these factors was the ways in which peoples of the time thought about their bodies, disease, and healing. In all three cultures—Native American, European, and African—these ideas were very different from the way we think about the human body today.

Premodern cultures shared some things in common. All three peoples who met in the American colonies believed that the body lived in balance with its environment. Weather, food, and emotions could all have an effect on a person's health. All three also believed that the functioning of the body was not a purely physical phenomenon. Spiritual elements had an important role in shaping health and disease. Finally, all three peoples used herbal medicines for cures and were eager to find new medicinal plants. While each culture manifested these traits in different ways, each recognized enough commonalities with the others to exchange medical knowledge.

Native Americans conceived of the body as naturally healthy but vulnerable to physical, spiritual, and magical forces. A healthy person lived in harmony with his or her community, physical surroundings, and supernatural beings. Disharmony could create disease in many ways. Offending a neighbor could bring on a direct magical attack or offend a spirit. Carelessness in the physical world created circumstances in which a person could be injured. An offended supernatural being could cause illness as punishment. Finally, among some peoples, especially the Iroquoian tribes, frustrated dreams or longings could cause disease. In this case, disease is the result of a lack of inner harmony.[8]

In all cases, the balance of health and disease rested on a network of relationships. For most Native American peoples, the natural world was imbued with spiritual power, and spirits and deities could have physical manifestations. Animals, plants, and the earth itself had agency and volition, and could be offended by bad behavior. It was crucial for human beings to have peaceful relationships with all. Just as human societies were made up of reciprocal relationships, so was the human relationship with the natural world. Health was a manifestation of maintaining the proper reciprocity with all one's surroundings.[9]

Disease resulted when any one of these relationships was disturbed. Many tribes shared a belief that the spirits of hunted animals or gathered plants must be appeased by performing prayers or songs, or by making an offering. If these rituals were ignored or neglected, the spirit would take revenge. Killing an animal unnecessarily or wasting its meat could bring similar results. Even inanimate things such as fire or water could cause disease if treated disrespectfully. For instance, among the tribes of southeastern North America, spitting or urinating into a fire would offend the spirit of the fire and bring misfortune. Every part of nature—plants, animals, fire, and water—that sustained human life could also take human life if treated badly.[10]

Human relationships were similar. Most indigenous societies emphasized the well-being of the whole rather than the individual. Being too greedy or ambitious could upset the balance of a family, tribe, or village and have serious consequences in both the physical and spiritual worlds. Disturbed human relationships could cause disease directly or indirectly. In the most extreme cases, an offended sorcerer could be to blame. Epidemics and mysterious, incurable diseases were most likely to be blamed on evil magic. In cases of individual illness, a sorcerer might send a snake, worm, or other small animal to invade the victim's body.[11]

Finally, each individual had to maintain a personal spiritual balance. An unfulfilled desire or ignoring an omen seen in a dream could cause illness. Dreams had special significance. Among the Iroquoian peoples, shamans specialized in interpreting dreams. Imagery in dreams could represent important spiritual or physical needs, or messages from deities and spirits. Ignoring the messages imparted by dreams was dangerous. Other peoples, such as the Huron, believed that the soul left the body during sleep and sometimes failed to return on waking. In other cases, the soul could actually be stolen by malevolent spirits or human sorcerers. "Soul loss" was fatal unless a shaman could summon the wandering soul back to its home.[12]

Indigenous American healing practices or "medicine" were only one part of a complex of spiritual beliefs. There was "medicine" to cure illness, but there was also "medicine" to ensure success in hunting. Unlike European cultures, most indigenous peoples did not distinguish between medical practice, religious ritual, and magic. Herbs, music, and ritual were involved in all three.[13]

The exact practices of the healer varied among indigenous peoples, but general principles were similar. The healer would address the spirits in some way by singing, shaking rattles, or playing drums. Some cultures "bathed" the patient in smoke from burning bundles of herbs such as sage, cedar, or tobacco. The healer would ask the spirits for guidance in diagnosing the patient and finding the correct remedy, which could be an herbal medicine, a special bath, or a particular ritual. The healer then followed the spirits' recommendations. The process sometimes required several visits.[14]

Healers came to their role in a variety of ways. Again, the general pattern was that a person had to be "called" to be a healer by a spirit or spirits. Some cultures initiated healers into secret societies or priesthoods whose rituals were known only to members. Healing shamans often carried bundles of herbs and other objects through which they channeled their power. These medicine bundles were unique to each individual. Some, but not all, healers were also herbalists, with extensive knowledge of medicinal plants and the proper rituals observed in gathering and preparing them.[15]

There were some exceptions to the rule that healing and religious ritual went hand in hand. While the healers in some cultures were members of elite medicine societies or priesthoods, this was not always the case. One scholar has noted that New England peoples did not follow this tradition.[16] Some kinds of practitioners, such as midwives, did not employ elaborate ritual in their practices. Similarly, there were ailments that did not require spiritual intervention, such as wounds or broken bones.[17]

Europeans shared the Native American idea of health as balance, but for them the balance was more internal than external. They believed that the body was made up of four humors: blood, phlegm, black bile, and yellow bile. In an ideal human being, each of these humors was in exact balance with the others. In most people, one or another of the humors predominated, which gave rise to temperamental differences. In fact, some of the words we still use to describe personality or mood have their origins in humoral medicine. For instance, the word "melancholy" comes from the Latin phrase for "black bile," a surplus of which was thought to make a person sad and out of sorts.[18]

This concept of health and disease had its origins in ancient Greece and Rome, and it dominated medieval and early modern medicine. The four humors were first described by the ancient Greek physician Hippocrates; the Roman physician Galen elaborated on and developed the concept. Humors were classified by degrees of "heat" and "moisture," which should also balance each other. In turn, each humor was associated with one of the four elements that made up the universe: fire, water, air, and earth. Each person's dominant humor stemmed from a variety of factors. Men were "hotter" than women; older people were "colder "and "dryer" than those who were younger. A person's living conditions, diet, and daily work also affected humoral balance. A healthy person was one who lived in an equilibrium unique to each individual.[19]

This paradigm of health and disease was tremendously resistant to change. While the seventeenth century saw the beginnings of the scientific revolution in Europe, many of the discoveries had little effect on day-to-day medical practice until the late eighteenth century. For lay people, the concept of the humors lingered even longer. The idea of balancing the body and purging excessive or putrid bodily fluids remained an important part of folk practice long after professionals abandoned the theory. During the Colonial period of American history, this medieval way of thinking about the body was shared by elite physicians, folk practitioners, and ordinary patients alike.

If health under the Galenic paradigm was a matter of equilibrium, disease was a matter of disequilibrium. When the balance of humors tipped too far, illness resulted. Medical practitioners looked for signs that a disease was "hot" or "cold," "wet" or "dry" to determine which humor was in excess and which was lacking. Most fevers, logically enough, were "hot" diseases; we still call an upper respiratory infection a "cold." This method of diagnosis suggested the proper counterbalancing treatment.[20]

Many things could upset a person's humoral balance. Being exposed to cold, wet weather could cause the body's humors to become too cold and wet. Eating too much of a spicy, "hot" food could cause excessive heat and dryness. An emotional upset could create melancholy both figuratively and literally. Factors such as diet and weather affected individuals, but there was room in the humoral paradigm for theories of contagious disease and epidemics as well. "Miasmas," or foul air, could cause many persons to fall ill at once. In fact the word for the disease we call malaria comes from the Italian for "bad air." Similarly, contact with a sick person could cause corruption of a healthy person's humors.[21]

While the theory of the humors provided a physical concept of health and disease, Euro-Americans also believed in spiritual and religious causes of illness. Like Native Americans, the European settlers believed that sickness could be a punishment for violating religious law. The strength of this belief varied by region. The pious Calvinists of early New England were especially likely to interpret illness as a message from God. The famous Massachusetts minister Cotton Mather wrote that those who suffered from toothache should remember that human-kind's original sin had been committed with the teeth, when Eve and Adam bit into the forbidden fruit. He suggested to those whose teeth were hurting that they "Think; The Teeth, wherein I suffer so much Torture; How much have I Sinned with them! ... I have Employ'd my teeth in Eating Irregularly, Inordinately; and Without a due Regard unto the Service and Glory of God ... "[22] While ministers like Mather are extreme examples, prayer and other religious ritual was a healing practice that Catholics, Anglicans, Baptists, and other Christian denominations practiced from New France to Mexico.

Europeans also shared a belief in witchcraft and sorcery with Native Americans. A witch or sorcerer could strike for no reason other than pure malevolence, but attack was more likely if the victim had offended or angered the witch. Among their many powers, witches could cause disease in animals or human beings. They were most likely to attack the weakest members of a family at their most vulnerable moments. Infants, children, and women in childbirth were the likeliest victims.[23]

Illness caused by God's hand or the spite of an offended witch required a different response from one that had a natural cause. Physicians and other practitioners assumed that most disease was natural, but if it failed to respond to treatment, they had to look to other causes. Repentance and prayer were the answer to an illness caused by sin; identifying and arresting the witch usually rendered her spells ineffective.

Unlike Native Americans and Africans, Europeans saw illness as primarily physical rather than spiritual. Healers—be they midwives, physicians, or more informal practitioners—looked first to the body as the cause of disease. The first matter of business was to examine bodily fluids for evidence of the humor that had poisoned the body. Healers looked at blood, urine, and even vomit to make their diagnosis. Once the offending humor had been identified, the practitioner determined a course of treatment.[24]

These treatments were aimed at restoring the body's natural balance. In most cases, the proper course of action was to purge the body of excessive humors. Taking blood from a vein, purging bile with powerful laxatives or emetics, and drawing fluid from the skin with blistering chemicals were all common treatments. One thing all early Euro-American medicines had in common was that they did not make the patient feel better immediately—indeed, most seemed sure to make the sick person even more wretched. However, patients looked for these unpleasant effects, believing that they were the mark of an effective drug. One of the most complimentary things a person could say about a prescription was that it was "a powerful purge, both upward and downward."[25]

Enslaved Africans in America brought their own beliefs about health and disease from their native countries. While it is sometimes hard to find records of African ideas about healing and disease, some indigenous African practices survived long enough to be recorded. Most of the sources we have on African American concepts of health and disease come from nineteenth-century records, but scholars have traced some similarities to West African practices. We can infer that these indigenous African practices were more common in the Colonial era.

African American beliefs about health and disease bore a strong resemblance to those of Native Americans. Both cultures saw a strong connection between spirituality, proper social behavior, and physical health. Supernatural forces were seen as an important cause of disease. In both cultures, healers were likely to have a religious role as well as a medical one.

The spiritual forces that affected human health had a dual nature. The same spirit could cause disease or cure it. While a spirit might act on its own, it could be harnessed by a human being and sent out to do work of helping or harming. Thus, an individual's health might not be entirely under his or her control. If an enemy sent a harming spirit, a person would fall ill. However, African cultures shared with Native Americans a belief that violating social mores or spiritual taboos could make one more vulnerable to spiritual attack. If one dishonored the family, for instance, ancestral spirits might take revenge by causing illness.[26]

Staying healthy was a matter of remaining "ritually pure" and in balance with the "cosmic equilibrium imposed by the spirit realm."[27] More specifically, "health" meant maintaining one's proper place in a network of relationships that included living people, such as one's family and the elders of one's community, one's own dead ancestors, and the spirit world. One historian has called this concept a "relational vision of health."[28] The health of individuals was closely tied to a healthy community, and vice versa.[29]

The idea of health as part of complex relationships did not mean that Africans lived in perfect harmony either in Africa or in American slave communities. African American healers acknowledged that human relationships were fraught with conflict, and that each individual had to manage that conflict in order to remain healthy. Disease resulted when the conflict got out of hand, and part of a healer's job was to restore the sick person to his or her proper place in the community.[30]

Like Native American healers, African practitioners were called by the spirits to their vocation. Their patients respected their special powers, in part because the power to heal could also be used to do harm. Healers were thus objects of both admiration and fear in their communities. Healers determined a diagnosis by communicating with the spirit world, and they prescribed remedies accordingly. A patient might be given an herbal medicine to take in conjunction with making offerings to a particular god, goddess, or spirit.[31]

However, the institution of slavery complicated these visions of health and disease. Slave owners had their own, very different ideas of what made a healthy slave. For these Euro-Americans, a healthy African was "sound." That is, he or she was physically capable of performing work in the tobacco, sugar, or rice fields. For women, soundness extended to reproductive capacity—a "sound" female slave was one who could bear children. Soundness also had a psychological dimension, in that a fully "healthy" slave would be docile and obedient with no desire to run away. All of these different aspects of slave "soundness" ultimately determined a slave's monetary value, either as a laborer or at auction. An unsound slave was one who failed one of these tests. A man with a bad back, a woman who could not conceive, or a slave who ran away were all "diseased" under this definition. In addition, slave owners often imposed their own ideas of healing on their slaves. Slaveholders viewed African medicine as "diabolical" or mere "superstition" and actively suppressed the practice.[32]

This definition of health, disease, and medicine often came into conflict with those of African Americans. One reason we know so little of the healing culture of slaves in the Colonial era is that they often hid their illnesses from whites to avoid European medicine. Similarly, whatever indigenous practices they brought from Africa were also kept secret. In addition, healing shamans had power within their own communities and were often at the center of rebellions, giving slave owners another reason to repress African healing methods and punish healers. Medicine and healing were a source of resistance to slavery and empowerment for the practitioners and as such had to be kept from the slaveholders.[33]

Despite these differences and conflicts, the three cultures were open to some exchange of medical knowledge. This was particularly true for Native Americans and Europeans. European healers sought out Native American herbal knowledge, believing that the cures to American diseases would be found in American plants. In addition, some Europeans disliked the harsh bleeding and purging that characterized Western medicine at the time and sought alternatives. While most Europeans rejected the religious aspects of Native American healing, they were more than willing to try indigenous herbs and surgical techniques.[34]

Under other circumstances, indigenous peoples sought the help of European healers, especially when new epidemic diseases struck. In New France, many Hurons accepted baptism from Jesuit missionaries during a smallpox epidemic, thinking it would reconcile them with the new deity who was causing the disease. Others took a more physical approach. In Massachusetts, the sachem Massasoit readily used medicines sent by the English settlers when he was sick and credited them with the cure.[35]

After some years of this exchange, European and indigenous practices merged into a new, synthesized folk medicine. Traveling "Indian Doctors" remained popular in New England well into the nineteenth century, and a Maine oral tradition has it that one of them saved the life of Hannibal Hamelin, Abraham Lincoln's vice president. Native peoples retained their own traditions but incorporated European drugs and western techniques into them.

LIVING CONDITIONS AND LIFE EXPECTANCIES

Diet, sanitation, and other living conditions formed another part of the health environment of early America. These conditions varied by culture and region, and the general health of various populations varied considerably. Overall, white settlers in New England seem to have been the healthiest, and enslaved people in the south the least healthy. Precontact Native Americans seem to have lived well, but the massive epidemics and their consequences had a long-term impact on well-being.

When Europeans first tried to establish settlements in America, the first few years were often disastrous. Two well-known examples are the English colonies at Plymouth in 1620 and Jamestown in 1607. In both cases, poor preparation combined with the rigors of a seventeenth-century sea voyage and lack of adequate shelter led to high death rates.

At Jamestown, the first arrivals came with the expectation that they could make their fortunes mining gold, as the Spanish had done in their Latin American colonies. What they did not do was plant crops, build sturdy houses, or dig wells. The water supply on the banks of the tidal James River was contaminated with seawater and almost undrinkable. Furthermore, the settlers' privies drained directly into their water supply, making the water full of "slime and filth."[36] Dysentery and other intestinal diseases soon followed. The English had brought little in the way of supplies, thinking they could trade or barter for food with the indigenous peoples. The English began to starve slowly. Starvation induces lethargy, making the inhabitants even less willing to do the work necessary to grow or hunt food. Finally, the makeshift shelters they did build were not enough to withstand the winter. One writer described the Jamestown settlers as "lying on the bare cold ground what weather soever came."[37] After a year, only 38 of the original 108 settlers were left alive.[38]

The first year at Plymouth colony had a similar outcome. The *Mayflower* settlers arrived in Massachusetts at the beginning of winter. They were already weakened by a long voyage and had little time to prepare themselves for the harsh climate of New England. They had only time to build seven houses by the end of December. Many of the *Mayflower*'s passengers and crew remained on board the ship, the best shelter they had available. The supplies they had brought ran short. Weakened by cold and malnutrition, and crowded together in the ship's cabins, the English began to succumb to disease. From December of 1620 to March of 1621, 44 of the original 102 passengers had died, and the ship's crew of 20 or 30 was reduced by half.[39]

However, these pioneer conditions did not last in Virginia or New England. Once Plymouth Colony was established, New England proved itself a relatively healthy environment. There were several factors that made this so. First, the climate and physical environment were healthier. The water supply was cleaner. The cool climate was not conducive to the long mosquito season that made malaria a serious threat in the south.

The second factor was the system of labor. In the south, much of the labor force was legally bound in some way, whether as white indentured servants (contracted to an employer for a term of five to seven years) or enslaved Africans. While indentured servants and slaves did exist in the north, neither made up the majority of working people. There was thus no large bonded population dependent on the whims of masters for food, clothing, and shelter, and they were not forced to work to exhaustion. As a result, life expectancies were long in New England. A man who reached adulthood could expect to live to 70; a woman to 63. While infant and child mortality remained high (about 25 percent), this was no better and no worse than the situation in the home country.[40]

As these facts suggest, English settlers in the Chesapeake and southern colonies of British North America were not as well off. Malaria and other infectious diseases took their toll. Nor can we ignore the living conditions for most white newcomers, who came as servants committed to a five- to seven-year term of unpaid labor. While the large landholders lived on enormous estates, most of the land was given over to tobacco production. Food was a secondary consideration. Landowners tried to maintain their servants with a bare minimum of food and shelter. Servants were housed in barns and tobacco sheds, or slept on the floor or unheated attics of houses. Their rations were made up of cornmeal mush, occasionally supplemented with a little salt pork, which was barely sufficient to maintain manual laborers who might work as long as 16 hours a day in season. In addition, the lack of variety made the workers vulnerable to nutritional deficiency diseases. Many new servants died in the first year of their indenture, and in 1700 the average age at death for Colonial English men in Virginia was 48.[41]

Eventually, of course, the labor system in the Chesapeake and south mutated from one based on temporarily bonded English laborers to permanently enslaved African laborers. For these workers, enslavement was a health catastrophe. The disaster began with the voyage from Africa to the Americas. All seventeenth and eighteenth century sea journeys were hard on the passengers, but conditions of the Middle Passage were worse than most. Slave traders employed doctors to examine slaves prior to embarkation and to select only the strongest and healthiest. Even so, mortality was high. Conservative estimates put the death rate at 50 percent; others calculate that the mortality was as high as 9 out of 10. Slaves were treated like any other cargo, crammed into dark, unsanitary holds where they were shackled hand and foot for the duration of the journey. Fresh water and food were hard to come by, and sanitation was nonexistent. Enslaved Africans died of dysentery, typhoid fever, scurvy, and dehydration, all compounded by despair.[42]

Slaves often became ill when they arrived at their destinations. The mortality rate in the first few months after arrival was almost as high as during the journey itself: 30 to 50 percent. Diseases such as tuberculosis and influenza preyed on their weakened bodies. Psychological distress played its part here as well, as slave owners deliberately denied slaves any remnant of their home cultures, separating slaves who spoke the same language and followed the same customs.[43]

For those who survived, living conditions improved slightly, but health problems remained. As was the case with indentured servants, plantation owners provided the bare minimum of food, shelter, and clothing to their slaves. Slave rations were cornmeal and salt pork. Historians have estimated that while there were adequate calories in this diet, many important nutrients were missing, even when slaves were able to supplement basic rations with produce from their own gardens. Plantation records indicate that "sore eyes," "sore mouth," and "black tongue" were common symptoms among slaves; all of these conditions are indicative of vitamin deficiencies. In addition, the amount of meat in the slave diet did not provide enough protein for people doing hard manual work, so "protein malnutrition" was also common.[44]

Housing was inadequate at best. Slave cabins were tiny, crowded, and often in poor repair. Tuberculosis and other respiratory disorders were common among slaves. Sanitary conditions were primitive even by the standards of the time. Some had no privies at all; others had shallow pit latrines that quickly contaminated the water supply. As a result, intestinal illnesses and parasites spread quickly, exacerbating nutritional deficiencies.[45]

It is not surprising then that African American life expectancies were lower than those for whites, even where white mortality was high. While many poor whites had primitive housing and monotonous diets as well, mortality statistics indicate that these conditions took a higher toll on blacks. Reliable numbers are hard to come by for the earliest periods, but in the nineteenth century black male life expectancy at birth was 32; for women, 34. These numbers remained stable even as mortality declined for whites during the same period.[46]

Native American living conditions and mortality were strongly skewed by the introduction of Old World diseases. The traditional lifestyle of most indigenous people seems to have been a relatively healthy one, but the changes brought about by the arrival of the Europeans created a crisis from which Native American populations never recovered.

Most of the Native populations of the Atlantic coast based their diet on horticulture and hunting, with the exception of the far north. Women cultivated maize, beans, and squash in large garden plots, while men hunted and fished. This system provided an adequate, balanced diet, although there was usually a "starving time" in the late winter and early spring when neither large game nor garden produce was available. The people lived in small villages near their farmland and moved on when the soil was exhausted or the hunting deteriorated. As a result, sanitary conditions were relatively good. There was never enough time for waste to build up and create conditions conducive to widespread disease. Before 1492, the Native American populations were probably the healthiest of the three ethnic groups that would come to populate North America. As we have seen, however, this changed once Europeans arrived.[47]

The impact of the post-1492 epidemics went beyond the immediate effects of the diseases. It is crucial to remember that these epidemics were not purely biological phenomena. Human agency and the stresses of invasion also played a role in the deteriorating health of the indigenous population. The arrival of Europeans brought not just disease but warfare, forced migration, enslavement, and environmental degradation. While not all these things happened everywhere, any one of them resulted in stress, social disruption, malnutrition, and lowered immunity. Even where relations between indigenous people and newcomers were relatively peaceful, the arrival of a new population brought with it disturbances in traditional subsistence systems.[48]

These disruptions were layered on top of terrible epidemics. While life expectancy statistics are hard to come by and hard to generalize, the population decline among Native Americans tells its own story. Clearly, a group who loses as many as 90 percent of its members over the course of a century is not a healthy population.

HEALTH AND DISEASE IN A TRANSFORMED AMERICA

The coming together of three peoples in North America truly created a New World for all of them. The three cultures each had their own concepts of health, disease, and healing; their own traditional diets and lifestyle; and their own inherent or acquired immunities to disease. These cultures exchanged disease germs, medicinal plants, and spiritual beliefs. The health environment in North America was brand new for all of them, whether from a biological or a cultural point of view.

NOTES

1. David S. Jones, "Virgin Soils Revisited," *William and Mary Quarterly*, 3rd Series, 60 (2003), 703–742. See also Colin G. Calloway, "Healing and Disease," in *New Worlds for All: Indians, Europeans, and the Remaking of Early America*. Baltimore: Johns Hopkins University Press, 1997, pp. 25–41.

2. Gary Nash, *Red, White and Black: The Peoples of Early North America*. Upper Saddle River, NJ: Prentice Hall, 2000, p. 21.

3. Alfred Crosby, *The Columbian Exchange: Biological and Cultural Consequences of 1492*. Westport, CT: Greenwood Press, 1973, p. 97; Nash, *Red, White and Black*, pp. 31–22.

4. Crosby, *The Columbian Exchange*, pp. 35–63.

5. Quoted in Nash, *Red, White and Black*, p. 92.

6. Jones, "Virgin Soils Revisited," p. 703.

7. Edmund Morgan, *American Slavery, American Freedom: The Ordeal of Colonial Virginia*. New York: WW Norton, 1975, 158.

8. Virgil J. Vogel, *American Indian Medicine*. Norman: University of Oklahoma Press, 1970, pp. 14–15.

9. Nash, *Red, White and Black*, p. 22.

10. Vogel, *American Indian Medicine*, pp. 14–15.

11. Nash, *Red, White and Black*, p. 23; Vogel, *American Indian Medicine*, pp. 15–16.

12. Vogel, *American Indian Medicine*, pp. 19–21; Kenneth Cohen, *Honoring the Medicine: The Essential Guide to Native American Healing*. New York: Ballantine Books, 2003, pp. 204–207.

13. Vogel, *American Indian Medicine*, pp. 24–25.

14. Ibid., p. 30.

15. Ibid., pp. 22–28.

16. Ibid., p. 31.

17. Ibid., p. 31.

18. Nancy G. Siraisi, *Medieval and Early Renaissance Medicine: An Introduction to Knowledge and Practice*. Chicago: University of Chicago Press, 1990.

19. Siraisi, *Medieval and Early Renaissance Medicine*, Chapter 4.

20. Ibid.; see also Rebecca J. Tannenbaum, *The Healer's Calling: Women and Medicine in Early New England*. Ithaca, NY: Cornell University Press, 2002.

21. Siraisi, *Medieval and Early Renaissance Medicine*.

22. Cotton Mather, *The Angel of Bethesda*, edited and with an introduction by Gordon Jones. Barre, MA: American Antiquarian Society and Barre Publishers, 1972, p. 62.

23. John Putnam Demos, *Entertaining Satan: Witchcraft and the Culture of Early New England*. New York: Oxford University Press, 1982, Chapter 3.

24. Tannenbaum, *The Healer's Calling*, Chapter 1.

25. Ibid., p. 6.

26. Sharla Fett, *Working Cures: Healing, Health and Power on Southern Slave Plantations*. Chapel Hill: University of North Carolina Press, 2002, pp. 38–42; Robert Voeks, "African Medicine and Magic in the Americas," *Geographical Review* 83 (1993), 66–78, p. 69.

27. Voek, "African Medicine and Magic," p. 69.

28. Fett, *Working Cures*, p. 6.

29. Ibid., p. 58.

30. Ibid., p. 6.

31. Fett, *Working Cures*; Voeks, "African Medicine and Magic," p. 69.

32. Fett, *Working Cures*, pp. 20–21; Voeks, "African Medicine and Magic."

33. Fett, *Working Cures*.

34. Calloway, "Healing and Disease."

35. Ibid.

36. Quoted in Karen Ordahl Kupperman, "Apathy and Death in Early Jamestown," *Journal of American History* 66 (1979), 24–40, p. 27.

37. Quoted in Kupperman, "Apathy and Death," p. 27.

38. Kupperman, "Apathy and Death." See also Nash, *Red, White and Black*, pp. 57–61 and Morgan, *American Slavery, American Freedom*, pp. 71–91.

39. James Deetz and Patricia Scott Deetz, *The Times of Their Lives: Life, Love, and Death in Plymouth Colony*. New York: W.H. Freeman and Company, 2000, pp. 59–60.

40. John Demos, *A Little Commonwealth: Family Life in Plymouth Colony*. New York: Oxford University Press, 1970, pp. 59–60.

41. Jane Kamensky, *The Colonial Mosaic*. New York: Oxford University Press, 1995, p. 34; Morgan, *American Slavery, American Freedom*, p. 160.

42. W. Michael Byrd and Linda A. Clayton, *An American Health Dilemma. Volume One: A Medical History of African Americans and the Problem of Race, Beginnings to 1900*. New York: Routledge, 2000, pp. 179–184.

43. Byrd and Clayton, *An American Health Dilemma*, p. 196.

44. Ibid., p. 226.

45. Ibid., pp. 224–225.

46. Ibid., p. 224.

47. Nash, *Red, White and Black*, pp. 7–24.

48. Jones, "Virgin Soils Revisited."

CHAPTER 2

Education and Training: Learned and Nonlearned

During the seventeenth and eighteenth centuries, there were a wide variety of medical practitioners with widely varied kinds of training. In Native American and African American cultures, healers followed a spiritual call into an apprenticeship with an experienced practitioner. In Anglo-American culture, a patient could choose a university-trained doctor, an apprentice-trained physician, a surgeon who honed his skills in the military, or a local woman with a lifetime of experience with herbs and care of the sick. All of these practitioners were highly skilled, and some, such as midwives, were recognized by all cultures as experts in their fields even without formal training.

By the mid-eighteenth century, formal education took on more importance in Anglo-American culture. This era saw the increasing influence of European medical science and the founding of the first American medical schools. However, lay practitioners remained important for all peoples and would continue to do so through the decades to come.

THE TRAINING OF NATIVE AMERICAN AND AFRICAN AMERICAN PRACTITIONERS

Native American and African American practitioners were trained in similar ways. Both groups stressed spirituality in their healing practices, and both had a long heritage of medical techniques that had been passed down through the generations. Training in these cultures combined both religious and secular elements. Novices usually learned their skills through training with an experienced mentor.

Native American Practitioners

The training of Native American healers took different forms. In some cultures, the training was lengthy and arduous. Among the Dine (Navajo), healers served a formal apprenticeship with a senior shaman. Dine healing rituals take place over several days and require the shaman or "chanter" to perform lengthy songs over that time. A mistake rendered the ritual useless. Most chanters specialized in one or two of the rituals, which could take years to learn. Healers of other cultures were members of special priesthoods, or "medicine societies" which required similar periods of apprenticeship before the healer was initiated.

While not all cultures required such structured training, most had some sort of informal apprenticeship for healers. In addition, many (though not all) cultures required that a potential healer have some sort of sign or call from the spirits. In some cultures, the position was hereditary, and only those of a certain lineage were eligible to become healers. For others, the call could come in a dream, a religious vision, or other supernatural experience.[1]

In the cultures of the Great Plains, young men wishing to become "medicine men" had to prove their bravery and spiritual worthiness through an elaborate and painful ritual. After an introductory ceremony, shamans made cuts in the muscles of the initiates' chests and calves, and inserted skewers through the cuts. Heavy weights, such as buffalo skulls, were attached to the skewers; or the initiates were hung from trees or posts. Those who passed through the ritual were deemed worthy of the high honor of practicing medicine. While this is an extreme example, it illustrates the importance of spirituality and personal virtue among Native American healers. Spirituality was as important as knowledge or skill in the practice of medicine.[2]

African American Practitioners

Spirituality also played an important role in African and African American medicine. In the cultures of West Africa, both diagnosis and healing required communication with the spirits, whether through trance, dreams, divination, or other rituals. While African and African American healers also used medicines and other techniques to treat the patient's physical body, none of these cures was effective without a religious element. The recruitment and training of African American healers reflect these cultural beliefs.

African American healers also needed to have a spiritual sign before they could begin their training. Some healers were chosen at birth, when they were born with a "caul" or amniotic sac over their heads. Healing seemed to run in families, and most healers were the sons or daughters of healers. No matter what, most felt that their abilities came from a divine or spiritual source, which could be an African deity or the Christian God. One nineteenth-century Georgia woman said "seems lak yuh jes' hab to be born wid duh knowledge." A male healer made a similar statement: "When the Lord gives such power to a person, it just comes to 'em."[3]

Still, healers had to learn to use their powers. At times, the training could come from supernatural sources. One woman claimed that her dead sister came to her in a dream and gave her instructions on how to treat a patient. A midwife related that her dead mentor came to her "in the spirit" to tell her how to handle a difficult labor.

In addition to these spiritual experiences, healers learned in more conventional ways. Many African Americans learned from family members and close neighbors. Groups gathered at sickbeds traded recipes and techniques with each other. The knowledge of the elderly was particularly respected. In families with healing traditions, knowledge was passed from parent to child. Many slave healers—both male and female—related learning their skills from their mothers. Midwives apprenticed with other midwives.[4]

In addition, some slaveholders trained chosen slaves in the practice of Anglo-American medicine. Landon Carter, an eighteenth-century Virginia planter and lay physician, trained his slave Nassau to assist him. Nassau prepared and administered medicines, reported symptoms to Carter and gave opinions on diagnosis, and performed therapeutic bleedings. Nassau treated his fellow slaves, white tenant farmers, and even Carter's own grandchildren. Nassau also assisted Carter with veterinary work and helped perform necropsies on animals that died. Nassau was one of the first documented cases of this practice, which would continue throughout the antebellum period. While Nassau was a man, many of the enslaved healers of the nineteenth century were women, described as "nurses" in the historical record. Like Nassau, these healers performed much of the day-to-day work of caring for the sick.[5]

ANGLO-AMERICAN TRADITIONS

English culture of the seventeenth and early eighteenth centuries recognized a wide variety of healers. Healers were categorized by gender, social status, and level of education as well as the type of service that they offered. In the earliest period, formal medical education was rare, although many "learned gentlemen" practiced medicine without an MD degree. By the mid-eighteenth century, formal education in medicine became more common.

Anglo-American Lay Healers

In the seventeenth and early eighteenth centuries, laypeople provided most of the medical care. Physicians with MD degrees were expensive and rare. However, this is not to say that lay practitioners were unskilled or untrained. On the contrary, most lay practitioners had a deep fund of knowledge and experience to draw on.

Household Medicine

The first people to intervene in any illness were members of the patient's family, especially the women members. Women learned nursing, herbal medicine, and diagnostic skills as part of their skills in "housewifery." Published housekeeping guides aimed at women included instructions in medical care and the making of medicines. In most families, though, the knowledge was probably passed on from mother to daughter in an oral tradition.

Some literate families kept records of their family medicinal recipes, which give historians a chance to see how kin and neighbors "trained" each other in medical practice. Such notebooks usually noted the origins of each recipe. For instance, one recipe is credited as "this receipt was given to my mother; from whom my aunt price had it whoe gave it to mee." Medical knowledge was a shared resource among female kin. Some women copied recipes from published medical books and then passed them on to other family members, and still others wrote down recipes they collected from formally educated physicians. As a result of this process, even the uneducated had access to some of the same medicines and techniques as the highest level of practitioner.[6]

While many of the medical recipes passed down were for everyday ailments such as bruises, minor skin complaints, and indigestion, household practitioners also learned techniques for treating more serious complaints. One household recipe book included recipes and instructions for caring for patients with the plague, "consumption," and childbed fever. A patient could look to his or her own family for sophisticated medical care under many circumstances.

Midwives

Midwives provided more specialized care than housewives. They delivered babies, dealt with the problems of newborn infants, and treated most "female complaints." During the seventeenth and eighteenth centuries, the only European institution to offer formal midwifery instruction to women was the Hotel Dieu in Paris. The Hotel Dieu's most famous alumna was Louise Bourgeois, who became midwife to the Queen of France in 1601. While no institution in England offered such training, some English midwives worked with surgeons or other male practitioners who took them on as apprentices. A few English midwives married surgeons and set up joint practices.[7]

However, there is no evidence that midwives in the American colonies were trained in this way. There were published guides to midwifery, most notably the widely circulated *Aristotle's Master Piece* and Jane Sharp's *Midwife's Book*, but it is not clear how many practicing midwives had read these works. Most American midwives learned their trade by attending other women at childbirth gatherings, gaining experience over time, and gradually taking a more active role. Many midwives were already known in their communities as skilled family healers and traded on that reputation when they entered midwifery.

In addition, most midwives were the mothers of many children. Having survived childbirth many times was an important qualification for a midwife. Age was another factor. Midwives usually did not begin practice until they had reached middle age and were done, or almost done, with childbearing. Age brought experience, wisdom, and compassion to a midwife's trade. It also brought the community respect that was necessary for a woman in such an authoritative position.

Other Lay Practitioners

Other women were also able to turn their household skills into a paying medical practice. There are many references in the colonial records to "doctoresses" and "doctor women" who saw both male and female patients and accepted payment for their services. One example is Anna Maynard of Marlborough, Massachusetts. Her family kept an extensive family recipe book, to which she contributed and from which she no doubt learned many remedies. In addition, her first husband, Samuel Brigham, was a physician. It is possible that she had apprenticed herself to him either before or during their marriage, just as English midwives worked in partnership with their surgeon husbands.[8]

Men also earned their livings as lay practitioners. Some traveled from town to town on a regular schedule, advertising their services as dentists and surgeons. While the advertisements sometimes made extravagant claims for the men's credentials ("Surgeon and Oculist to Her Royal Highness Princess Dowager of Wales"), these were likely hyperbole.[9] Most of these men had probably learned their skills in much the same way as the doctoresses and midwives: family tradition, informal apprenticeships, or life experience that lent itself to medical practice. For instance, the dentist John Greenwood was the son of a dentist, so he no doubt learned some of his skills by assisting his father. However, as a young man he did not practice dentistry. He started his working life as an apprentice cabinetmaker and spent several years as a maker of nautical and scientific instruments before practicing dentistry. His skills as a craftsman came into play when he changed careers. Greenwood became especially well known as a maker of high quality dentures and dental tools.[10]

In all likelihood, many of the itinerant surgeons and dentists of the colonial period "trained" in the same way—learning skills appropriate to one trade and applying them to another. Military service and seafaring were jobs that lent themselves to training in medical matters. In both cases, men might pick up skills such as therapeutic bleeding, minor surgical procedures, or dentistry without formal apprenticeship or credentials.

Other lay practitioners claimed a wide variety of credentials and training. Some, such as Isaac Calcott, advertised himself as a "seventh son of a seventh son." The circumstances of his birth endowed him with magical healing powers. Still other Anglo-American practitioners marketed themselves as "Indian Doctors." Their cures were loosely based on the practices of Native Americans, and many, such as John Salse, claimed that he would cure cancer with "a method he acquired whilst [living] among the Indians." It is hard to say how accurate these claims were. Many Indian Doctors made and sold herbal medicines based on plants native to North America such as sassafras and Seneca snakeroot; it is possible that they were remedies used by Native Americans. However, these same medicines often were often made using methods that resembled those of European practitioners. The majority of Indian Doctors were probably self-taught entrepreneurs who used some knowledge of Native American medicine to create remedies that drew on both Native and European traditions.[11]

Learned Practitioners

The line between learned and lay practitioners was often blurred in the early years of the Colonial period. High-status, educated men with extensive private libraries often practiced medicine and were accorded respect as physicians, even though they had no formal medical training. On the other hand, physicians and surgeons usually learned their trade through apprenticeships rather than academic training. By the eighteenth century, academic credentials became more important, setting the stage for the professionalization of medicine in the century to come.

Learned Gentlemen

Medical practice did not require a medical degree. A broad general education, community respect, and access to medical books were enough to qualify as a physician. In New England, ministers often added medical practice to their pastoral duties. Other educated gentlemen also used their knowledge and libraries to teach themselves medicine. A wealthy, well-educated, and respected man earned trust through his social status as well as his education, and many of these self-taught physicians had extensive practices.

Landon Carter of Virginia, discussed previously as the mentor of Nassau, was one of these practitioners. He owned a large collection of medical books and took it upon himself to doctor his family, neighbors, tenant farmers, and slaves. His practice resembled that of contemporary physicians. Carter used herbal drugs as purges and emetics. He also performed bleedings or had Nassau perform them. His prickly personality probably did not do his medical practice much good—Carter's diary is full of entries in which he complains that his family members would not follow his prescriptions.[12]

In colonial Connecticut, Governor John Winthrop, Jr. had an extensive medical practice in addition to his political career. Winthrop had studied law at Trinity College, Dublin. However, Winthrop considered himself a scientist and spent much of his life reading medical and scientific texts, performing experiments, and presenting papers to the Royal Society in London, where he was a member. One of Winthrop's great interests was alchemy and chemistry, and he created a number of medicines based on alchemical principles. Patients from throughout the colony consulted Winthrop in difficult cases that local healers could not cure, more evidence of the respect the populace had for Winthrop's intellectual credentials.

Apprenticeships

The most common career path for a physician or surgeon was through apprenticeship. In this, medicine resembled other skilled trades. Boys were apprenticed in their early teens and committed to six or seven years of study. An apprentice usually lived in his mentor's household as a member of the family. During this time, he would shadow his mentor on rounds, read books from his preceptor's library, and assist in procedures. The eighteenth-century physician Benjamin Rush remembered compounding medicines, doing follow-up visits with patients, and keeping his master's accounts as part of his apprenticeship. Similarly, Alexander Anderson of New York City recorded his duties in his diary:

> Jan. 8. Made Syrup of Licorice root. After-noon— ... went in quest of yellow-dock root—got a small supply in a lot near the Battery . . . Took medicine downtown . . .
> Feb. 8—Fore-noon—went with Dr. Smith to see some patients. I bled Mr. Blair—seiz'd with Pleurisy . . .[13]

Many apprentices did menial tasks as well, such as cleaning instruments, looking after the master's horse, and harassing patients for unpaid fees.

This is not to say that apprentice-trained physicians were uneducated. For boys who were apprenticed young, instruction in basic literacy was part of their education as physicians. These skills were then put to use. Many preceptors had extensive libraries and eagerly awaited the latest medical texts from Europe. Reading these texts, and perhaps even committing passages to memory, was an important part of an apprentice's training. One medical apprentice noted in his diary that he read 80 medical books during his training. Another recorded reading two books that had been published in Europe just a few months earlier.[14]

The training of surgeons followed a similar course. Medicine and surgery had been considered separate skills for many years in Europe and required different training. In the colonies, there was less of a distinction, and many practitioners thought of themselves as both physicians and surgeons. However, in some apprenticeships, there was more of an emphasis on one set of skills than the other.

John Hartshorn was apprenticed to the prominent Boston surgeon Silvester Gardiner in the 1750s. His diary, like that of Alexander Anderson, records his duties and the skills he learned. Although Gardiner pronounced the diagnosis, prescribed the treatment, and performed the most complex surgeries, he left it up to his apprentices to carry out the day-to-day care of the patients. Hartshorn described accompanying Gardiner on visits to patients and then making follow-up appointments to dress wounds, perform bleedings, lance abscesses, and check on progress. When Gardiner operated, Hartshorn "handed the instruments" while another apprentice "held the tourniquets." When Gardiner amputated a leg, Hartshorn and his fellow apprentice "brought the leg home and . . . dissected it," taking advantage of the opportunity for further education.[15]

The military provided another opportunity for surgeons to acquire and develop skills. James Thacher had just finished his medical apprenticeship when the Revolutionary War broke out. He joined the Continental Army, applied for the post of surgeon's mate, and was duly examined by a committee of established military surgeons. He was accepted as an assistant to the well-known surgeon John Warren. While Thacher had already served an apprenticeship, he saw his military service as an opportunity for education as well as patriotic duty. Thacher knew he was young and inexperienced, and he hoped to gain more medical skills in the army: "My contemplated enterprise [medical practice] it is true, requires the experience and resolution of riper years than twenty-one." In his wartime diary, Thacher took note of the many complex injuries he saw during his time in the military and recorded the techniques he learned from Warren and other senior medical officers. While he was careful always to express his sympathy for the terrible suffering he saw, he also could barely conceal his excitement at what he was learning: "A military hospital is peculiarly calculated to afford examples for profitable contemplation." In addition to learning surgical techniques (including a method of repairing injuries from a scalping) Thacher learned how to inoculate patients for smallpox, and treat typhus and other epidemic diseases that ran rampant through military camps.[16]

CHANGES IN THE EIGHTEENTH CENTURY

The mid- to late eighteenth century saw an expansion of formal medical education both in Europe and America. Medical science took on new prestige in European universities, and American students who could afford to do so traveled abroad to take advantage of the new opportunities. These experiences inspired the young European-trained physicians to found medical schools in America.

European Training

For young men of wealthy families, European medical training was important preparation for a medical career. London and Edinburgh were the most common destinations. In London, medical students focused on clinical experience in a kind of extended apprenticeship with famous English physicians. At Edinburgh, students enrolled in a formal degree program and concentrated on pure science and medical theory. It was common for Americans to start a medical education in London with practical instruction then round it off in Edinburgh with a taste of state-of-the-art science.

Medical students in London did not attend a university but instead served a clinical apprenticeship supplemented with lectures from some of the leading figures of the day. Many Americans studied with John Hunter, one of the most influential surgeons of the eighteenth century. Hunter was a pioneering experimental scientist as well as a practicing surgeon and encouraged his students to do experimental research. One of his most famous British pupils was Edward Jenner, inventor of the smallpox vaccine. When Jenner wrote to his former mentor, asking advice on his hypothesis that inoculation with cowpox could provide immunity to smallpox, Hunter replied, "Why not try the experiment?" Hunter's American students included John Morgan, Benjamin Rush ("The American Hippocrates"), William Shippen, and Philip Syng Physick ("Father of American Surgery"), all of whom brought home Hunter's techniques and experimental philosophy.[17]

American students in London divided their time between treating patients at the hospital, dissecting cadavers, and listening to lectures from their mentors. Benjamin Rush described a typical day during his stay in London like this: "Rose at six, operating 'til eight, breakfast at nine, dissected 'til two, dined 'til three, dissected 'til five, lectured 'til seven, operated 'til nine, supper 'til ten, then bed." In addition, Rush wrote of his long informal conversations with his preceptor John Hunter, whom he remembered with fondness.[18]

The program at Edinburgh was attached to a university and awarded formal degrees in medicine. The Edinburgh curriculum became the model for the first American medical schools. It consisted of a three-year course, during which the students attended lectures in anatomy, chemistry, theory of medicine, practice of medicine, materia medica (what would now be called pharmacology), midwifery, and medical botany. Some of the professors included William Cullen, who made the first modern attempt to classify diseases, and whose textbook was used for over 150 years; Francis Home, who first described and named diphtheria; and Alexander Monro, pioneering professor of anatomy and surgery.

While there were only a few European-trained physicians in America during the Colonial period, their influence was out of proportion to their numbers. The physicians trained abroad founded medical societies, brought new treatments to America, and eventually founded the first American medical schools.[19]

THE FIRST AMERICAN MEDICAL SCHOOLS

As medicine became more based in science and experiment, some American doctors began to see the need for formal medical education in the colonies. Two schools were founded in the years before the Revolution by American doctors who had been educated abroad: the medical school at the College of Philadelphia (later the University of Pennsylvania), which admitted its first class in 1765; and the King's College Medical School (later Columbia University) in New York City in 1767.

The Medical College of Philadelphia was founded by William Shippen and John Morgan, two graduates of the University of Edinburgh who wanted to establish a similar institution in their hometown. Such a project would encourage the development of medical science in America, increase the supply of credentialed physicians, and (not incidentally) boost the careers of its founders.

Shippen and Morgan first came up with the idea while they were still students in Scotland. They based the curriculum on the one in Edinburgh, and appointed themselves and their friends to be the faculty. Morgan would teach the theory and practice of medicine, Shippen would be professor of anatomy and obstetrics, Shippen's brother-in-law Arthur Lee would teach medical botany, and their friend Theodorick Bland would handle materia medica. Morgan's London mentor, Dr. John Fothergill, donated a set of anatomical illustrations to help the enterprise along.

Of course, putting the plan into practice took some time. When Shippen returned to Philadelphia from Europe in 1762, he began a series of anatomy lectures that were not affiliated with the college. He specifically marketed them to "those whose Circumstances and Connections will not admit of their going abroad." The success of these lectures indicated that there was a demand for formal medical education in Philadelphia and helped establish Shippen's reputation as an up and coming young doctor.[20]

When John Morgan returned home, he made his proposal for a medical school to the trustees of the College of Philadelphia. In May of 1765,

Morgan gave a commencement speech at the college in which he out-
lined his vision of the ideal medical school. He began by outlining the
ideal curriculum for medical study. Not surprisingly, it closely
resembled the course he had followed at Edinburgh. The student had
to begin with anatomy as the basis of all medicine, followed by materia
medica and medical botany, which allow students to understand the
functioning of the body and the effects of drugs. After this preparation,
the student would be ready to learn the theory of medicine, including
physiology and pathology. Only then could the student move on to
learning the actual practice of medicine, which included diagnosis
and treatment.

Morgan also made a case for the establishment of a medical school in
the colonies. First of all, it was essential that physicians learn medicine
in an academic setting rather than the traditional apprenticeship. In
an apprenticeship, a student learns only what his mentor teaches
him—which "confines a man to a very narrow circle and limits him to
a few partial indications in the cure of diseases." If the mentor's own
knowledge is limited, the student "soon gets through his little stock of
knowledge" and finds that "he has exhausted all the resources of art."
A medical school would ensure that all the students received a broad
education. Establishing a medical school in America would also ensure
that more American physicians would have access to this kind of education, and establishing it in Philadelphia would bring "world wide
fame to their city."[21]

Morgan ended his speech with a call for specialization in medicine. He
wanted a return to the old European system in which physicians, surgeons, and apothecaries stayed within their own specialties. In America,
most practitioners ignored these boundaries out of necessity—there
simply were not enough specialized practitioners to go around. Morgan
hoped that the establishment of an American medical school would
rectify this situation.

The school admitted its first class in November of 1765 with Morgan
and Shippen as the first professors. Three years later, Adam Kuhn was
appointed professor of materia medica and botany, and in 1769,
Benjamin Rush became professor of chemistry. With a full complement
of faculty, the college was able to offer two degrees in medicine: the
bachelor's degree (BM) and the doctoral degree (MD) Recipients of
the MD had to complete the bachelor's program, practice for at least
three years, and then return to present and defend a doctoral thesis.
The first bachelor's degrees were awarded in June of 1768.

The school in Philadelphia was soon followed by one in New York
City. Like John Morgan and William Shippen, Samuel Bard had studied

at Edinburgh and wanted to transplant that model of medical education to America. In 1767, he assembled a medical faculty and asked his influential father to convince the governing board of King's College to establish a medical school. The original faculty included three professors who were prominent senior physicians from New York, all of whom had European education; and three recent Edinburgh graduates, including Samuel Bard.

The curriculum at King's College Medical School was similar to that of the College of Philadelphia. It included anatomy, surgery, obstetrics, theory and practice of medicine, chemistry, and materia medica. Samuel Bard went on to write the first American obstetrics textbook as well as influential articles on diphtheria and yellow fever.

Some historians have argued that King's College should be considered the first American medical school. In contrast to the College of Philadelphia, it opened with a full complement of faculty, most of whom were already distinguished in their fields, meaning that its entering class had earlier access to a full curriculum. However, most historians give the Philadelphia school priority because it admitted students first.[22]

Teaching a full Edinburgh-style curriculum presented its own problems. As was the case in Europe, it was difficult to obtain cadavers for dissection in anatomy classes. Rumors soon spread that medical students were robbing graves to supply material for anatomy classes. There was truth to the gossip. African American burial grounds were especially vulnerable. There were incidents in both Virginia and New York City in which medical students "ravaged" African American cemeteries.[23]

Anatomy professors made weak attempts to reassure the public, usually by insisting that the "better class" of citizens need not worry. (African Americans and poor whites received no such promises.) For instance, William Shippen assured the citizens of Philadelphia that all the cadavers in his classes were individuals who "had willfully murdered themselves, or were publickly executed, except now and then one from the Potters Field." Not surprisingly, community resentment and suspicion continued to grow.[24]

Such resentments came to a head in an incident known as the Doctor's Mob of 1788. It began with a tasteless student prank, in which some apprentice surgeons at New York Hospital dangled a cadaver arm out a window. When they noticed a boy playing in the street below, they called out to him that it was his mother's arm. As it happened, the boy's mother had recently died, and when he told his father of the incident, the father immediately checked her grave. It was empty.

Enraged, the father gathered a group of his friends and marched on the hospital to retrieve her body.

The riot lasted four days. The mob burst into the anatomy lab, destroyed the equipment and books, and confiscated all the cadavers and anatomical specimens they could carry. They loaded the bodies onto a cart and "[i]nterred them the same evening." The rioters then turned their attention to finding the physicians and students who had been working in the dissection room. Luckily for the doctors, the mob did not find them—the sheriff had located them first and put them in jail for their own protection. The crowd dispersed for the day but reassembled the next morning to forcibly search the houses of every doctor in the city for further evidence of graverobbing.[25]

Soon after, the New York legislature passed a series of laws designed to prevent future riots. One law made graverobbing for the purposes of dissection punishable by a heavy fine, a sentence to the pillory, and a term of imprisonment at the judge's discretion. On the other hand, the legislature passed a second act explicitly donating the bodies of executed criminals to medical schools for the purpose of instruction. The public was reassured that the graves of their loved ones would remain undisturbed, and the medical schools had a legitimate source of cadavers. However, finding adequate anatomical specimens for medical training would remain a problem into the nineteenth century and beyond.

Despite these difficulties, more and more colleges began adding medical schools, and free-standing schools began to appear. In Boston, the local medical society had been advocating for a medical school at Harvard since shortly before the Revolutionary War. One physician bequeathed the school 1,000 pounds sterling to establish a professorship in medicine, but the Harvard governors did not think the sum adequate. During the war, the subject was raised again, this time more seriously. The Boston Medical Society held a special meeting in 1780 at which Dr. John Warren presented a proposal for a medical college. The original plan included a faculty of three; however, two of the three professors nominated withdrew their names. Warren presented his proposal directly to the members of the Harvard Corporation in 1782, and this time his plan was accepted. Harvard Medical School opened its doors in October of 1783.

Two more American schools opened before the turn of the nineteenth century, a free-standing school in Baltimore, founded in 1790 by Andrew Wiesenthal and George Buchanan, and Dartmouth Medical College, founded in 1797 by Nathan Smith. As was the case with Pennsylvania, King's College, and Harvard, the founders of these schools were all Edinburgh graduates who wanted to transfer the Edinburgh model to the United States.

While these projects were ambitious, they met with mixed success overall. On the one hand, the early schools made great strides toward standardizing American medical education and defining what training a physician needed to have. In doing so, the early medical schools represented an important step toward creating the modern medical profession. On the other hand, the young United States did not have the hospitals, university-trained physicians, or other facilities to make the Edinburgh model work exactly as it did in Scotland. In addition, the professors at the early colleges were young and inexperienced themselves. Much of the education at the early medical colleges was, in the words of one historian, "watered down Monro and Cullen rather than original material based on the experiences of [the] professors." While the four college-affiliated schools survived and eventually became elite scientific institutions, it took some time before they achieved that status.[26]

Medical education and training in early America reflected the diverse nature of Colonial healers. While all healers received training and learned skills, the quality varied greatly. The early medical schools were one attempt to standardize medical training, but it was a project that would take most of the next century to complete.

NOTES

1. Donald Sander, *Navaho Symbols of Healing*. New York: Harcourt Brace Jovanovich, 1979, pp. 26–30; Virgil J. Vogel, *American Indian Medicine*. Norman: University of Oklahoma Press, 1970, p. 22–30.

2. David Dary, *Frontier Medicine: From the Atlantic to the Pacific: 1492–1941*. New York: Alfred A. Knopf, 2008, p. 10.

3. Quoted in Sharla M. Fett, *Working Cures: Healing, Health, and Power on Southern Slave Plantations*. Chapel Hill: University of North Carolina Press, 2002, p. 53.

4. Quoted in Fett, *Working Cures*, p. 55.

5. Landon Carter, *The Diary of Colonel Landon Carter of Sabine Hall: 1752–1778*. Jack P. Greene (Ed.), Charlottesville: University Press of Virginia, 1965.

6. Quoted in Rebecca J. Tannenbaum, *The Healer's Calling: Women and Medicine in Early New England*. Ithaca, NY: Cornell University Press, 2002, p. 24.

7. Nicky Leap, "Midwifery." In Stephen Lock, John M. Last, and George Dunea (Eds.), *The Oxford Companion to Medicine*. Oxford University Press, 2001. Oxford Reference Online. Oxford University Press. Yale University. 1 June 2011 http://www.oxfordreference.com/views/ENTRY.html?subview=Main&entry=t185.e309.

8. Tannenbaum, *The Healer's Calling*, p. 13.

9. Quoted in Peter Benes, "Itinerant Physicians, Healers, and Surgeon Dentists in New England and New York: 1720–1825." In Peter Benes (Ed.), *Medicine and Healing, Dublin Seminar for New England Folklife Annual Proceedings 1990*, Boston: Boston University Press, 1992, p. 97.

10. David Krasner, "John Greenwood," *American National Biography Online*. Retrieved June 21, 2010 from http://www.anb.org/articles/12/1200350.html.

11. Benes, "Itinerant Physicians, Healers, and Surgeon-Dentists," pp. 105–106.

12. See, for example, July 24, 1766, in Carter, *Diary*. This case is also discussed in Rhys Isaac, *The Transformation of Virginia: 1740–1790*. New York: Norton, 1982, p. 49.

13. Quoted in Genevive Miller, "Medical Apprenticeship in the American Colonies," *Ciba Symposia*, 8 (January 1947), p. 502.

14. Helen Brock, "The Influence of Europe on Colonial Massachusetts Medicine." In *Medicine in Colonial Massachusetts: 1620–1820*. Boston: The Colonial Society of Massachusetts, 1980, pp. 106–107.

15. John Hartshorn, "Tucker's Wife's Leg." In A. Scott Earle (Ed.), *Surgery in America: From the Colonial Period to the Twentieth Century*. New York: Praeger, 1983, p. 19.

16. James Thacher, "A Military Journal during the American Revolutionary War: from 1775 to 1783." in Earle, *Surgery in America*, pp. 44–46.

17. Harold Ellis, *The Cambridge Illustrated History of Surgery*. Cambridge: Cambridge University Press, 2001, p. 57.

18. Quoted in Ellis, *Cambridge Illustrated History of Surgery*, p. 62.

19. Brock, "The Influence of Europe," pp. 107–109.

20. Martin Kaufman, *American Medical Education: The Formative Years: 1765–1910*. Westport: Greenwood Press, 1976, p. 19.

21. Genevive Miller, "Medical Schools in the Colonies," *Ciba Symposia*, 8 (1947), p. 527.

22. Kaufman, *American Medical Education*, p. 24.

23. Ibid., pp. 29–30.

24. Ibid., p. 29.

25. Jules Calvin Ladenheim, "The 'Doctor's Mob' of 1788," *Journal of the History of Medicine and Allied Sciences*, V (1950), 23–43, p. 30.

26. Kaufman, *American Medical Education*, p. 28.

CHAPTER 3

Faith, Religion, and Medicine

All three culture groups in Early America—European, Native American, and African American—recognized a supernatural element in disease, health, and healing. The "supernatural" had several manifestations. Gods or other deities could cause or cure illness, as could evil spirits or demons. A person's health could be affected by magic wielded by a benign healer or a malicious witch. In addition, clergy played a role in healing in all three cultures.

Of course, the beliefs of the culture groups varied. Christians saw illness as a test of faith or as God's punishment for sin. While ministers could tend the body as well as the soul, medicine was not their primary task. European American culture put more emphasis on natural factors as a cause of disease, while in African American and Native American societies, all illness had a spiritual component. Similarly, in African American and Native American culture, shamans and "medicine men" saw healing as one of their most important spiritual tasks.

CHRISTIANITY AND HEALING

Christianity was the dominant religious belief among European Americans, and Protestantism was the dominant sect among English colonists. While most early American Christians were of European descent, missionaries and evangelists converted many Native Americans. Slave owners expected their slaves to become Christian and many did,

although African American Christianity was inflected by African traditions and beliefs.

Christian beliefs about illness changed over time. The seventeenth
and early eighteenth centuries were dominated by harsh, even punitive
beliefs about sickness and sin. However, as the eighteenth century progressed, more liberal sects emphasized God's healing powers rather
than divine wrath.

Sickness, Suffering, and Sin

Even though there was a diversity of Christian sects, most seventeenth-
and early eighteenth–century American Christians shared core beliefs
about the relationship between sickness, health, and sin. While New
England Puritans wrote most extensively about the relationship
between spiritual and physical health, Catholic priests and Protestant
ministers of other sects preached similar doctrine. The English Book of
Common Prayer (the spiritual handbook of the Anglican church) prescribed repentance and prayer as a remedy for illness, much as
Puritan ministers did. Catholic doctrine stated, "bodily infirmity is
sometimes caused by sin" and encouraged believers to call a priest
before they called a physician.[1]

For most Christians, disease and ill health were the result of humanity's sinful nature. Before Adam and Eve were expelled from Eden,
there was no sickness; original sin brought physical suffering into the
world. "Sin was that which first brought sickness upon a sinful world,"
wrote Boston's Reverend Cotton Mather, "and which yet continues to
sicken the world with a world of diseases." Disease was an evil in and
of itself, placed in the world to cause suffering, test the faith of the
pious, and bring the sinful to repentance.[2]

While the existence of disease was evidence of humanity's collective
sin, disease that affected an individual was punishment for that person's specific sins. God made his displeasure with individuals known
through visible misfortune; a sinner's cows might die while his pious
neighbor's prospered. Similarly, God might strike a person with sickness to bring community attention to her misconduct.

A striking example of this kind of thinking took place during the
religious upheaval in Massachusetts known as the Antinomian
Controversy of 1635 to 1638. Religious dissident Anne Hutchinson dis-
puted the received doctrine of the Puritan church. Hutchinson acquired
a following large enough to challenge not only the religious establishment but the colony's political leadership as well. However, two medical events—one involving one of Hutchinson's close allies and one that

affected Hutchinson herself—were seized upon by ministers and magistrates alike as evidence of God's disapproval, and did much to discredit Hutchinson's ideas.

The first of these occurred in October of 1637. Mary Dyer, a close friend and supporter of Hutchinson, gave birth to a stillborn baby that observers described as "monstrous and misshapen." John Winthrop, governor of the colony and Hutchinson's bitter adversary, noted, "that very day Mistris Hutchinson was cast out of the church for her monstrous errors." Winthrop connected the "monstrosity" of Hutchinson's ideas with the "monstrosity" of her follower's stillborn child; God was giving clear evidence of his displeasure with Mary Dyer, and by extension, Hutchinson. When Hutchinson herself suffered a miscarriage a few months later, Winthrop and his supporters placed a similar interpretation on the event. The 30 "deformities" identified on the fetus were interpreted as symbolic of Hutchinson's 30 theological errors. God had spoken once more by punishing Hutchinson with a miscarriage for her sins.[3]

Individuals did not need to be as notorious as Anne Hutchinson for their illnesses to be interpreted as God's judgment. Ministers encouraged parishioners to interpret sickness as a "correction" from God for their sins and seek forgiveness. Religious writers noted that God often gave clues to the particular sin by the nature of the illness. For some diseases, such as venereal disease, the sin was obvious: "Wretches, Because you would not remove your way far from the strange woman, you are now mourning at the last, when your flesh and your body are consuming." But even more mundane symptoms were divine messages: "Let thy Head-ache bring into thy head such thoughts as these: Lord, My Head has been too destitute of those thoughts which are proper to be lodged in a temple of God!"[4]

The proper response to such messages was, of course, repentance and prayer. Many believers wrote in diaries and other personal documents of how a serious illness had renewed their faith. Minister Stephen Sewall wrote that a month-long illness had inspired him "to serve God better." Another man, who had recovered from smallpox, declared to his church "God visited me with the small pox yet I thought it nothing in comparison with the sickness of my soul."[5]

Even for those who lived virtuous lives, illness was an important time for religious reflection. The sick were reminded of the Biblical book of Job, in which God allowed Satan to send afflictions to a righteous man to test his faith. To pass this test, it was crucial that the patient accept the illness as the will of God. Submission to God's will was an important act of faith for Colonial-era Christians. Sickness was a chance to prove that a person had put himself or herself completely in God's hands. When a Cambridge, Massachusetts, man was suffering from a bladder stone (a notoriously painful ailment) friends and neighbors gathered around his sickbed worried that he would not recover because "he could not in the extremity of the paine submit with cheerfulnesse to the will of God." Eventually, however, the man found spiritual peace and told a friend that God had spoken words of comfort to him.[6]

Communities, as well as individuals, could suffer God's wrath in the form of sickness. An epidemic was chastisement for a community who had strayed too far from God's plan. The sins of a community were often manifold. One clergyman made a list of misconduct he believed had brought on a smallpox epidemic: "pride, covetousnesse, animositys, personal neglecte of gospelizing our youth, and of gospelizing of the Indians . . . drinking houses multiplyed."[7]

Collective guilt required collective repentance. Ministers and government officials often organized official days of prayer and fasting during epidemics, a practice that had been common in England since the Reformation. Special daylong church services begged God for forgiveness and asked for his blessing to end the epidemic. Public prayers for the sick were believed to be especially effective in bringing about a recovery.

Clergy as Healers

The Christian response to disease had a physical as well as a spiritual component. Many ministers were called to care for the physical as well as the spiritual health of their congregations. When a clergyman visited a sick parishioner, he came primarily to offer prayers, but most could offer medical skills as well.

While early American Christians believed in a spiritual element to health, they also believed that most illnesses had physical causes. God may have created disease to remind humankind of its sins, but He sent the disease through the agency of the physical world. Thus, while prayer and religious ritual were important in healing, medicines and surgery were equally important. As a result, ministers and other clergy often provided medicine as well as spiritual counsel.

In Medieval and Renaissance England, a Catholic priest's education usually included some reading in medical texts, and most formally educated physicians had taken religious vows. While medical education became increasingly secular as time went on, many clergy, both Catholic and Protestant, continued to study medicine. The tradition was still strong during the time of European settlement in the Americas.

Spanish Catholic missionaries made medical practice a part of their religious proselytizing. Franciscan missions in Baja California provided the local people with medical care in addition to religious instruction. Many of the priests incorporated indigenous treatments into their medical practices, which made the missions a more appealing source of care. However, the medical missions may have done more harm than good; gathering the sick together inside the missions alongside a healthy population may have done more to spread disease than cure it.[8]

Spanish missionaries authored the first medical books printed in the Americas. Two Jesuit priests, Francisco Bravo and Alonso Lopez de Hinojosis, wrote books on New World medicine and surgery, respectively, in 1570. Nine years later, another Jesuit brother wrote a book on anatomy, surgery, and medicine, which included many cures used by the Aztecs. Unfortunately, the central church authorities disapproved of promulgating "pagan" cures, and discouraged further publications.[9]

In England, clergy of both the established Anglican Church and the dissenting Puritans believed that ministers had a duty to provide medical care to their flocks. Ministers of both sects brought this belief to the American colonies. One Anglican writer wrote that since it was "easie for any Scholer to attaine to ... a measure of Physick ... by seeing one Anatomy, reading one Book of Physick, having one Herball by him," there was no reason every minister should not be a physician as well. In addition, medical care would help the congregation appreciate the "manifold wisdom of God" in providing humankind with medicinal plants to relieve their suffering. Puritan clergy saw the study of medicine similarly. They also believed that it was a minister's duty to serve his community in whatever way he could, including providing physical and material relief to his parishioners.[10]

Some clergy had other motives as well. Ministers were not well paid (especially in comparison to other university-educated men), and in New England, their salaries depended on the goodwill of their flocks. For some, practicing medicine became a lucrative sideline, or even a full time job when preaching to a quarrelsome congregation became too difficult. Harvard graduate Michael Wigglesworth served as both a minister and a doctor in his early career, but he eventually gave up the ministry for medicine. He complained that his flock was "most unjust" to him and that they held "a very low esteem of my ministry." He resigned his post and took up the practice of medicine full time, noting that medicine was a more reliable source of income and community respect.[11]

Ministers' wives also played an important role in the medical care of their husbands' flocks. Most women had extensive healing skills, especially high status women. Ministers' wives saw community healing as part of their duty to support their husbands' careers. Most of these women remained in the shadows, giving all the credit for their cures to their husbands. Elizabeth Davenport, wife of minister John Davenport of New Haven, Connecticut, is one minister's wife whose healing practice is well documented. Davenport tended the citizens of New Haven whenever they were sick but was especially active during epidemics. Other ministers' wives, such as the wife of Boston minister John Cotton, practiced in much the same way. The presence of the minister's wife at a sickbed reminded parishioners that the minister was looking out for their welfare—and bolstered the minister's position within the community.[12]

Alternatives to Mainstream Christianity

There were some alternative voices within Christian culture. Early on, some practitioners combined religious ritual with folk magic. As the Colonial period wore on, Christian sects proliferated, and they often brought a different view of healing as well as a different view of theology.

Early English settlers included a number of folk magic practitioners known as "cunning folk." Cunning folk offered a number of services in addition to healing, fortune telling and the finding of lost objects among them. Much of the cunning folk's magic had a religious or Christian element to it. For instance, one cunning man's cure for toothache involved writing out "In Nomine Patris, Filii, et Spiritus Sancti ["In the name of the Father, Son, and Holy Spirit"]" on a piece of paper and having the patient wear the paper in a charm around the neck. Another cunning man cured fevers by inscribing letters on pieces of bread and having the patient eat one piece a day until he or she recovered. This "spell" recalled the use of bread in the Christian ritual of communion.[13]

Clergy universally opposed the practices of cunning folk and condemned them from the pulpit. Most ministers saw this sort of practice as magic and believed all magic was a tool of the devil. However, most laypeople used healing magic and still thought of themselves as good Christians. Magic and prayer were two different ways of invoking supernatural powers, and most ordinary people did not see any conflict, especially if the charms and spells they used had Christian elements. As time passed, the cunning folk scattered or went underground, although healing charms and spells persevered as part of folklore through the nineteenth and early twentieth centuries.

In the eighteenth century, the number of Protestant sects increased. Some of these sects moved away from the harsh theology that had dominated earlier periods and advocated a different attitude toward healing. One sect from the late eighteenth century, the Shakers, demonstrated some important differences from what had come before.

The Shakers were founded in America by "Mother" Ann Lee, who emigrated from England in 1774. Shakers lived in closed, celibate communities. They dedicated themselves to living "simply," holding property in common, rejecting marriage, and striving toward spiritual perfection. Lee was an extremely charismatic leader and attracted thousands to her sect during the late eighteenth century.

While the Shakers used medicines and physicians, they also practiced faith healing. Ann Lee herself was a faith healer. In 1783, she cured a young convert of a cough by administering wine and water, and laying on hands. Lee's brother William acquired a reputation for healing through prayer alone. Sarah Kendall, suffering from "violent vomiting," described William Lee's technique:

> Oh he spoke with such power of God one would think the heavens and earth were coming together. Thus he spoke for about 10 minutes; you cannot imagine the power of his word. His gift was the power of eternal life to my soul and healed my body at that time.

Other Shakers took up the faith healing tradition. One Shaker elder healed a fellow believer's broken ankle through the laying on of hands. Shakers believed that such miracles were "evidences of ... divine work."[14]

While faith healing was important to the Shakers, it was not the only kind of healing they practiced. Shaker communities set up infirmaries to care for sick members, staffed by members who felt a call to be nurses. One infirmary, in Alfred, Maine, received patients from surrounding Shaker communities for special care. The nursing members cared for patients, prepared medicines, and even performed surgery. By 1821, some Shakers had prohibited seeking care from a "world's doctor" and employed only Shaker practitioners.[15]

The Shakers' practice of faith-based medicine hinted at future developments. Their faith in God's power to heal contrasted strongly with the previous generation's emphasis on sickness as God's punishment. As the nineteenth century went on, many new Christian sects developed their own philosophy and theology of healing. The Shakers' use of faith healing and rejection of non-Shaker physicians foreshadowed such sects as Christian Science, which rejected physicians and medical practice altogether.

NATIVE AMERICAN PRACTICES

Unlike Christians, the Native Americans who followed their traditional religions saw no distinction between body and spirit. With the exception of injuries and childbirth, bodily maladies were always a manifestation of spiritual malaise, and vice versa. It was impossible to heal the body without also healing the soul. Medical practitioners were spiritual practitioners as well. There was no difference among the priest, the magical practitioner, and the physician.

The Shaman or "Medicine Man"

For most Native Americans, the ability to heal was an expression of spiritual power. The concept European observers translated as "medicine" referred to all sorts of supernatural abilities. Thus, for Native Americans, the practice of medicine included "clairvoyance, ecstasism, spiritism, divination, demonology, prophesy." The "medicine man" is not just a healer but "the diviner, the rain-maker, the prophet, the priest." It should come as no surprise that many Native American political and military leaders were also medicine men. The wielding of spiritual or divine power had many cultural manifestations.[16]

There were several different kinds of healing shamans. The Ojibwa people recognized four kinds of practitioners: members of the elite Midewiwin society, the highest ranking priesthood; the Wabenos, who specialized in magic for success in hunting, courtship, and healing; Jessakid, who were primarily diviners; and the herbalists, who used medicinal plants as well as magic to drive out the demons that caused illness. Other peoples, such as the Zuni, had as many as 13 types of shamans. While not all tribes had such specialized practitioners, these categories indicate the wide variety of religious and medical services shamans provided.

Many shamans had a set of personal equipment that they used to call the spirits and direct their power. One of the most common tools was the "medicine bundle" used in many cultures, including the Miami and the Potawatomis. A typical medicine bundle was made of animal skin, often the skin of a shaman's totemic animal. It contained small objects of personal significance, which could be animal parts (such as deer tails), stones, or dried plants. The bundle "contained" and channeled the user's personal power and could be used in any kind of ritual. Sometimes shamans made charms or bundles for their patients as well.

A wide variety of artifacts were used in healing rituals. Some shamans wore special robes or masks. Some cultures used "medicine sticks" to direct power or spirits toward the afflicted body part; others used objects such as snake fangs to make ritual cuts in a patient's body as well as direct the power of the snake spirit to heal. Shamans also carried such mundane tools as mortars and pestles for grinding herbs and syringes for therapeutic enemas.

Healing Rituals

Healing rituals themselves centered on driving away the malevolent powers that caused illness, invoking helpful powers, or calling back the patient's wandering soul. Most ceremonies involved physical manipulations of the patient as well as some sort of invocation of spirits or deities. Physical manipulations could include hot or cold baths, herbal medicines, massage, or "smudging" with smoke. However, most peoples believed that these methods would not work without the blessing or intervention of supernatural powers.

The details of healing rituals varied by culture. The Winnebagos of the Great Lakes region scattered tobacco, feathers, or other sacred substances while reciting prayers to drive away the spirit of disease. Tobacco was used in the rituals of many cultures. The Seminoles believed that tobacco could ward off harmful spirits of all kinds, including those who caused illness. Singing, chanting, and drumming was another common element, so common that one historian commented that it "seems to be universal." Use of music in Native American healing rituals was documented by some of the earliest English settlers. One Jamestown chronicler wrote: "To cure the sick, a man with a Rattle and extreame . . . showting, singing . . . will sucke out blood and flegme from the patient." The singing and drumming added an element of the sacred to the otherwise mundane actions of the shaman.[17]

The use of medicinal herbs would seem at first glance to have no religious element. However, as was the case with all Native American medicine, drugs used on the body were imbued with spiritual or magical significance. One French missionary described the process among the Miamis. The entire village would gather, and the shaman "declares he is going to provide good store, the virtue of healing of all sorts of wounds, and even restoring the dead to life. He falls immediately to singing." Through this ritual, "the medicinal quality is communicated to the plants." In other cases, the physical action of the plants was given a supernatural significance. Many herbs used by Native Americans were strong emetics or purges; those who used them, such as the Ojibwa, believed that such medicines were as unpleasant to disease-causing spirits as they were to the patient. Using them would literally drive the illness from the patient's body.[18]

Many outside observers were surprised to see how much comfort the rituals brought the patients, and how effective they were at easing pain and improving symptoms. However, as is the case with all religious rituals, the positive effect of community involvement and personal religious belief cannot be discounted. As one historian has commented: "The strong connection between these rites and the whole religious and tradition of the tribe produce certain . . . advantages for the medicine man which the modern physician lacks."[19]

AFRICAN AMERICAN RELIGION AND HEALING

Religion among African Americans was complex. Most enslaved Africans brought their own religious traditions with them to the Americas. However, slave owners actively discouraged such practices, and African religions went underground. As a result, while African religions did not entirely die out, they changed considerably. The Africans who adopted Christianity incorporated many of their older traditions into the new religion. All of these cultural adaptations had an effect on the relationship between healing and religion in African American culture.

There is little documentation for African American religious practices during the earliest days of the Colonial period. Therefore, many of the following examples come from nineteenth-century sources. However, from the reactions of the slaveholders, it seems that the practices were common from the beginning of slavery in the Americas. Many early plantation owners in the West Indies spoke with fear and contempt of the "obeah" among the slaves. As late as the immediate antebellum period, slaveholders on the North American continent complained of the "superstitions" of slaves and the dangers of "conjurers." From this evidence, it seems reasonable to infer that African religions and traditions were widely practiced during the early period and maintained their existence for many years.

African Religions and Healing

Like Native American religions, those of Africans regarded healing as a spiritual practice. Gods and spirits could cause illness or cure it; a person's spiritual state had a direct influence his or her health. Most "physicians" were also shamans, diviners, or magicians, even if they also used physical means to help the patient.

Most West African religions did not divide deities into powers for good and powers for evil. Most spirits had the ability both to cause harm and provide blessings, and to create and destroy. Similarly, most medicines could both cause and cure illness. As one African scholar put it at the turn of the twentieth century, deities and the medicines they ruled could "cause sickness in a man and also to remove it. To destroy, to kill, to benefit . . . to look after their owners and to visit retribution upon them." By extension, any effective healer was also an effective poisoner and witch. The power to heal could not exist without the equivalent power to cause harm.[20]

The healing shamans, called conjurers, obeah, root doctors, or hoo-doos (as well as other names) among African Americans, were thus objects of fear as well as respect and admiration. As one former slave put it, "I wouldn't trust dem sort of folks cause if dey can cyore you dey can kill you too."[21] A shaman's "Left-handed work" would cause illness, but "right-handed work" would remove curses and cure dis-ease. Often the first step in curing an illness was finding the person who had cast the spell that caused it. As a result, a successful conjure doctor had to have not just medico-religious skills, but a good under-standing of social networks, friendships, and enmities in his or her community.[22]

Like Native American shamans, African American practitioners had special tools that helped them channel their power and which marked them as a conjure doctor. Conjure doctors used special power bundles filled with charms, herbs, and other magical materials. Many carried a crooked cane, which acted as both a badge of office and as a "medicine stick." Some conjurers filed their teeth to sharp points, or had ritual tat-toos or scars.

Conjure doctors used both magic and physical means to enact cures. They often made charms and amulets to ward off evil spirits. Such charms could both prevent and cure disease. These methods were com-bined with prayers and other invocations of the deities. Many conjurers healed by touch, in a similar fashion to Christian faith healers. In addi-tion, these practitioners used enemas, emetics, and fasting to "purify" the blood and drive illness from the body.

Most West African deities could play some role in healing. For exam-ple, the pantheon of the Yoruba people (many of whom were enslaved and sold to the Americas) included the following gods and goddesses, each of whom had dominion over specific diseases, body parts, and medicinal plants. Osanyin was the "god of the leaves" and thus especially important in medicine since he imbued medicinal herbs with their power to heal. Oshum, goddess of beauty, had dominion over sweet smelling plants and medicinal baths. Babalu-Aye, often portrayed as disfigured, governed smallpox and skin diseases. His great healing powers earned him the name "doctor of the poor." Yemaya, goddess of the ocean, was associated with intestinal complaints and tuberculosis. Even the trickster god, Ellegua, had a role in healing. As the god of doorways and crossroads, he had the power to "open the door" to good health. Conversely, his impulsive and spiteful nature made him likely to afflict those who offended him with illness; thus, those who were sick were well advised to cultivate his good will. Medicinal plants associated with Ellegua reflected his character: they often had nasty thorns as well as healing powers.[23]

In the Americas, followers of these deities often had to hide their practice behind a Christian façade. Enslaved Yoruba who worked in Catholic colonies associated each deity with a Catholic saint. Babalu-Aye became St. Lazurus, for instance, and those who wished to propitiate him could openly pray at a St. Lazarus shrine or make an offering there.[24] Even for those who did not have such an easy way to disguise their faith, the practice of African religion went on.

African American Christianity and Healing

Christianity also had a strong influence on African American beliefs about medicine and healing. Many enslaved people practiced Christianity and African traditions simultaneously, while others turned away from the conjure doctors completely. Nonetheless, African concepts of divine power and spirituality continued to influence African American religious culture.

One Protestant concept that meshed well with African ideas was the belief that God sends illness as a punishment. African deities often sent illness to the mortals who offended them. During a nineteenth-century Virginia smallpox epidemic, slaves noted that the "cruelest" whites were most likely to die, while "not a single slave" came down with the disease. This phenomenon was interpreted as divine justice for the mistreatment many had received: God "made up his mind to punish the white folks."[25]

More often, Christian African Americans looked to God for healing rather than vengeance. Many African American folk healers credited the Christian God for successful cures. One healer described herself as "an instrument in God's hand." Many hymns emphasized God's healing power as well: "He kin cure/Glory Hallelujah/Doctor Jesus, hallelujah." Both of these attitudes mesh with African traditions of religious healing, in which the deities "call" some mortals to be healers, and in which healing is accomplished only with the intervention of the gods.[26]

Both Christianity and traditional African religions came together to create a unique African American healing culture. All healing in African American communities had what one historian has called "a sacred basis." Religion, whether Christianity or some other faith, was an integral part of the understanding of disease and medicine.[27]

WITCHCRAFT AND DEMONIC POSSESSION

All three cultures in early America believed that supernatural forces could cause disease. Sometimes these forces were directed by a malevolent human being—a witch or sorcerer—and other times a demon or evil spirit could act on its own. In Native American and African American cultures, almost any disease could be of supernatural origin; while in Anglo-American culture diseases caused by demonic possession or witchcraft had more specific symptoms.

Witchcraft and Possession Native American Cultures

Supernatural attack by malevolent and angry spirits was a common diagnosis among Native Americans. In most cases, these spirits acted without the direction of human sorcerers; however, they could be offended or provoked by human action. For instance, a hunter who did not adequately propitiate the spirit of a hunted animal might find himself attacked by the spirit of that animal. In some cultures, such as the Creek, all diseases were thought to be caused by animal spirits. The Creeks named diseases for the animal spirits thought to cause them.[28]

Human ghosts could also cause illness. Among the Inuit, the spirits of the dead were believed to linger around the houses of their relatives for several months. All food and drink had to be covered so that the living did not accidentally ingest the ghost; to do so was inevitably fatal. The Alabama believed it was dangerous to linger too near a grave for similar reasons. In other cultures, only certain kinds of ghosts could cause illness, such as the spirits of tortured war captives. Ghosts could also cause illness indirectly by luring away the souls of the living.[29]

A spell cast by a malevolent sorcerer or evil shaman was another possible cause of disease. A sorcerer or witch could send a disease spirit into a victim through magic. The Iroquois believed that witches were themselves possessed by evil spirits who used the witch's body to do

their will. Other cultures proposed a more active role for the witch or
sorcerer. Epidemic disease, in particular, was commonly believed to
result from witchcraft. Jesuit missionaries in New France were often
suspected of being sorcerers when epidemics followed their arrival; as
a result, some were attacked and killed. The Zuni of what is now
Arizona had similar beliefs. Persistent illness in an individual or sudden epidemics in communities were signs of witchcraft. As is the case
in many cultures around the world, the solution was to kill or exile
the witch.

Shamans played a role in curing illness caused by witchcraft or
demonic possession. Shamans used their skills to dislodge the afflicting
spirit from the body part it had infested. Sometimes the evil spirit took
a physical form. Shamans in many Native American cultures performed rituals in which they appeared to remove a small animal or
object from the patient. The invader could take many forms but was
often in the shape of a lizard, snake, or worm. Inanimate objects such
as pebbles or twigs could also enter the body through supernatural
means. Shamans used special tools such as hollow tubes of bone to
remove the objects; in other cultures, they used their mouths.

Native Americans were not unique in their conviction that supernatu-
rally inserted objects could cause illness. It was a common belief among
Africans and African Americans as well. In addition, there are some
records of European Americans sharing the same idea. One man visited
a healing spring in Pennsylvania to cure a chronic illness; after drinking
from the spring, he "discharged from his bowels a living monster,
described by some who saw it as a lizard, by others as a crab, with legs,
claws, etc., and of considerable size." It may be that cultural exchange
among the peoples of colonial America led to this shared belief.[30]

Witchcraft in African American Culture

In African American culture, if an illness did not respond quickly to
treatment, it was likely to have been caused by magic. Some of the hall-
marks of diseases caused by "conjuring" or "tricks" were chronic pain,
mysterious lumps or swellings, paralysis, and wasting away. Mental
illness could also be caused by hoodoo. Sometimes patients had a sudden realization that their complaints were caused by a conjurer's spell:
"I went home and I knew I was conjured," said one man who was
afflicted by sudden pain in his legs and head.[31]

Those who thought they had been conjured could often identify the
moment and the means. One method for cursing involved leaving an
object in a place where the victim would step over it or near it—under

a doorstep or on a frequently used path. When the victim passed by, the magic would take effect. One woman remembered walking past a discarded bottle: "Right den and deah I took sech a misery in muh lef side an den uh swell up al obuh." Sometimes an object was not necessary. The conjurer only needed to touch a spot on the ground where the victim walked.[32]

As is often the case with witchcraft, the victim often had an argument or other conflict with the conjurer shortly before the spell was cast. A story collected in the nineteenth century related the tension that arose when one housekeeper was replaced by another. The new housekeeper soon drank from a mysterious bottle left in the kitchen and fell sick. Despite the efforts of a white physician, the housekeeper did not recover until another conjurer lifted the spell. In another story, a group of children who tormented a disabled man all lost the ability to walk. Most common were situations in which young women rejected the advances of older men. In one case, a man tried to court a woman by helping her hoe the garden. She turned him down: "When that gal went back ter the field the minute she touches that hoe she fell dead."[33]

One symptom of conjure illness that distinguished it from others was the presence of animals or objects under the skin of the patient. If not removed by another conjure practitioner, the animals would remain until the patient died. Usually the procedure involved lancing or poulticing the patient: "He come and put a plaster on her. It draw to a head and it bust after a week or two. A lizard came out after it bust." Other ways of driving out the spell included special broths or purges to dissolve the invaders from the inside out.[34]

Witchcraft and Demonic Possession in Anglo-American Culture

Like African Americans and Native Americans, English settlers believed that some illnesses and deaths were the result of malevolent supernatural forces. Witches could cause disease in human beings and animals. Demons could invade human bodies and cause similar symptoms. Cures included prayer, folk magic, and criminal proceedings against the witch.

Witches, in Anglo-American belief, were most likely to be quarrelsome middle-aged women (although men were also accused). Witches gave their souls to the devil in exchange for the power to harm their enemies with magic. Thus, any misfortune that took place after a conflict with a neighbor might be the result of witchcraft.

Anglo-American witches chose the most vulnerable as their victims. Children and women in childbirth were most likely to be attacked by a witch. One of the most tragic examples of a death "caused" by witchcraft took place in Hartford, Connecticut, in 1661. Eight-year-old Elizabeth Kelly developed a stomachache one Sunday afternoon after sharing some soup with a neighbor woman, Goodwife Ayres. Elizabeth's parents tried some herbal remedies, but her pain only worsened. In the middle of the night, Elizabeth began screaming: "Goodwife Ayres is upon me she chokes me, she will break my bowels, she pinches me, she will make me black and blue." Elizabeth suffered for two more days before she finally died. Her last words were "Goodwife Ayres chokes me." The Kellys initiated criminal proceedings against Ayres, but Ayres fled Hartford for New York and was never prosecuted.[35]

The Kelly case is unusual, however. In most cases, victims of witchcraft suffered terrible symptoms but did not die. The most famous example of the signs of bewitchment is the symptoms of the "afflicted children" of the Salem witch trials of 1692. They contorted their bodies into "odd postures," lost the ability to speak or spoke only in gibberish; and they fell into convulsions or "fits." The local physician, William Griggs, examined them and found no natural cause. Eventually, the children recovered their ability to speak. When they did, they began having visions of local women pinching, biting, and strangling them, much as Elizabeth Kelly did 30 years earlier.[36]

If the victim could not identify the tormentor, there were other ways of identifying the witch. One of the most common was the "touch test," used during the Salem trials. A suspect was forced to touch the victim; if the touch alleviated the symptoms, the suspect was guilty. Other methods for finding a witch were more elaborate. When a young man named Michael Smith fell ill with suspicious symptoms, some of his neighbors collected some of his urine, placed it in a bottle, and sealed the bottle with a cork. A woman named Mary Hale, who had recently quarreled with Smith, arrived at Smith's house and did not leave until the bottle was uncorked and the urine discarded. To those who had conducted the "experiment," this event confirmed the suspicion that Hale had bewitched Smith.[37]

Once the witch was identified, the patient could be cured. Arresting the witch seemed to put a stop to a victim's symptoms. If that was not possible, a cunning man or woman could offer other methods. The victim's urine was placed in a pot along with "crooked pins" and placed on the fire. When the urine came to a boil, it would "give Punishment to the wicked . . . contriver of this . . . affliction," and force the witch to withdraw the spell.[38]

Sometimes demons could afflict a person without a witch's participation. Young women and children were most likely to be affected. The symptoms of demonic possession were similar to those of bewitchment: convulsions, distorted speech, odd body postures, and the sensation of being strangled. Some victims also experienced mysterious pain: "She cried out oh my legs! And clapped her hands on them, [then] immediately, oh my breast!" Unlike victims of bewitchment, however, victims of possession did not have visions of the witch who tormented them. Instead, they spoke in the voice of the demon itself. The voice might be inarticulate, and "roar" or "scream"; at other times, the possessed person might make animal noises, such as barking like a dog. When the possession was at its height, the demon would speak clearly through the body of the victim, often to insult the others in the room: "Oh! You are a great rogue!" one "demon" said to a minister who was praying with the victim. Observers noted that when the demon spoke, the victim's tongue and mouth did not move, and the voice "was hollow, as if it issued out of her throat."[39]

If observers suspected that a person was possessed, the first step was to rule out natural causes. Sometimes epilepsy and mental illness were confused with possession. If purging, bleeding, and other remedies did not work, the next step was to cast out the demon. Protestant New England did not have a formal rite of exorcism. Instead, a minister would pray with the victim and encourage her (most victims were female) to search her soul for sinfulness. Secret sins and an "obstinate heart" were thought to give demons entrée into a person's body and soul. Once the victim had thoroughly repented and pledged to reform, the demon would no longer have a foothold in the person's body.

Supernatural factors were an important part of Colonial America's views of health and healing. Whether caused by sin, a conjurer, or an offended spirit, illness almost always had a religious as well as a physical cause. Clergy and physicians were thus equally important in curing disease.

NOTES

1. Patricia A. Watson, *The Angelical Conjunction: The Preacher-Physicians of Colonial New England*. Knoxville: University of Tennessee Press, 1991, p. 10.

2. Cotton Mather, *The Angel of Bethesda: An Essay on the Common Maladies of Mankind*, edited by Gordon W. Jones. Barre, MA: American Antiquarian Society, 1972, pp. 5–6.

3. Quoted in David D. Hall, *Worlds of Wonder, Days of Judgment: Popular Religious Belief in Early New England*. Cambridge, MA: Harvard University Press, 1989, pp. 100–101.

4. Mather, *Angel of Bethesda*, pp. 118, 121.

5. Quoted in Hall, *Worlds of Wonder*, p. 199.

6. Ibid., p. 199.

7. Quoted in Watson, *The Angelical Conjunction*, pp. 14, 15.

8. David Dary, *Frontier Medicine: From the Atlantic to the Pacific: 1492–1941*. New York: Alfred A. Knopf, 2008, p. 15.

9. Dary, *Frontier Medicine*, p. 14.

10. Quoted in Watson, *The Angelical Conjunction*, p. 29.

11. Ibid., pp. 57–58.

12. Rebecca J. Tannenbaum, *The Healer's Calling: Women and Medicine in Early New England*. Ithaca, NY: Cornell University Press, 2002, pp. 71–84.

13. Quoted in Richard Godbeer, *The Devil's Dominion: Magic and Religion in Early New England*. New York: Cambridge University Press, 1992, p. 41.

14. David Richards, "Medicine and Healing among the Maine Shakers: 1784–1854." In Peter Benes (Ed.), *Medicine and Healing: The Dublin Seminar for New England Folklife Annual Proceedings: 1990*. Boston: Boston University Press, 1992, p. 143.

15. Margaret Moody Stier, "Blood, Sweat, and Herbs: Health and Medicine at the Harvard Shaker Community: 1820–1855." In Peter Benes (Ed.), *Medicine and Healing: The Dublin Seminar for New England Folklife Annual Proceedings*. Boston: Boston University Press, 1992, p. 158.

16. Virgil J. Vogel, *American Indian Medicine*. Norman: University of Oklahoma Press, 1970, p. 26.

17. Vogel, *American Indian Medicine*, p. 32.

18. Ibid., pp. 31–32.

19. Ibid., p. 34.

20. Quoted in Sharla M. Fett, *Working Cures: Healing, Health and Power on Southern Slave Plantations*. Chapel Hill: University of North Carolina Press, 2002, p. 41.

21. Quoted in Fett, *Working Cures*, p. 41.

22. Herbert C. Covey, *African American Slave Medicine: Herbal and Non-Herbal Treatments*. New York: Lexington Books, 2007, p. 58.

23. Robert Voeks, "African Medicine and Magic in the Americas," *Geographical Review*, 83 (January 1993), pp. 71–72.

24. Ibid.

25. Quoted in Fett, *Working Cures*, p. 40.

26. Ibid., p. 54.

27. Ibid.

28. Vogel, *American Indian Medicine*, pp. 14–16.

29. Ibid., pp. 18–19.

30. Ibid., p. 17.

31. Quoted in Fett, *Working Cures*, p. 93.

32. Ibid., p. 93.

33. Ibid., p. 91.

34. Quoted in Covey, *African American Slave Medicine*, p. 63.

35. "The Kellys Describe Their Daughter's Fatal Illness." In David D. Hall, *Witch-Hunting in Seventeenth-Century New England: A Documentary History: 1638–1692*. Boston: Northeastern University Press, 1991, pp. 152–153.

36. Paul Boyer and Stephen Nissenbaum, *Salem Possessed: The Social Origins of Witchcraft*. Cambridge, MA: Harvard University Press, 1974, pp. 2–3.

37. Godbeer, *The Devil's Dominion*, pp. 7–8.

38. Ibid., p. 45.

39. "A Servant Possessed." In Hall, *Witch-Hunting*, p. 208.

CHAPTER 4

Women's Health

Women's health in Colonial America was understood to focus on sexuality and reproduction. In Euro-American cultures, a woman's social role was defined by her status as a wife and mother. Women's experience of their bodies and health followed this model as well. A married woman in the seventeenth century could spend as much as two thirds of her reproductive years either pregnant or breastfeeding a child.

If asked for her greatest health-related fear, a white Colonial woman might well have answered "childbirth." Women and men thought of childbirth as a terrifying ordeal. Women preparing to give birth made clothes for the baby and washed and ironed their special "childbirth linen"; at the same time, they set aside lengths of cloth for their own shrouds. Maternal mortality was high enough to make these fears legitimate, and religious ideas confirmed that women's suffering was God's punishment for the sin of Eve.

Scientific and popular ideas about the female body followed these lines. Female bodies were "colder," "moister," and "less perfect" than male bodies. A woman's cold, moist nature also defined her sexuality—she craved the "heat" of the male body and thus was more "lustful" than a man.

African American and Native American women shared the biological experiences of sexuality, pregnancy, and childbirth with their European counterparts. There were many commonalities in their experiences. For instance, all cultures called on women to attend other women in childbirth, and all used similar techniques to deal with the problems that sometimes arose. Cultural differences, however, ensured that women understood their bodily functions somewhat differently. Enslaved African women feared not just childbirth but the intervention of the master; Native American women saw birth as a test of their courage.

BELIEFS ABOUT WOMEN'S BODIES: MENSTRUATION, SEXUALITY, AND CONCEPTION

A popular early American medical guide stated that "women are but men turn'd outside in."[1] This quotation illustrates two basic beliefs about sexual differences among Euro-Americans. First, that women and men's bodies were essentially the same. Each reproductive organ had its counterpart in the opposite sex. Medical experts and laypeople alike believed that the vagina and ovaries were internal versions of the penis and testicles. Men and women were more alike than different when it came to anatomy.

The second belief was that, despite these similarities, women's bodies were weaker, more prone to disease, and generally inferior to men's. Female bodies lacked the essential "heat" to grow their genitalia externally. As a result, their bodies were imperfect versions of the ideal (male) human body. These beliefs reflected and confirmed the general notion that women were designed by God to be subordinate to men.

Another belief that related to ideas about anatomy was the idea that women needed sex for their health and well-being. Women were widely believed to desire sex more than men did and to have less control over their sexual desires. Women who remained celibate were subject to "strange diseases," including hysteria (long thought to be a disease of the womb) and a malady called "green sickness" in which the face turned greenish, the arms and legs swelled, and the patient experienced heart palpitations. The cure for these diseases, naturally, was marriage. Marriage (and regular sexual activity) would add needed "heat" to a woman's cold nature and help keep her system in healthy balance.

Sex (and pregnancy) was also "good" for women's health because it prevented the build-up of menstrual blood in her body. People of the time understood menstruation to be the purging of excess blood from a woman's body. Women's "cold" bodies could not transform this excess blood into other bodily material, and it thus needed to be expelled, or, as was preferable, used to form or nourish a fetus.

Colonial era people also recognized a disease called "suppressed" or "obstructed" menses in which the blood was retained within the body. Suppressed menses could make a woman very sick if it was not treated.

We do not know for sure how Anglo-American women dealt with menstrual disorders such as cramps or bloating. Somewhat surprisingly, remedies for such discomforts are rarely mentioned in the recipe books of Colonial era women, and never in the records of male physicians. It is likely that Colonial era women did not menstruate as often as women of later times. Once an Anglo-American woman was married, she would be pregnant or breastfeeding so often that years could go by between menstrual periods.

Among Native Americans, many tribes observed some sort of isolation for menstruating women. Women of the peoples of modern North Carolina, for instance, lived in a separate house during their periods and prepared their food separately from the rest of the village. European observers noted that Native American women used a variety of herbs for menstrual discomforts. The Rappahannock people of Virginia used pennyroyal and spicebush tea for menstrual pain.

Seventeenth- and eighteenth-century knowledge of the process of conception was primitive even among the most elite scientists. Experts debated whether the man provided the vital seed and the womb was merely a field in which it would grow, or whether men and women both contributed to the physical makeup of a fetus. *Aristotle's Masterpiece*, a popular medical and sex education book, leaned toward the second explanation. Men and women each made their own contribution of "seed," which mixed together with menstrual blood in the womb to form the fetus. Men also contributed the physiological "heat" that allowed this process to take place.

While pregnancy within marriage was valued, there is some evidence that Colonial era peoples practiced some forms of birth control, at least to space births apart. The most common method was probably extended breastfeeding, a technique used by Native Americans and African Americans as well as European settlers. Anglo-American women nursed their babies for one to two years; among most Native American peoples, breastfeeding lasted three or four years and as long as five or six in some cultures. Breastfeeding suppresses ovulation and thus has a contraceptive effect. Passages from eighteenth-century diaries suggest that women knew that nursing prevented pregnancy. Philadelphia matron Elizabeth Drinker comforted her daughter after a difficult birth by saying that "she was now in her 39th year, and that this might possibly be the last trial of this sort, if she could suckle her baby for 2 years to come as she had several times done heretofore etc."[2]

There were other techniques available in addition to extended breast-feeding, including male withdrawal, herbal remedies, and condoms. All of these contraceptives were associated with illicit sex—condoms, for instance, were most often used by urban "rakes" when visiting prostitutes and were usually intended to prevent venereal disease rather than pregnancy. However, there is some evidence that married couples used some form of birth control. In eighteenth-century Philadelphia, for instance, the number of children per couple was well below what might be expected from "natural" fertility, and the fertility rate continued to decline through the first half of the nine-teenth century. While we cannot know what technique was used, we can assume that Philadelphia couples were using some form of contraception.[3]

Birth rates among Native American peoples were consistently lower than among European Americans. Early twentieth-century anthropologists have documented numerous contraceptive practices among Native American peoples in addition to extended breastfeeding. Many cultures had taboos against intercourse at certain times. Others, including the Cherokee, Comanche, and Nevada peoples, used roots and herbs that later investigation showed to inhibit ovulation. Other wild plants "regulated menstruation" but may also have induced mis-carriage early in pregnancy. While this data was collected in the twen-tieth century, it seems likely that the remedies had a long history behind them. These remedies, or ones very like them, were probably in use during the Colonial period.

PREGNANCY

Early pregnancy was an ambiguous state. Colonial people knew that menstruation ceased when a woman became pregnant, and they knew that pregnancy lasted nine months. However, in a time long before sci-entifically accurate pregnancy tests, there was no way to know if a woman was pregnant or whether her symptoms were the result of a different disorder, such as obstructed menses. The symptoms of obstructed menses were similar to those of early pregnancy: nausea, a swollen abdomen, and fatigue.

In Anglo-American culture, folklore and home medical guides pro-vided dubious tests for pregnancy. A woman might urinate on seed corn or other seeds, and if the seeds sprouted, she was pregnant; simi-larly, the urine of a pregnant woman left to sit in a bottle for a few days would spontaneously generate tiny animals. Another test was to exam-ine a particular vein in a woman's lower eyelid—this vein was said to swell when the woman was pregnant. However, when all was said and done, the only to way to confirm a pregnancy definitely was the presence of fetal movement, which is usually first noticed in the fourth or fifth month of gestation.

The ambiguity of early pregnancy allowed for a number of home remedies that may have produced abortions. One recipe from a family recipe book in Massachusetts is titled "To Cleanse the Womb." It contains a number of herbs that later researchers discovered could induce uterine contractions or miscarriage. However, when reading these recipes, it is clear that they were intended as remedies for obstructed menses, not abortifacients. Abortion before "quickening" or fetal movement was not illegal, but it was widely condemned as immoral. Most of the women who used these recipes probably did not think of them as inducing abortion, but menstruation. However, it is also possible (though not provable) that some of these remedies were passed on from woman to woman with a knowing look or a sly whisper.[4]

For women who carried their pregnancies to term, there was little of what we would call prenatal care. Euro-American women were pregnant so often—every two years, on average, from marriage to menopause—that pregnancy did not seem like an unusual state requiring special care. There were, however, a large number of medical beliefs and folk practices concerning pregnancy. Most centered on the idea that a woman's mental state and emotions could have an influence on a fetus's development. For instance, many believed that it was important for a pregnant woman to indulge her food cravings. Stories circulated that a woman who craved strawberries and did not get them gave birth to a baby with a large red birthmark. Similarly, sights that left a deep impression on a woman could change the appearance of her fetus. One of the most common cautionary tales concerned a woman who looked at a painting of John the Baptist wearing hairy animal skins; her daughter was born covered with coarse hair.

Enslaved African American women had an especially difficult time with pregnancy. Some masters allowed more food and reduced workloads for pregnant women, but many did not. Nor did pregnancy mean that the woman was immune from harsh physical punishments. Many women miscarried after being whipped or beaten.

Like white women, African American women had knowledge of herbs that would "regulate menstruation" or induce an abortion. As is often the case with the history of abortion, it is hard to tell who used these remedies or how often. However, slaveholders were deeply suspicious of any miscarriage and interrogated or punished women who failed to bring their pregnancies to term.

CHILDBIRTH

Pregnancies, of course, lead to childbirth. All cultures have a set of practices and rituals surrounding birth as well as specialized practitioners to assist the woman in labor. These practitioners had a variety of techniques to cope with protracted labor or a malpositioned fetus, ranging from herbal medicines to physical manipulation of the mother or infant.

Among Anglo-American women, childbirth was a dreaded ordeal. Most Christians of the time believed that a woman's suffering in labor was divinely ordained as punishment for Eve's role in original sin. Clergy reinforced this belief from the pulpit and in their writings. One New England minister wrote of pregnant women: "For you ought to know your death has entered into you."[5] With these cultural definitions echoing in their minds, it is no wonder that women feared giving birth.

These fears were not unfounded. About 20 percent of women died as a result of childbirth.[6] While birth is a normal biological process, many things can go wrong, and since most women gave birth 8 to 10 times in their lifetime, the chances that one of those births would end in disaster were high. During birth, the placenta can separate early and cause hemorrhage; if the fetus is in a position that prevents it from emerging, the mother can die of exhaustion or uterine rupture; or a woman may have seizures from pregnancy-induced high blood pressure (pre-eclampsia and eclampsia). However, even more deadly than these causes was postpartum infection, or "childbed fever." During birth, the open birth canal provides a pathway for bacteria to enter the body. The resulting infections progress rapidly to septic shock and death.

A good birth attendant was one that was skilled in preventing these catastrophes and (perhaps more importantly) reassuring the patient. In European American cultures, all births were attended by a midwife assisted by a group of female neighbors and relatives. The practice of "social childbirth" (as many historians call it) was so widespread that the phrase "she called her women together" was a common euphemism for giving birth. When a woman was sure she was in active labor, she would send for the midwife first, and then for her closest female relatives and neighbors. Men and young children were banished from the house or room where the birth took place.

The assembled women would help the expectant mother to walk around the room (believed to encourage labor). They often prepared food and drink for her, and performed other tasks to help make her as comfortable as possible. When the birth was imminent, the "helpers" supported the patient's back and legs while she pushed the baby out.

In uncomplicated births, the midwife's role was to "catch" the baby, cut the umbilical cord, and deliver the afterbirth.

If things took a turn for the worse, most midwives had techniques to correct the problem. Many midwives knew how to manipulate a mal-positioned fetus so that it could be born more easily. For instance, some midwives used a technique male physicians called podalic version, in which the birth assistant manipulates the fetus internally into a feet-first (breech) position, allowing the practitioner to pull on the infant's legs to help it emerge. If the woman began to bleed heavily after delivery, midwives packed the birth canal with linen bandages to stop the hemorrhage. They also knew recipes for herbal medicines that could stimulate uterine contractions, speed up a slow labor, or slow bleeding.

Only if labor were so obstructed that the mother, child, or both seemed likely to die would a midwife call a male physician. Unfortunately, there was little even a formally educated doctor could do. If it seemed that the mother had died but the infant might still be alive, a surgeon could perform a crude Cesarean section and at least save the baby. (In the days before anesthesia, good bleeding control, and sterile technique, abdominal surgery was a death warrant for the patient.) If the situation were reversed and the infant was dead or dying, a doctor might perform a gruesome procedure to save the mother, cutting up the fetus inside the woman's body and extracting it piece by piece.

Anglo-American midwives wielded social as well as medical authority. Women often approached midwives to mediate conflicts informally, without involving the courts. Midwives also had formal legal authority in some areas. If a baby was born out of wedlock, it was the duty of the midwife to question the mother about the father's identity. She then reported her findings to the authorities, who held the man she named liable for child support. Midwives also had the respect and affection of their patients. In cases where a midwife found herself in legal trouble, women signed petitions testifying to her good character.

By the late eighteenth century, however, physicians had begun to participate in normal births. For the most part, they attended the wealthy urban women who could afford their services. These patients felt that male doctors could provide services that the traditional midwife could not: pain relief, in the form of laudanum (an opiate), and the use of forceps to assist difficult deliveries.

Obstetrical forceps were in common use in Europe by the 1730s. Forceps are a tool shaped a bit like a pair of salad tongs. A doctor uses the forceps to grasp the baby high in the birth canal. The practitioner can then either ease the baby out or reposition it so that it can be born. Elite American physicians who had trained in European medical schools brought forceps back with them. Of these doctors, the most famous is William Shippen. Shippen learned his obstetrical techniques at the famous medical school in Edinburgh, Scotland, and made it his mission both to offer them to patients and instruct other American doctors in their use. The first reference to the use of forceps in the United States mentions Dr. Shippen. Elizabeth Drinker wrote in her diary that during the labor of her daughter Sally, "Dr. Shippen told me that he thought he should have occasion for instruments, which he said I have in my pocket, clapping his hand on his side, when I heard them rattle."[7]

Drinker and her daughter were members of one of Philadelphia's most prominent and wealthy families and thus were not typical. However, such families set the fashion for others. As time passed, and as doctors like Shippen trained their students in obstetrics, more women chose physicians for their deliveries. This change was not without controversy, however. Midwives defended their profession by calling on tradition, contrasting the gentleness of their hands with the "hands of iron" (or forceps) used by their competitors. They emphasized the gruesomeness of some obstetric procedures, such as the dismemberment of dead fetuses. Other supporters of midwives expressed concern that women's modesty would be compromised by having a male doctor in the birthing room. Physicians, for their part, derided midwives as unscientific and unsafe. Physicians stressed the safety that their new techniques could provide for mother and child.

For many years, midwives and physicians practiced in parallel. Women who could afford to do so called both a midwife and a physician when they were in labor. For the poor and those in isolated rural communities, midwives remained the only option. The process of replacing midwives with physicians for normal deliveries took many years of uneven change. The change began in the late colonial period, but was not complete until the early twentieth century.

If all went well, the new mother would "lie in" anywhere from a week to a month. Lying in meant just that—staying in bed and recovering from childbirth. The same relatives and neighbors who attended the birth would help the new mother with chores and help take care of her other children. Childbirth was not "officially" over until the new mother was "back in her kitchen" after the lying in period.

Among Native American peoples, women also were in charge of childbirth. However, there were fewer attendants—usually just a midwife or one female relative. One anthropologist documented practices among the peoples of what is now the southwestern United States. Women gave birth squatting or on their hands and knees, supported by their helpers. Sometimes they pulled on a rope or strap fastened to a tree or pole, a technique that helped them expel the baby more easily. Midwives of the Arikara people of the Great Plains used external manipulation to change an infant's position, rather than the internal techniques used by European midwives. Like Euro-American midwives, Native American midwives had a large herbal pharmacopeia. The root of a species of Trillium became known as "squaw root" or "papoose root" among Europeans because of its widespread use by Native American women to encourage slow labor.[8]

European observers were astonished by what they perceived as the unusual ease with which Native American women gave birth. They were shocked that indigenous women did not scream or moan during labor, and that they did not observe a period of lying in like European women. Some actually believed that indigenous women did not feel pain during labor. However, one French missionary noted that the women he observed felt it would be a "disgrace" to show pain or fear. Their cultures deemed it proper to remain stoic during childbirth and to return to daily activities quickly, just as the opposite was proper among Europeans.[9]

Childbirth was especially fraught for enslaved African American women. On the one hand, any child born to a slave would grow up to a lifetime of slavery; on the other hand, children were cherished and loved. Like their mistresses, enslaved women were attended by midwives. During the early Colonial period, the midwife was likely to be white. Slaveholders preferred to have male slaves on their land, and the sex ratio was so imbalanced that an African woman might be the only female of her race for miles. By the eighteenth century, the situation was more balanced. Large plantations were likely to have a woman who worked as a "granny" or midwife among her fellow slaves. The physical skills African American midwives had were similar to those of their Native American and European American counterparts: skill in delivering malpositioned babies, knowledge of medicinal plants to induce or hasten labor, and techniques for delivering the afterbirth.

Like other African American healers, a granny saw her job as both a spiritual and secular calling. Some felt "called" by spirits to their vocation, or had been identified by an omen or sign such as being a seventh child or a twin. For others, midwifery was a tradition passed down from mother to daughter and ran only in that family. Midwifery was not just a skill to be learned but a gift from the spirits. Granny midwives understood the important African traditions involved in handling the afterbirth or the amniotic sac. If these rituals were not performed properly, the baby or the mother would be in danger.

Slaveholders did their best to control the reproduction of their slaves. While midwives (white and black) attended most births, slaveholders reserved the right to call practitioners of their choice. Slave owners had an economic interest in the "increase" of their slaves, as well as in the health of the mother. They saw it as both duty and necessity to supervise all medical procedures performed on their human "property" and condemned many practices of African American midwives as "superstition" or "quackery." Some slaveholders tried to ban such practices. African American women, however, resented and feared this interference. Some women went so far as to give birth in secret to avoid it.

BREASTFEEDING AND BREAST HEALTH

Breastfeeding infants was a universal practice in the Colonial period. Women of all three cultures fed their babies this way unless there was no other choice. As a result, care of the breasts and medicines to increase the flow of breast milk were part of every woman's medical knowledge.

Despite the acknowledged importance of breast milk for infants, a European American baby was not put to its mother's breast immediately after birth. It usually takes two or three days after childbirth for the body to start producing milk. Until then, the breasts secrete a fluid called colostrum. Modern medicine has discovered that colostrum contains important vitamins, minerals, and antibodies. However, in the seventeenth and early eighteenth centuries, colostrum was thought to be an "unclean purgation" that would harm the infant. Breast milk itself was thought to be a "purified" form of the menstrual blood that had nourished the fetus in the womb. Colostrum was an intermediate product that had not been sufficiently processed, and was thus dangerous.[10]

Midwives had a variety of techniques to encourage a new mother's body to start producing "true" milk. Herbal remedies were the first choice, as usual—teas and extracts of hops or nettles, for instance. The use of hops was taken one step further by the common practice of having nursing mothers drink beer. Others recommended such humble remedies as eating a bowl of lentil soup or a cup of fish stock. Midwives were also known to massage their patients' breasts and nipples to stimulate flow. Some even suckled the woman's breasts themselves to draw out the colostrum. Another technique employed nursing puppies or kittens to perform this task. Since suckling does indeed encourage the body to make more milk, these methods were probably effective.

In the meantime, newborn infants were nursed by another woman, either a paid wet nurse or a relative or friend of the mother. The prominent Boston judge Samuel Sewell noted after the birth of one of his children in 1677: "The first Woman the Child sucked was Bridget Davenport," a family servant. Mrs. Sewall did not begin nursing her infant until five days after the birth.[11] If a wet nurse was unavailable, babies were given cow or goat milk dripped from a rag, sweetened wine, or, in some cases, nothing at all.

Extended wet nursing was frowned upon, however. It was common in Europe during this time for the nobility and other wealthy families to send their infants out to a wet nurse, where the baby would be cared for in the nurse's home. Often the child would stay with the nurse for a year or more and return home only after being weaned. However, this practice was not common in America and was frowned upon in many circles. In New England, Puritan ministers preached that maternal breastfeeding was God's will and cited Biblical precedents from Sarah (Abraham's wife) to Mary (Jesus' mother). Others pointed out that God had given every creature the means to feed its young. Denying an infant its own mother's milk would be denying God's providence. Finally, breastfeeding an infant was thought to be the ultimate expression of unselfish love. Some ministers went so far as to compare a nursing mother's love for her baby with the love of Christ for humankind. A woman who could not love her own child in this way was condemned as an unnatural and selfish mother.

Nursing women had many remedies for the problems that sometimes crop up during breastfeeding. The most common were cracked and sore nipples, which were treated with salves of herbs, beeswax, and honey. The worst potential problem was mastitis, or an infection of the breast. Bacteria from the baby's mouth can enter the breast and cause painful abscesses, sometimes accompanied by fever. Midwives used hot poultices to "draw" the infection out. In the worst cases, a surgeon could be called in to lance the abscess.

If an infection made it impossible for a woman to continue nursing, the options were limited. Infants who were "hand fed" on animal milk with bottles made of animal horn or pewter usually did not live long. Unmodified cow or goat milk does not contain the right balance of nutrients for a human infant, and unsterilized feeding bottles no doubt caused babies to sicken. The other option was to hire a wet nurse, but this was filled with its own dangers. It was believed that babies would acquire the characteristics of the women who nursed them. Thus, it was important that the wet nurse be a virtuous woman with no physical defects. The list of characteristics to avoid ranged from alcoholism to red hair. In addition, wet nurses were scrutinized for the "right" breast size and shape. Then there was the matter of the nurse's own infant. Since many believed that a woman's milk adapted itself to the infant, a nurse should suckle only a baby of the same age and sex as her biological child. The fear was that a woman who had given birth to a boy and then suckled a girl would pass on "masculine" characteristics to her charge, and vice versa. Finding a willing wet nurse who fulfilled all of these conditions was a difficult task for most families.

While the image of the slave wet nurse is a common one, it is not clear how common the practice actually was in the Colonial era. In the nineteenth century, antislavery activists used the image of black women nursing white women's children as an example of the ways in which slavery exploited women, destroyed black families, and made white women into "unnatural" mothers. Some interviews with former slaves, conducted in the early twentieth century, describe women on plantations who nursed the white children, and white southerners wrote nostalgic accounts of their black "mammies." There is not much direct evidence about the practice during the Colonial era. Indirect evidence suggests that the practice existed but was not common. Given the imbalanced sex ratio among Colonial era slaves (more men than women), there probably were not enough enslaved women available for the practice to be widespread. Furthermore, the belief that a wet nurse would pass her personality and physical characteristics to her charge might have discouraged whites from employing a racial "inferior" to nurse their children. If a white slaveholding woman was physically unable to nurse her infant, however, she might well have turned to the most readily available substitute—one of her own slaves.

As for the slaves themselves, they had no choice but to nurse their own children. Slave owners varied in the allowances they made for the health and well-being of nursing mothers. Some provided extra rations and reduced workloads for women with young infants, but others did not, or provided inadequate allowances. Women doing field work, for instance, might be allowed only two 15-minute breaks a day to feed their babies—not enough time for an infant to finish nursing. A woman's milk supply might dwindle without enough calories to support both heavy physical labor and the demands of an infant. In addition, breast infections and other problems are more common when breastfeeding is rushed or the infant is not given the opportunity to empty the breast at each feeding. As was the case with many other aspects of health, enslaved women lived under much worse conditions than other women of their time.

Tumors of the breast were treated surgically. Breast tumors were easily detected, and mastectomies were not as dangerous as abdominal or thoracic surgery, although, like all Colonial era surgeries, they were performed without anesthetic or sterile technique. Removal of a cancerous breast could give a patient months or even years of life. John and Abigail Adams's daughter Abigail Smith was diagnosed with breast cancer and underwent a mastectomy a year later. She survived the operation and lived two more years until the cancer returned. Other patients were luckier: Fanny Burney, an English woman who had her breast removed while living in France, survived for 30 years after the procedure.[12]

FERTILITY AND INFERTILITY

Childbearing was valued in all three American cultures. For white women, childbearing was a social duty and a potential road to religious redemption. Birth rates for Anglo-American women in particular were high. Although fertility rates were lower in both Native American and African American communities, children were valued and cherished in those cultures, and mothers were honored. However, childbearing also had profound effects on women's health.

Anglo-American women of childbearing age gave birth about every two years. A typical woman married in her late teens or early twenties, and she could expect to spend two thirds of her life from then until menopause either pregnant or nursing a baby. Childbearing and nurturing defined both her social role and her health. Pregnancy, childbirth, and nursing were a married woman's normal biological state.

Despite this normalcy, frequent childbearing could take a toll on a woman's health. Even if she survived her frequent deliveries, there was always the possibility of childbirth injury. Of these, the worst were what modern physicians call obstetrical fistulas. Fistulas are holes in the vaginal wall. They develop during prolonged labor, when the pressure of the baby's head cuts off circulation to a piece of tissue. The dead tissue sloughs away, leaving a channel between the bladder and vagina, or even worse, between the rectum and the vagina. Women with obstetrical fistulas are left permanently incontinent. While these injuries were the worst, there were others that could cause chronic pain or incontinence, such as a prolapsed (or fallen) uterus, pelvic nerve damage, or scar tissue from tears or lacerations.

Yet women's fertility was highly valued. The highest praise a woman could win was to be called "a fruitful vine," and to be a grandmother and great grandmother. While pain in childbirth was seen as just punishment for the sin of Eve, being the mother of many children was a road to redemption. Cotton Mather wrote that producing healthy children meant that the "Curse is turned into a blessing."[13] Ministers also quoted the Bible directly on this matter, especially the New Testament verse which states ""But women will be saved through childbearing—if they continue in faith, love, and holiness with propriety."[14] There was secular value in women's fertility as well. A large family was seen as the sign of a happy marriage, and the mother of many children was regarded as a virtuous woman.

As might be expected, infertility carried a stigma for women. A small or nonexistent family brought suspicion that the wife had somehow "unmanned" her husband. Another suspicion was that God was punishing her for some secret sin. Childlessness was thought to create resentment and bitterness in women, and women with no children were more likely to be accused of witchcraft. A common accusation in these circumstances was that the "witch" killed or sickened other women's children out of jealousy. Interestingly, a woman with fewer children than average was more likely to accuse others of witchcraft, perhaps because she felt she had to prove her own piety by accusing others of sin. Both of these statistics likely stem from the same cause: a woman who did not bear children was an imperfect woman in this culture.[15]

Women desperate to have children tried a variety of remedies to conceive. Some straddled the line between folk medicine and folk magic. For instance, one remedy for infertility was oil of mandrake root. Mandrakes had a long association with magic and witchcraft in Europe, where they were believed to grow under gallows where criminals had been hanged, and to shriek with a human voice when harvested. Part of the evidence against Massachusetts midwife Jane Hawkins at her heresy trial in 1638 was her use of mandrake for women who could not conceive.[16] Other remedies were less controversial. Many women wore lodestones (naturally magnetic rocks) around their necks to prevent miscarriage.

While children were valued and cherished in other early American cultures, there was not quite so much emphasis on frequent childbearing. In many Native American cultures, prolonged breastfeeding combined with common cultural taboos against intercourse during lactation ensured that women gave birth much less often. Less frequent births meant that Native American women were less vulnerable to childbirth injuries or perinatal death than Anglo-American women.

African American women valued their own reproductive capacity—and so did slave owners, for different reasons. In African cultures and the African American cultures that they influenced, children were desirable for the happiness and love that they brought to their parents. They were also bearers of the family name and traditions, a role that took on increased significance under slavery, where masters stripped slaves of their names and culture. Slaveholders, on the other hand, saw the children of their slaves as an important economic resource and slave reproduction as a way of increasing their wealth.

Enslaved women saw regular menstruation as key to fertility. There is evidence that women kept track of their periods by noting the phase of the moon. If menstruation became irregular, they used herbal medicines to remedy the problem. If the herb did not bring on a period at the proper time, the woman assumed she was pregnant.

African American women had fewer children, spaced farther apart, than white women. A study comparing the childbearing patterns of white and black women in Loudoun County Virginia between 1760 and 1820 found that while black women usually had their first child two to four years earlier than white women, they gave birth to about three fewer children over the course of their childbearing years (five as opposed to eight). In addition, black women had children at two-and-a-half-year intervals, instead of the two-year spacing of white women.[17]

There are several possible reasons why this might be so. Unlike European women, African American women believed that bearing children too close together was detrimental to the health of both mother and child. Like white women, African American women used breastfeeding as a contraceptive. African American women's lower fertility rate may also have stemmed from general poor health. Malnutrition, heavy work, intestinal parasites, and other chronic illnesses may have rendered many women infertile.

Women's health in the Colonial period was inexorably bound up with women's social role. At a time when a woman's crowning glory was to be the mother of many children, her physical health rested most on her fertility and ability to survive multiple childbirths. A woman who did so could take justified pride in her many descendants.

NOTES

1. Quoted in Vern Bullough, "An Early American Sex Manual or Aristotle Who?" *Early American Literature*, 7 (1973), p. 243.

2. Entry for October 23, 1799, in Elaine Forman Crane (Ed.), *The Diary of Elizabeth Drinker*, Vol. 2. Boston: Northeastern University Press, 1991, p. 1227.

3. Susan E. Klepp, "Lost, Hidden, Obstructed, and Repressed: Contraceptive and Abortive Technology in the Early Delaware Valley." In Judith A. McGaw

(Ed.), *Early American Technology: Making and Doing Things from the Colonial Era to 1850*. Chapel Hill: University of North Carolina Press, 1994, pp. 94–95.

4. "To Cleanse the Womb," *Charles Brigham Account Book*, Folder Four, American Antiquarian Society, Worcester, Massachusetts. (Despite its title, the *Charles Brigham Account Book* is a handwritten medicinal recipe book kept by the women of the Brigham family.)

5. Cotton Mather, *The Angel of Bethesda*, edited by Gordon W. Jones. Barre, MA: Barre Publishers, 1972, p. 237.

6. John Demos, *A Little Commonwealth: Family Life in Plymouth Colony*. New York: Oxford University Press, 1970, p. 131.

7. Entry for October 24, 1799, in Crane, *The Diary of Elizabeth Drinker*, p. 1228.

8. Virgil J. Vogel, *American Indian Medicine*. Norman: University of Oklahoma Press, 1970, pp. 234–235.

9. Quoted in Ann Marie Plane, "Childbirth Practices among Native American Women of New England and Canada: 1600–1800." In Peter Benes (Ed.), *Medicine and Healing: The Dublin Seminar for New England Folklife Annual Proceedings: 1990*. Boston: Boston University Press, 1992, p. 16.

10. Quoted in Paula A. Treckel, "Breastfeeding and Maternal Sexuality in Colonial America," *Journal of Interdisciplinary History*, 20:1 (Summer 1989), p. 27.

11. Entry for April 1, 1677, in M. Halsey Thomas (Ed.), *The Diary of Samuel Sewall: 1674–1729*, Vol. 1. New York: Farrar Strauss and Giroux, 1973, p. 41.

12. Marilyn Yalom, *A History of the Breast*. New York: Alfred A. Knopf, 1997, pp. 231–235. Yalom's text includes quotations from Fanny Burney's first-person account of her surgery.

13. Mather, *Angel of Bethesda*, p. 236.

14. I Timothy 2:14.

15. On the connections between infertility and witchcraft accusations, see John Demos, *Entertaining Satan: Witchcraft and the Culture of Early New England*. New York: Oxford University Press, 1982, pp. 72–73.

16. Carol F. Karlsen, *The Devil in the Shape of a Woman: Witchcraft in Colonial New England*. New York: Norton, 1987, p. 16.

17. Brenda E. Stevenson, *Life in Black and White: Family and Community in the Slave South*. New York: Oxford University Press, 1996, p. 246.

CHAPTER 5

Infants' and Children's Health

Childhood was a precarious time of life in Colonial America. Infant mortality ran from 25 percent among those of European descent to as high as 50 percent among African Americans; and even for those who survived their first year, up to 40 percent would die before reaching the age of 10. There were many causes for these statistics. Chief among them were infectious diseases such as diphtheria, scarlet fever, measles, and gastrointestinal infections. Children also died from accidents and injuries: open fireplaces, uncovered wells, and kettles of scalding water all contributed to child mortality.[1]

Colonial parents did their best to keep their children healthy and safe. Childrearing practices were designed to protect children from disease and shape them into healthy and strong adults. Special precautions surrounded times Colonial era people thought of as especially dangerous, such as the first few weeks of life, teething, and weaning.

INFANT AND CHILD CARE IN NATIVE AMERICAN CULTURES

Care for an infant's health began shortly after birth. Many Native American cultures took special care of an infant's umbilical stump, putting substances such as puffball (among the Cherokee) or pollen (among the Pimas) on a baby's navel to protect it and prevent swelling and infection. Among Algonquian peoples of the Northeast, the umbilical cord was carefully preserved and kept in a ceremonial sack around the infant's neck. One French missionary noted, "If they were to lose it their children would be dolts and lacking in sense."[2]

After the cord was cut, birth attendants often gave infants a symbolic first meal of animal oil or melted fat. The oil was often derived from a clan's sacred animal, and created a bond between the new baby and its people's guardian spirit. Physically, the oil acted as a mild laxative to purge the meconium, or fetal bowel movement, from the baby's digestive tract.

Most Native American newborns also had a bath shortly after birth, and the water was infused with plants that had medicinal or spiritual significance. Peoples of the Northeast usually bathed the baby in cold water, which seventeenth-century French and English observers interpreted as a ritual to strengthen the infant and make it accustomed to hardship. More recent scholarship has interpreted these rituals as a symbolic separation of the child from its mother. In either case, the ritual had hygienic rationale as well. This interpretation is borne out by the antiseptic properties of some of the herbs (such as goldenseal) that were infused in the bath. The Arikara people bathed not only the infant's skin but also its mouth, nostrils, and eyes with berry juice.

After its bath, the baby was wrapped in soft animal skins or cloth lined with moss or cattail fluff (this absorbent material served as an easily changed "diaper") and, among the many peoples that used them, strapped into a cradleboard. Cradleboards were infant carriers made of leather and wood that could be strapped onto an adult's back, laid flat on the ground, or even hung from a tree. They were used by a wide variety of cultures, from the Northeast Woodlands to the Great Plains. Infants were kept swaddled on the cradleboard until they were able to walk. Many peoples believed that the cradleboard allowed the baby's legs and back to grow straight and thus made for strong, agile adults. In addition, the cradleboard allowed the infant's body to be shaped according to the beauty standards of its people. Among tribes that preferred feet with turned in toes, the baby's feet were positioned so that they would grow in the appropriate shape. The Choctaw and Catawba shaped the heads of infants by applying clay to the forehead and back of the skull. Other peoples pierced babies' ears and inserted porcupine quills, wampum, or feathers.

Native American children were breastfed much longer than their European American counterparts—usually until the child was three years old, and as long as five or six years in some cases. While young children ate solid food as well, the long nursing period had several important effects. Extended breastfeeding ensured that a child had an adequate supply of nutrition, even when food was scarce. It also had a contraceptive affect on the mother, ensuring that the baby would have its mother's exclusive attention and would not have to compete with a younger sibling for care or resources. Europeans noted that Native American children seemed healthy and strong, free from the rickets that often disabled children in Europe. One observer wrote that indigenous children in North Carolina escaped "Disasters that Proceed from the teeth, with many other Distempers which attack our Infants in England, and other Parts of Europe. They let their Children suck until they are well grown."[3] Once a child was ready for solid food, and for some time after weaning, he or she ate meat broth, corn porridge, and other foods that were easy to chew and digest.

As the child grew older, many peoples stressed the development of stoicism and the ability to endure physical hardship. Mohawk children were left naked year-round to learn to tolerate cold. Coming of age rituals at puberty often included periods of starvation and forced exercise to test endurance and to induce visions. Among the peoples of southern New England, children selected for tribal leadership were subjected to a series of increasingly harsh physical tests, which sometimes included beatings and other painful rituals. Those who passed all the tests were honored and respected.

INFANT AND CHILD CARE IN ANGLO-AMERICAN CULTURES

Colonial era Anglo-Americans believed that babies and children required conscious shaping into acceptable adults. This shaping included education and discipline but extended to the child's body as well. Without intervention, a newborn infant might never grow properly, or even become fully human. The process of molding an infant into a proper member of society began at birth.

The midwife cut the umbilical cord when she delivered the baby. If the baby was a boy, the stump was left long; if a girl, it was cut short. A baby boy with a short cord might grow up weak and effeminate; a girl with a long cord, rebellious and sexually promiscuous. An infant's umbilical cord must never touch the floor, or the baby would never be toilet trained. The stump was then anointed with herbs or other medicines (myrrh, for those who could afford it). Just as in Native American cultures, the next step was to bathe the infant. Warm water was the usual bath. Midwifery manuals recommended warm wine, although it seems doubtful that any but the most wealthy families would follow this practice.

Soon after the bath, the midwife began the process of turning the infant into a human being. Since many infants' heads become misshapen during the birth process, the first job of the midwife was to mold the skull back into a "natural" shape. Once the skull was properly rounded, the midwife bound the baby's head with a strip of cloth to keep it that way. Another strip of cloth covered the umbilical stump.

As in Native American cultures, Anglo-Americans thought it important to ensure that a baby's arms, legs, and back grew straight, tall, and strong. In Anglo-American society, swaddling took the place of the cradleboard. Babies were wrapped tightly in strips of linen that bound the legs in an extended position, kept the back aligned, and pressed the arms tightly to the side of the torso. In the words of one historian, "The end result was an immobile little mummified package about the size and shape of a loaf of bread."[4] Because of the frequency of rickets and other diseases that resulted in crooked legs and backs, parents were especially anxious to ensure that their children grew up with straight limbs. Swaddling was thought to "train" the growth of a child's bones, much as a vine or tree could be "trained" into shape with pruning and binding.

Swaddling served other purposes as well. It kept the baby warm in inadequately heated houses. The absorbent linen cloth was an excellent diaper. As the child grew, the swaddling bands kept it immobile—and thus safe from the many dangers that surrounded young children. A busy mother could put a swaddled infant down in its cradle or on a bed and know that it would be right where she left it when she returned. Swaddling also meant that a young sibling could be put in charge of watching the baby without fear.

Infants were kept swaddled for 12 to 24 hours at a time. When the bands were removed, the infant was bathed again in warm water. Because of the difficulty of doing laundry, swaddling bands were not washed often. Those that were merely wet, rather than soiled, were hung to dry in front of the fireplace and then reapplied. It is not surprising that many infants suffered from severe diaper rash and other skin conditions, and that medicinal recipe books were full of remedies for infants' skin. To prevent these problems, some mothers rubbed infants' skin with grease or oil before reswaddling.

While the child was free of swaddling bands, the mother would "exercise" the baby's arms and legs by bending, stretching, and rubbing them. This practice, like swaddling, was designed to ensure the proper shape of the child's body, and to strengthen the muscles needed for standing and walking.

At four to six months of age, the swaddling bands came off and were replaced by a bodice and petticoat (for boys and girls). When the child began to walk, parents put a padded cap or headband called a "pudding" on its head. The pudding cap protected the toddler from falls and other accidents.

Swaddling fell out of favor by the end of the eighteenth century. Under the influence of Enlightenment ideas about childrearing, parents now believed that nature should be allowed to run its course. Clothing for infants and young children was loose and light to allow freedom of movement. Children would naturally strengthen their bodies if allowed to exercise their arms and legs without impediments. Swaddling and other restrictive practices were thought of as old fashioned, associated with the "ignorant" at best and downright dangerous at worst. Affluent parents (who were among the first to adopt these new ideas) cautioned each other to beware of nursemaids who clung to the old ways.

The eighteenth century brought about other childrearing practices as well. It became common practice to keep infants and toddlers as lightly dressed as possible, give them only light blankets, and bathe them in cool or even cold water. Many eighteenth-century physicians thought that exposure to cold would enable children to endure hardship and discomfort, and strengthen their ability to fend off disease.

One practice that did not change was the feeding of infants. Infants were breastfed almost exclusively. Only under the most dire circumstances were babies "hand fed." However, babies were not put to their mothers' breasts immediately after birth. Women do not produce milk immediately; instead, the breasts secrete a fluid called colostrum. Colonial era people believed that colostrum was "impure" and dangerous for the baby. Newborn infants were nursed by female friends, relatives or servants of the mother. If none were available, the baby was sometimes given a little water or gruel dripped from a feather or left unfed until the mother's milk came in, usually three or four days after childbirth

Anglo-American infants were nursed until they were 18 months to two years old. Up until then, breast milk was supplemented with mashed food from the family table, or "pap," bread soaked in milk or water. When the time came to wean the baby from the breast, the baby was not allowed to "taper off"; instead, weaning was complete and sudden. Some women took a "weaning journey" without the child, leaving it in the care of relatives while she spent a week or two elsewhere; a related practice was to send the child on a visit for the same time period. The separation of mother and child was thought to make weaning easier on both parties.

Colonial era parents regarded weaning as a dangerous time in a child's life. Weaning was best done in the spring or fall, rather than the summer. Parents feared that summer weaning would make the child vulnerable to "summer flux" or diarrhea, a potentially deadly illness for a young child. Gastrointestinal complaints were indeed more common in the summer, and shifting a toddler from relatively clean breast milk to potentially contaminated water might well have resulted in illness. Similarly, if a child seemed ill, parents put off weaning until it had recovered. Breast milk would keep up the child's strength; weaning the child while ill could weaken it still further.

Teething was also thought to be an especially dangerous time. Colonial era parents believed that teething could cause fevers, runny noses, and diarrhea, as well as other illnesses. Philadelphia matron Elizabeth Drinker wrote of a servant's infant in 1795, "Her bowels much disordered, I suppose she is teething . . . I sent . . . Medicine etc. for the poor little Child . . . "[5] Despite the medicine, the baby died a few days later. Well into the nineteenth century, "teething" was listed as a cause of death for infants. Parents watched their teething children carefully, and regulated their diet and exposure to the weather. Many babies wore a necklace of red coral beads since coral was thought to aid in teething and ward off disease. Finally, if the teeth did not erupt quickly enough, parents sometimes made an incision in the child's gums to allow them to emerge. Once the toddler had passed through the twin crises of teething and weaning, parents breathed a sigh of relief—the most dangerous stage of infancy had passed.

INFANT AND CHILD CARE IN AFRICAN AMERICAN CULTURES

The care of African American infants was shaped by two factors: the material conditions of slavery and parents' memories of African traditions. African American infants were also twice as likely to die in their first year as Anglo-American infants. Enslaved African American women bore fewer children and saw fewer of their infants live to adulthood than Anglo-American women.

As was the case in all American cultures, a newborn's umbilical cord and umbilical stump were treated with care. As late as the nineteenth century, African American midwives followed traditions that had their origins in Africa. The baby's umbilical stump was daubed with ashes or mud to protect it. This practice, while rooted in a long tradition, carried dangers. Soil or mud can carry tetanus, and many infants died of the disease as a result of this practice.

Enslaved midwives also looked for signs that the infant might have special powers, such as the ability to see and talk to spirits. A baby born with the caul, or amniotic sac still over its head, was thought to possess these powers, as was a baby born in the breech position, or feet first. If a baby was born with a caul, the caul itself had to be carefully preserved, or the infant would lose its powers.

Like all Colonial infants, African American babies were breastfed. However, the desires of the slave owner to maximize labor and the needs of the mother and infant were in conflict. Enslaved women were expected to get back to work as soon as possible after giving birth, sometimes within days. Often a woman's work was lightened for the first few weeks postpartum—she might be assigned spinning or weaving work instead of field labor. However, by the time her baby was a month or six weeks old, she would be back at her usual tasks. What happened to the baby while the mother was working depended on the size of the plantation and the number of slaves. On small farms, where there were few slaves, the mother might strap the baby to her back in a sling, another practice that originated in Africa. On larger plantations, infants and children too young to work were left in the care of a slave "nurse," usually an elderly or disabled woman who was incapable of field work.

Nursing mothers were given limited time to feed their babies, usually 15 minutes to half an hour, two or three times a day. This time was rarely adequate for a nursing infant's needs. Young babies need to be fed every two to three hours to get the nutrients they need. The limited number of times mothers were allowed to feed their infants (Anglo-American and Native American infants were fed whenever they got hungry) and the limited time they had to do so set African American babies on a road to malnutrition while still in infancy.

Slave owners encouraged early weaning, usually around one year of age, although many mothers continued to breastfeed their infants at night. For newly weaned toddlers in the care of slave nurses, food usually consisted of cornmeal mixed with milk or water, sometimes sweetened with a little molasses. This diet was occasionally supplemented with a little bit of meat, usually salt pork. This basic diet was deficient in protein and many vitamins. While some American slaves were allowed to supplement their rations by planting their own gardens or hunting their own game, these supplements were often not enough to improve the nutritional status of children. Nutritional deprivation stunted growth and weakened immune response.

Children were put to work around the age of six. Small children weeded gardens and gathered vegetables, cared for poultry, carried water to adults in the fields, and helped with cooking and cleaning in the house. Girls were taught to sew and spin, and boys learned to care for livestock, and herd cattle and sheep. Children who were careless in their work or who were perceived as "lazy" were beaten.

All of these factors—early weaning, malnutrition, and physical labor—meant that African American children were much more vulnerable to disease and death than their Anglo-American and Native American counterparts. Slave children often suffered from chronic diseases such as yaws, a bacterial skin condition. These ailments were not life threatening in themselves but made children more vulnerable when the next epidemic of measles or gastroenteritis came along. While good data is hard to come by, estimations of infant mortality (deaths among infants up to a year old) among African Americans during the eighteenth century ranges from 28 to 50 percent. Child mortality (children from one year to 10 years old) was also high—40 to 50 percent.[6]

Some slave owners blamed mothers for the deaths of infants. Many plantation records note the deaths of infants by "smothering" or "overlaying." Since most infants shared the mother's bed, slave owners assumed that the mother had accidentally suffocated the baby by rolling over on top of it. While this is one possibility, it is also possible that some of these deaths were due to undiagnosed disease, or to what we now call sudden infant death syndrome. However, there are some records that suggest that some enslaved mothers killed their children, perhaps to spare them a life under slavery. Infanticide remains another possible contributing factor to the high mortality rate among African American children.

ACCIDENTS AND INJURIES

Accidents were another factor accounting for the high death rates of children from all cultures. In large families, it was easy for one child to escape the supervision of an adult and stumble into a dangerous or even deadly situation. The hard work expected of children in Anglo-American families or under conditions of slavery created its own dangers, as did the harsh physical punishments typical of the time period.

Conditions in Anglo-American households were not childproof, to say the least. Most houses had large open fireplaces, many had lofts reached by trapdoors or rickety ladders, livestock such as pigs and cows roamed free, and small children and toddlers were often under the supervision of siblings not much older than themselves. Colonial court records are full of descriptions of these dangers and their consequences. Children drowned in tanning pits and millponds, were severely burned in boiling wash kettles or fireplaces, or fell through trapdoors and down ladders.

Children's health was also affected by the work they did or the conditions under which they did it. In all cultures, children began working young, whether in the fields, in the house, or in the workshop. The health and safety of servants and apprentices were often neglected. Hugh March of Newbury, Massachusetts, became severely ill while serving an apprenticeship to a blacksmith. Hugh became severely lame during his apprenticeship, either due to an injury or an infection. His knee swelled and he developed a weeping rash on his legs. The blacksmith's family refused to care for him and left him to languish in an unheated room with only a cotton blanket for warmth. Luckily, his parents were able to break his indenture and take him home to convalesce.

Enslaved African American children were especially vulnerable to work-related injuries and to severe physical punishments. Children were set to work in heavy agricultural labor; hoes, rakes, axes, and hatchets were all potential sources of injury. Young boys assigned to care for cattle and other livestock could be kicked, bitten, trampled, or gored.

But perhaps the biggest source of injury for African American children was the brutal punishments meted out by slave owners and overseers. Whippings could leave deep lacerations and permanent scars, but other punishments could also result in injury. One boy recalled his mistress pinching his ears until they bled; a girl had scars on her arms from being cut with the sharp edge of a china plate she had dropped. In one particularly horrific episode, a girl was punished for stealing a piece of candy by having her head placed under the rocker of a chair and rocked on. This punishment shattered her jaw so that she could not chew solid food for the rest of her life.

INFECTIOUS DISEASE

While all age groups were vulnerable to infectious disease, some illnesses particularly affected children. Diphtheria, scarlet fever, and measles all had periodic outbreaks in the colonies. For infants and toddlers, gastrointestinal disorders were an endemic threat.

Diphtheria

Diphtheria is a bacterial disease that primarily affects children under 12. The primary symptoms are sore throat, fever, and lethargy, followed by a growth of a grayish membrane on the throat and tongue. This membrane gave the disease one of its eighteenth-century names, putrid sore throat. The membrane is thick and hard, and can become widespread enough to obstruct the trachea. The bacteria also secrete a toxin that can damage the heart, kidneys, and nerves. The severity of the symptoms varies considerably from person to person, with some victims experiencing only mild effects while others have much more severe symptoms. While diphtheria in the modern world is easily prevented with a vaccine, and an antitoxin is available to ameliorate symptoms, when outbreaks occur death rates can still be as high as 10 percent.

The Reverend Cotton Mather described an epidemic in 1659 that probably was diphtheria, although the diagnosis cannot be certain. Mather called the disease "the Malady of Bladders in the Windpipe" and noted that it "removed many children." Another minister, Samuel Danforth of Roxbury, Massachusetts, recorded the deaths of all three of his children from the illness "within the space of a fortnight."[7]

The first epidemic that can be confidently identified as a diphtheria outbreak began in the winter of 1735 in New Hampshire, and over the next three years made its way slowly southward through New England and the mid-Atlantic. In New Hampshire alone, there were over a thousand deaths over the course of 14 months, and 80 percent of those were children under 10. One historian described the outbreak as "the plague among children," noting that "many families lost three or four children—many lost all." In town after town and colony after colony, observers lamented the terrible toll the disease took on children. Over and over again, these writers spoke of entire families of children taken by the disease. In December of 1735, the governor of Massachusetts declared a public day of fasting and prayer to ask God to abate the epidemic. The proclamation noted the "great Numbers" of "younger People" who had "been removed by Death" and asked God to "spare his unworthy people."[8]

Treatments for diphtheria reflect the desperation many parents must have felt when their children fell ill with such a serious disease. Cotton Mather recommended a mixture of human urine, molasses, olive oil, and nutmeg; if that was not enough, parents and physicians applied irritating substances to the outside of the throat to raise blisters on the skin in the hope that the "putridity" associated with the disease would be drawn to the outside of the body. In addition to these remedies, victims of diphtheria were subjected to the seventeenth- and eighteenth-century standby treatment of strong laxatives and emetics.

Scarlet Fever

Scarlet fever resembles diphtheria in some of its symptoms and was often confused with it. Like diphtheria, it most often affects children.

Both diseases were called quinsy or putrid sore throat in the Colonial era. Scarlet fever, while serious, is not as deadly as diphtheria, however. Scarlet fever is caused by the streptococcus organism and usually follows a case of strep throat. After the initial sore throat and fever, the patient develops the bright red rash that gives the disease its name. The rash begins on the chest and spreads to the rest of the body. Skin on the fingers and toes may peel off like sunburn. The tongue also turns scarlet, and a "strawberry tongue" is one of the diagnostic symptoms.

Outbreaks of scarlet fever occurred periodically throughout the Colonial period. One of the most severe occurred in Boston and coincided with the New England diphtheria epidemic of 1735 to 1736. From descriptions of the symptoms, however, it seems that the disease that affected the city was scarlet fever and not diphtheria, as diphtheria does not cause a rash. The death rate was also much lower—one in 40, as opposed to one in four during the New Hampshire diphtheria epidemic.[9]

The main danger with scarlet fever, as with any streptococcus infection, is the possibility of rheumatic fever. Rheumatic fever is an abnormal immune response to the streptococcus organism in which the body attacks its own tissues, sometimes weeks after the patient recovers from the initial illness. In this case, the heart and joints are most affected. Children who have rheumatic fever can suffer heart damage that can lead to congestive heart failure or heart rhythm problems later in life.

Measles

Measles was another epidemic disease associated with children, although in Colonial America measles did not affect children exclusively. Measles is a highly contagious viral disease characterized by high fever, a distinctive blotchy rash, and red swollen eyes. While many people who contract measles recover, complications can include pneumonia or encephalitis, which can lead to brain damage and permanent disability. Both of these complications can be deadly. If a pregnant woman contracts the disease, measles can cause miscarriage.

Measles was often confused with smallpox during the Colonial period. Some historians believe that measles was responsible for many deaths attributed to smallpox among Native Americans during the early years of European contact. Like smallpox, measles can be especially deadly to previously unexposed populations. An 1874 outbreak on Fiji killed 40,000 indigenous islanders of all ages. Jesuit missionaries in Quebec recorded an outbreak among Native Americans in 1687, which spread to New England tribes as well.

Epidemics among European Americans affected mostly children, although adults did contract the disease. In 1713, Joseph Green of Salem, Massachusetts, noted that all seven of his children had survived measles, but that a number of families in his town had not been so lucky. During an epidemic in New York, one man wrote that "four of our children have had the Measles two almost quite recovered, two Sick as yet . . . we have three children more . . . which we Expect every day to have them." However, in 1717, a Virginia man named Philip Ludwell noted in a letter that "measles hath been epidemical amongst us this winter." Ludwell listed those who had died in his neighborhood, and almost all the victims were adults, including one of his own slaves, "a young Negro woman." African Americans seemed especially vulnerable to the disease—the New York man who described the illness of his children also mentioned that he expected his three African American slaves to contract the disease. Measles would not become a disease exclusively of children until it became more established in the America, late in the Colonial period. When epidemics were separated by long time periods, enough adults remained vulnerable to make measles a significant threat to all age groups.[10]

In a time characterized by harsh bleeding and purging, therapies for measles were surprisingly mild. Wait Winthrop of Boston recommended a tea of sage, saffron, and balm, and he urged practitioners to "let nature have time to work without too much forcing." Similarly, Cotton Mather's advice to those treating measles was "Don't kill 'em . . . with mischievous kindness—" in other words, do not overtreat the disease. Mather's advice came from hard experience. In the space of two weeks, he had lost three of his children to measles.[11]

Whooping Cough

Other children's illnesses were much milder. Epidemics of whooping cough were common and were almost an accepted part of childhood. Whooping cough begins like a mild cold, with a runny nose, mild sore throat, and slight cough. After a week or so, the patient develops a more severe cough that comes in spells or spasms. The patient is often unable to take a deep breath during these spells so that when they are over, he or she inhales suddenly with the characteristic "whoop" noise. The disease is unpleasant but not serious in older children, but infants and toddlers can have severe cases and can stop breathing completely during a coughing spell.

Outbreaks were recorded as early as 1659 in Boston, but the most serious epidemics seem to have occurred during the eighteenth century in the south, especially South Carolina. A 1738 epidemic affected adults as well as children and had an unusually high death rate. The *South Carolina Gazette* pleaded with the public to send in "Recipes and Instructions tending to cure that violent and present reigning Disorder, called the Whooping-Cough." The disease caused deaths in other areas as well. In Philadelphia in 1769, one diarist noted that "one of our neighr. Children [is] dead of the Hooping Cough, almost all of the children in the neighborhood bad with it." However, for the most part, whooping cough epidemics were noted this way in Colonial records: "No Sickness excepting Colds and the . . . Whooping Cough."[12]

Gastroenteritis and Intestinal Parasites

Gastrointestinal illness had a greater or lesser impact depending on the age of the victim. Older children and adults can survive an attack of gastroenteritis that could kill an infant or toddler. When epidemics of dysentery or other severe gastroenteritis struck in Colonial America, young children were in the most danger, although adults suffered as well. The Reverend Samuel Danforth of Massachusetts noted that a 1669 epidemic of "flux" (diarrhea) "proved mortal to many infants and little children." In 1715, a severe epidemic in Charleston killed many persons, but as one physician noted, "children most chiefly."[13]

Infants and toddlers were at the most risk because they can dehydrate so easily. Diarrhea and vomiting drain water from the body. Babies' small body size means that they have smaller reserves of water to begin with, and many infants refuse to nurse when they are ill, so the water that is lost is not replaced. Severe dehydration can kill a small child quickly, sometimes in a matter of a day or even a few hours. Even when no epidemic existed, infants could develop a severe illness from a passing virus that might have little or no effect on an older person.

The recommended remedies for diarrhea and vomiting probably did more harm than good to very young patients. Laxatives and enemas were often prescribed for diarrhea, using the logic that the poison that was causing the symptoms should be purged from the body. Patients were often given emetics for the same reason. Other, less harsh, remedies included poultices laid on the abdomen and bits of toasted bread soaked in olive oil.

Parasitic worms caused intestinal problems as well. One of the most common was infestation with ascaris, or roundworms. They are especially prevalent in areas where people defecate on the ground or use human waste as fertilizer—two practices which were common in early America. While both adults and children can be affected, children are more likely to have severe infestations and to suffer complications. The worms live in the intestine, draining nutrients from the host's body. Children who are malnourished are more vulnerable to other infections and diseases; in addition, severe infestations can cause intestinal obstruction. The worms can also cause a form of pneumonia.

Roundworms, hookworms, and pinworms were especially prevalent in the South, and African American folk medicine prescribed a number of remedies for worms. Slave medical practitioners used an assortment of herbal remedies to cure infested children, including garlic, rhubarb, and the highly toxic jimson weed. All cultures recognized parasites as a problem and had their own remedies for them. The Cherokee people used a plant called Carolina pinkroot, which their Anglo-American neighbors quickly adopted. Other Native American remedies included the roots of wild plum trees or the leaves of horsemint. In addition to adopting pinkroot from the Cherokee, European Americans brought their own traditional remedies, including a plant called wormwood for its common use for this purpose. More learned physicians prescribed mercury or sulfur derivatives.

All parents feared greatly for their children during this time of high infant and child mortality. The many strange remedies and practices associated with Colonial era childrearing are only examples of concerned parents doing the best they could with the knowledge that they had.

NOTES

1. Brenda E. Stevenson, *Life in Black and White: Family and Community in the Slave South*. New York: Oxford University Press, 1996, pp. 105, 249.

2. Quoted in Ann Marie Plane, "Childbirth Practices among Native American Women of New England and Canada: 1600–1800." In Peter Benes (Ed.), *Medicine and Healing: The Dublin Seminar for New England Folklife Annual Proceedings: 1990*. Boston: Boston University Press, 1990, p. 19.

3. Virgil J. Vogel, *American Indian Medicine*. Norman: University of Oklahoma Press, 1970, p. 237.

4. Karin Calvert, *Children in the House: The Material Culture of Early Childhood: 1600–1900*. Boston: Northeastern University Press, 1992, p. 21.

5. Entry for June 29, 1795 in Elaine Forman Crane (Ed.), *The Diary of Elizabeth Drinker*, Vol. 1. Boston: Northeastern University Press, 1991, p. 697.

6. W. Michael Byrd and Linda A. Clayton (Eds.), *An American Health Dilemma: A Medical History of African Americans and the Problem of Race:*

Volume One, Beginnings to 1900. New York: Routledge, 2000, p. 286; Stevens, *Life in Black and White*, p. 249.

7. Quoted in John Duffy, *Epidemics in Colonial America*. Baton Rouge: Louisiana State University Press, 1953, pp. 115–116.

8. Ibid., pp. 117, 118.

9. Ibid., p. 131.

10. Ibid., pp. 168–170.

11. Ibid., p. 167.

12. Ibid., p. 181.

13. Ibid., pp. 215–218.

CHAPTER 6

Infectious Disease

Infectious disease was one of the top killers during the Colonial era. In the days before antibiotics and vaccination, any illness could rapidly prove fatal. Epidemic disease devastated populations at the beginning of the Colonial period. For Native Americans in particular, the epidemics that arrived with the Europeans proved to be a demographic disaster. For European settlers, new diseases introduced from trade with Africa and other tropical countries meant that every new arrival had to cope with a period of "seasoning" to the new disease environment.

Diseases from all over the world came to the Americas during the time of colonization and settlement. From Europe came smallpox, measles, whooping cough, several forms of dysentery and one form of malaria. Tropical diseases from Africa included a more serious form of malaria and yellow fever. While most of these diseases are now understood and can be treated with modern drugs or prevented by vaccines, none of the Colonial era peoples had the knowledge or skill to treat them effectively. The introduction of these diseases made the North American disease environment very different—and much more dangerous—than it had been before 1492.

The growth of the white population and increasing urbanization brought about changes in disease patterns as well. In the eighteenth century, periodic outbreaks of smallpox and yellow fever took their toll on the populations of the growing cities. On a more positive note, new diseases also gave rise to new scientific writings and medical practices. American doctors debated the merits of inoculation to prevent small-pox and wrote treatises on the cause and cure of yellow fever. Epidemic disease also prompted city governments to pass pioneering public health laws that laid the groundwork for more ambitious measures in the nineteenth century.

FIRST CONTACT EPIDEMICS

The arrival of Europeans and Africans in the Americas was a historical event of immense significance, but it was also a significant medical and biological event. The newcomers brought viruses and bacteria as well as trade goods and missionaries. The microorganisms established themselves in the new environment and triggered a series of epidemics during the early years of European exploration and settlement.

Smallpox

Of these new diseases, probably the most devastating was smallpox. While smallpox has been eliminated in the modern world, it was one of the most feared diseases in history, with gruesome symptoms and a high mortality rate. The virus spread quickly. Most cases were airborne—a healthy person inhaled virus particles exhaled by the sick—but the disease could also be communicated through direct physical contact. Scabs and dried bodily secretions from smallpox victims could contain active virus for months, so someone sweeping the room where a patient has been could contract the disease from breathing dust. Once a person was infected, the virus replicated asymptomatically for a week to 10 days before it struck.

Symptoms began with fever, headache, and muscle aches. Then the rash began. It started as red blotches but quickly developed into the characteristic raised, fluid-filled blisters. The pustules could cover the entire body, from the soles of the feet to the palms of the hands. They erupted inside the mouth and throat, making swallowing difficult or impossible. They could affect the eyes, leading to blindness. In some cases, the virus took a hemorrhagic form, leading to massive internal bleeding and quick death. Otherwise, the prognosis depended on the extent of the pustules. In the worst cases, they blended into one another, causing layers of skin to peel off completely—this was another quick route to death, with a 60 percent mortality rate. If the patient was luckier, the blisters remained discrete, with some healthy skin in between. In either case, the blisters exuded a distinctive foul smell. After two weeks of this horror, the pustules began to scab over. If the patient survived to this stage, recovery becomes more likely, although secondary bacterial infection and dehydration could still take their toll, and the patient remained contagious. Finally, a month after the original infection, the last scab fell off and the patient recovered—albeit with deep, distinctive scars where the pustules were. Those who were fortunate enough to survive, however, would never have to suffer this way again. Infection guaranteed lifelong immunity.

The Native American Demographic Disaster

The first Europeans to colonize North America, the Spanish, triggered a smallpox epidemic in Mexico that was a major factor in the fall of the Aztec empire. In late 1518, a smallpox epidemic struck Spanish outposts in the Caribbean, killing between one half and one third of the Native Americans there. By 1520, the disease had spread to Mexico. At the time, Hernan Cortés was engaged in an ongoing battle with the Aztec army. Cortés and his men besieged the city of Tenochitlan. At the same time, smallpox broke out within the city walls. Many of the warriors fell deathly ill, along with other inhabitants, including the newly crowned emperor, Cuitlauac, Montezuma's brother. Aztec chroniclers described the horror and devastation of the disease: "There was a great havoc. Very many died of it. They could not walk; they only lay in their resting places and beds. They could not move, they could stir; they could not change position, nor lie on one side; nor face down, nor on their backs. And if they stirred, much did they cry out. Great was its destruction. Covered, mantled with pustules, very many people died of them."[1] Starvation and despair soon drove the few survivors to surrender.

Elsewhere on the continent, the story was much the same. Everywhere European settlers and conquerors arrived, epidemic disease soon followed. European observers did not always record the name of the disease that was wreaking havoc on the indigenous population, but smallpox was a likely culprit in many of the epidemics. Measles and influenza are other possibilities. No matter what the disease was, the effects were devastating.

French missionaries to the Atlantic coast of Canada in 1616 wrote that the indigenous peoples there were "dying fast."[2] Thomas Hariot, one of the English settlers who established the Roanoke colony in 1587, noted that whenever the English visited an Indian village, "within a few days after our departure . . . people began to die very fast, and many in a short space; in some towns about twenty, in some forty, in some sixty . . . The disease was so strange that they neither knew what it was nor how to cure it; the like by report of the oldest men in the country never happened before, time out of mind."[3] The tragic sequence of events would repeat itself over and over. By some estimates, 95 percent of the Native American population died by the end of the sixteenth century.[4]

Why was this the case? Why were Native Americans so susceptible to these diseases? Why did the epidemics carry off people from all age groups, instead of targeting the very young and the very old, as most infectious diseases do? The answers to these questions are complex and not entirely understood. What seems certain is that a combination of biological and social factors was necessary to create this demographic disaster.

It seems likely that Indigenous Americans shared some sort of biological vulnerability to these diseases. There are several possible ways this could be so. One possibility is that centuries of isolation had created a genetically homogeneous population that was especially vulnerable to viral diseases. Ninety to 95 percent of people of Indigenous American descent have type O blood, which is a remarkable lack of variation. In contrast, only 55 to 60 percent of people of Western European descent have type O blood.[5] Some viruses, such as measles, can adapt to the immune system of their hosts. If a population lacks genetic diversity, the virus becomes more virulent with each victim, and mortality rates rise. This may have been one factor in the impact of new viral diseases on the Indigenous American population. Similarly, genetic homogeneity combined with isolation from Eurasian disease could also allow inherited immunological deficits to spread throughout a population. Historian David S. Jones notes that modern populations of Navajo and Jicarilla Apaches have increased incidence of inherited immune deficiency. However, there is not enough evidence to prove either of these hypotheses. Modern studies have shown that Native American groups mount normal immune responses to disease. Furthermore, the immune deficiencies seen among the Navajo and Jicarilla peoples are not seen among other groups; nor do we know when this genetic variation emerged. Whether these factors affected indigenous populations in the sixteenth and seventeenth centuries can only remain a matter of speculation, and some historians have dismissed the idea of genetic vulnerability completely.[6]

The most likely biological explanation of Native American vulnerability is environmental rather than genetic. In Europe, diseases such as smallpox and measles were endemic—that is, regularly found there.

While these illnesses killed many in Europe—and smallpox was universally feared—they did not have the same devastating effect on the population. Most Europeans were exposed to these viruses at an early age. If they survived, they acquired lifelong immunity. Thus, the majority of the adult population would have at least partial immunity to many dangerous diseases, although they could carry the germs and spread them to others. However, the Native American population had no acquired immunities at all. When Europeans arrived, they brought with them deadly stowaways in their own bodies, invaders against which Native Americans had no defenses.

INFECTIOUS DISEASE AND COLONIAL SETTLEMENT

The problem of epidemic disease did not go away after first contact. African and European immigrants also had to confront a new disease environment. Malaria, smallpox, dysentery, and yellow fever took their toll on natives and newcomers alike.

New Immigrants, Malaria, and "Seasoning"

While Europeans and Africans did not die in the same numbers as Native Americans, the infectious disease environment of the American colonies raised mortality rates for new immigrants. Newcomers came off the ship already weakened by weeks of seasickness, poor diet, and unsanitary and crowded conditions on shipboard. They were thus prime targets for pathogens. Landholders in Virginia were advised to give new indentured servants and slaves only light work for the first year after they arrived so that they could become "seasoned" to conditions in America. Nevertheless, mortality rates remained high.[7]

It is not entirely clear what the diseases that killed the settlers were. However, one possibility for which there is good evidence is malaria. While a mild form of malaria was endemic to some parts of England, ships trading in Africa and the Mediterranean brought new strains of malaria parasite and its vector mosquitoes with them to the Caribbean and to what would become the southeastern United States. The disease quickly established itself there, with severe consequences for those who had not previously been exposed to it.

Malaria is caused by a microscopic parasite that infects the red blood cells, liver, and lymphatic system. The parasite is carried from victim to victim by the anopheles species of mosquito and does not spread person to person. There are four strains of the malaria organism, only two of which commonly infect human beings: *Plasmodium vivax* and *Plasmodium falciparum*. Vivax results in a relatively mild disease, with a low mortality rate, but falciparum can be deadly. Both types are unpleasant, causing high fever, shaking chills (the "fevers and agues" described by many Colonial people), headaches, abdominal pain, nausea, and diarrhea. A person who recovers from either acquires temporary immunity for some years thereafter, and subsequent cases are likely to be mild.

Exposure to a new strain, however, can have serious consequences. The milder form, vivax, is more common in temperate areas and was most likely the strain endemic in England. Vivax probably came to America with the first Europeans, and while it caused much illness and debility, mortality rates were relatively low. Patterns of disease in early Virginia bear this out. Accounts from the first years of English settlement describe the seasoning that affected newcomers to the swampy coastal region as "two or three fits of a fever and ague."[8] While most recovered from this initial illness, malaria weakens the body and makes a person more vulnerable to other diseases, and no doubt contributed to the reputation of Virginia as a "death trap."

The situation changed in the 1680s. The falciparum strain of the parasite is endemic to Africa and other warm climates. As English planters imported more slaves to America, the ships that brought the slaves also brought falciparum malaria. Suddenly the mild seasoning turned into a deadly plague. Even those who had survived vivax would have no immunity to falciparum. In South Carolina, where the disease was especially prevalent, shiploads of French immigrants died within weeks of landing. Others, seeing how widespread sickness was in the city of Charleston, got back on the boat and settled elsewhere, possibly bringing the disease with them. Large planters in South Carolina abandoned their coastal rice plantations during the mosquito season and spent their summers in the highlands to avoid disease. By the mid-eighteenth century, falciparum was well established in other southern colonies and carried off new immigrants, children, and pregnant women. Some scholars believe that malaria was the primary reason that life expectancy for Europeans varied so much between colonies.[9]

Smallpox and Immigrants

Once European settlement was well established, the pattern of American epidemics changed. Smallpox remained a widely feared disease among both European colonists and Native Americans, flaring up periodically and killing many. Most Europeans who survived to adulthood would have been exposed to smallpox in childhood and have acquired immunity. However, in North America, smallpox never achieved a permanent foothold. Instead of being a constant presence, the disease erupted in periodic epidemics and killed adults, the elderly, and children alike. The reasons for this difference lie in the nature of the disease. Smallpox cannot exist without a human host. To be endemic, the virus must have a constant supply of new, nonimmune victims. In the large cities of Europe, the dense population combined with a high birth rate, a constant stream of migrants from the countryside, and active international and domestic trade to maintain the virus as a continuing presence.

In the American colonies, however, the early epidemics left the remaining population either dead or immune. The virus died out for a time, until there were enough vulnerable people to sustain an epidemic. African Americans were also vulnerable to smallpox. Although smallpox had been known in Africa for some time, many Africans had not been exposed. Slaveholders preferred to purchase captives with pockmarks, knowing that the scars were a sign of immunity. Nonetheless, many enslaved Africans remained vulnerable.

When a ship carrying sick passengers docked at an American port, the disease spread, first into the port cities and then to the countryside. Such was the case throughout the late seventeenth and early eighteenth centuries. For instance, New England experienced smallpox outbreaks about every 10 years or so, starting in 1648. The epidemics usually started in a port city—Boston, most often, but also Salem; Newport, Rhode Island; and New London, Connecticut. Sometimes the disease spread through the city and died out. People fleeing to the countryside to avoid contagion, however, could bring the disease with them. In the epidemic of 1689 to 1690, for instance, smallpox entered through the Boston port but spread as far as Canada.

Low population density and lack of good transportation networks kept epidemics infrequent and isolated in the south. Charleston, South Carolina, was one of the few good ports in the region. For this reason, most smallpox epidemics began and ended there. Other regions of the south, such as Virginia, suffered much less, although they were not completely immune.

The middle colonies—New York, Pennsylvania, and New Jersey—saw the most frequent epidemics. New York City and Philadelphia were major ports, and rivers and roads offered easy access to the interior for both traders and the smallpox virus. Epidemics in these colonies took place about every five years rather than every 10. New York was a major area of trade with Native Americans, and smallpox followed the fur traders along the Hudson River and into Canada. Even after the initial epidemics of smallpox devastated Native American populations, new waves of disease continued to roll, leaving little time for populations or cultures to recover.

Finally, warfare did its part to spread smallpox through the continent. Both the Seven Years' War (1754 to 1763) and the Revolutionary War were accompanied by outbreaks of smallpox. Both wars brought boatloads of soldiers from Europe to America, and among those soldiers were inevitably those who carried smallpox. Troop movements helped move the virus from place to place, and the disruptions and stresses of war rendered the population even more vulnerable to illness.

Yellow Fever

Like malaria, yellow fever is a mosquito-borne illness endemic to the tropics. Also like malaria, yellow fever was probably first brought to North America by ships trading in Africa and the Caribbean. However, the symptoms it causes are quite different, and the mortality rate can be as low as 12 percent, or as high as 80 percent. The mosquitoes that carry the yellow fever virus cannot survive winters in North America, so the disease took on an epidemic form rather than remaining as a permanent threat. The first outbreak took place in Boston in 1693 and recurred in the port cities periodically throughout the eighteenth century. The most devastating outbreaks occurred in New York, Charleston, and Philadelphia.

Yellow fever is a viral hemorrhagic fever. It comes on suddenly with a high fever, nausea, and sometimes a nosebleed. The fever rises again in a few days, with more nausea and vomiting. At this point, some patients go into remission and many recover. However, in about 15 percent of patients, the remission ends and the disease enters a more severe phase. Bleeding begins all along the digestive tract, and the liver begins to shut down. The patient develops the jaundice—yellow skin and eyes—that gives the disease its name. There may also be hemorrhages into the skin and eyes. The patient may vomit blood, either fresh blood or black clots like coffee grounds. This symptom gave the illness one of its eighteenth-century names, the black vomit. Organ failure, coma, and death follow rapidly for about half of those whose disease has progressed to this level.

As one might imagine, the disease caused widespread panic when it appeared. In 1699, Charleston and Philadelphia were struck simultaneously. In Charleston, the deaths came so rapidly that there was no time for proper funerals—the dead were simply loaded onto carts and buried quickly and without ceremony. Nearly half of the members of the Colonial assembly died, as did the chief justice of the Colonial court. As one witness described it, "The Distemper raged, and the destroying Angel slaughtered so furiously with his revenging Sword of Pestilence, that there died . . . 14 in one day."[10] The colonial government and most of the city's businesses shut down for over a month. A similar reaction prevailed in Philadelphia. The people withdrew to their homes in fear, leaving the streets empty and the cities like ghost towns. As soon as the first frost came, killing the mosquitoes—October in Philadelphia and November in Charleston—the disease vanished as mysteriously as it came. About 7 percent of Charleston's population and 5 percent of Philadelphia's had perished.[11]

The pattern was to repeat itself multiple times. An outbreak began in late summer and raged until the first frost, killing quickly and in great numbers until the cold weather brought it to a halt. Many people of the time noted that the disease rarely spread beyond the city limits, even when city dwellers fled for the country. This pattern differed from smallpox, and baffled contemporary observers. Yellow fever seemed to be a disease of cities in the summer, and the more affluent urban residents began to leave their homes for the country each summer. When an outbreak struck, anyone who could fled the cities in a mass exodus. Those who remained were the slaves, servants, the poor, and the ministers, physicians, and merchants who were brave enough to serve them or greedy enough to profit from the lack of competition.

FIGHTING EPIDEMIC DISEASE IN THE COLONIAL CITY

The emergence of these devastating diseases motivated physicians and lawmakers to take action. Physicians introduced the controversial method of inoculation to prevent smallpox and debated cures for yellow fever. City councils and other officials introduced quarantine and other measures to stop the spread of epidemics. The 1793 yellow fever epidemic in Philadelphia brought all these efforts together in ways that foreshadowed the emergence of modern public health measures.

Smallpox, Isolation, and Quarantine

Americans took several measures to prevent smallpox from spreading. One was the ancient practice of quarantine. When outbreaks occurred, all the British colonies had laws in place to require the quarantine of ships. These laws compelled ships arriving from infected ports to wait 10 to 20 days before unloading passengers or cargo. Other colonies, such as Virginia, had internal quarantine laws on the books as well.

If a person had smallpox, all members of his or her household were placed under house arrest for one month. Massachusetts required infected households to hang red cloth on their doors as a warning to others.[12]

The New England colonies and South Carolina took quarantine laws one step further in the early eighteenth century by building government-funded quarantine hospitals or "pest houses" to isolate the sick. Usually these buildings were put on islands to protect the rest of the community from accidental exposure. Some individuals who had already survived smallpox ran private isolation hospitals. Mary Hale, a "doctoress" who practiced in Boston, specialized in caring for patients with contagious or "noxious" diseases. She charged a weekly sum that covered food, linens, and medicines. Families sent infected members to Hale to keep the disease from spreading within the household and to avoid the stigma of isolation.[13]

The Smallpox Inoculation Controversy

At the turn of the eighteenth century, a new way of preventing small-pox appeared: the practice of inoculation, or variolation. Inoculation is not the same as vaccination, although the practices are related. In vacci-nation, a weakened or closely related virus is injected into a patient to produce immunity; in inoculation, the full-strength virus is used. The eighteenth-century practice consisted of injecting pus or scabs from smallpox victims under the skin of healthy patients. In most cases, those who were inoculated contracted a very mild case of smallpox but still developed full immunity. Scientists are still not sure why this practice usually resulted in a mild, survivable disease, whereas catch-ing the disease "naturally" had a high mortality rate. Those who devel-oped the disease through inoculation, however, are just as contagious as any other smallpox patient, and those who catch the disease from them are just as vulnerable to complications and death.

Inoculation had been used throughout Asia and Africa for centuries but did not reach Europe until around 1700. In England, the practice was first popularized by the noblewoman Lady Mary Wortley Montagu. Montagu was the wife of the British ambassador to Turkey. While living in Istanbul, Montagu learned of the practice and was deeply impressed: "The small-pox, so fatal, and so general among us, is here entirely harmless."[14] Montagu persuaded her friend Caroline, the Princess of Wales, to have her own children inoculated. In America, the minister Cotton Mather first learned of inoculation from his African slave, Onesimus. Mather had a lifelong interest in medicine and science. When he read of inoculation in a British medical journal, he wrote to the Royal Society (a professional organization of elite scientists in London) describing what Onesimus had told him. Once he confirmed that the practice was the same as that described by Montagu, Mather determined to begin inoculating the people of Boston.

In 1721, just as a smallpox epidemic began in Boston, Mather and his friend Dr. Zabdiel Boylston began their experiment in inoculation. The first subjects were Boylston's six-year-old son Thomas and two of his slaves. Three weeks later, Boylston inoculated seven more people, including another of his sons. The experiment was successful: all of the subjects survived and did not develop smallpox again, even as the epidemic raged around them.

However, the practice of inoculation was not universally accepted. This was not an example of a "miracle drug" bursting onto the scene and saving thousands of lives; quite the opposite. Mather and Boylston's advocacy of inoculation triggered a bitter medical, political, and religious controversy. Ironically, many of the arguments against inoculation were religious. Despite Mather's standing as a man of God, many Bostonians saw inoculation as a questioning of God's will. One minister wrote that inoculation was evidence of a sinful "distrust of God's overruling care."[15] Others argued that inoculation was a heathen remedy that should not be used by good Christians.

Mather countered with his own religious reasoning: other medical practices were acceptable to God, so why not this one? Furthermore, since God had put this remedy into human hands, rejecting it was a sinful rejection of God's blessings. As the controversy raged, one inoculation opponent decided to take matters into his own hands: a gunpowder grenade was thrown through a window of Mather's house, with this note attached: "Cotton Mather you dog, damn you, I'll inoculate you with this, with a pox to you."[16] Luckily for Mather and his family, the bomb was a dud.

The medical debate proceeded less violently but no less passionately. Inoculation was dangerous, both by eighteenth-century standards and those of modern times. Some reports from Europe noted that patients had died after inoculation, and others did not develop the promised immunity. Many physicians resented the intrusion of the clergy onto their turf. The most vocal opponent of inoculation in Boston, Dr. William Douglass, raised ethical concerns. He maintained that it was wrong for a doctor deliberately to make a patient sick.

The most important of these dangers was the contagiousness of inoculated patients. These people often developed such a mild case of smallpox that they felt well enough to see friends or even go out in public.

Opponents were quite correct in seeing a danger to public health—one careless inoculation patient could trigger a major epidemic.

As the controversy raged, it came to the attention of the selectmen (city council) of Boston. They sided with Douglass and the other opponents of inoculation and ordered Boylston to halt his inoculation experiments immediately. Other cities and colonies followed suit. Charleston forbade the practice within the city limits in 1738; the governor of New York issued a proclamation making inoculation a crime. Public opinion was firmly on the side of banning the practice. Dozens of petitions arrived at the Virginia House of Burgesses denouncing inoculation and asking the legislators to make it illegal.

However, by mid-century the tide turned. The anti-inoculation laws on the books were repealed or left unenforced, and inoculation became a much more common practice. Many Colonial leaders, including Benjamin Franklin, voiced their support. The practice had become so widespread that in July 1776, while her husband John met with the Continental Congress to declare independence, Abigail Adams had herself and her four children inoculated.[17]

Dysentery, Typhoid, and Sanitation

Diseases of the digestive tract, known to the colonists as the "flux" or the "bloody flux" were some of the most common causes of illness, disability, and death. Most of the organisms that cause these diseases are spread through contaminated water or food. Sanitary practices of the time were not adequate to the task of keeping the water supply clean, especially in the cities.

While hundreds of organisms can cause serious gastroenteritis, including viruses, bacteria, and protozoa, among most serious are shigellosis (bacillary dysentery), amoebic dysentery, and typhoid fever. Shigella and typhoid are bacteria, and the amoeba that causes dysentery is a protozoan very similar to the ones beginning biology students study in a drop of pond water. Shigella and amoebas cause severe intestinal cramps, watery diarrhea, and blood and mucus in the stools. Typhoid's symptoms are somewhat different: a high fever (102 to 104 degrees Fahrenheit), which can last as long as a month; diarrhea and abdominal pain; and a dark pink, spotted rash. In all cases, the organisms spread by the fecal–oral route. That is, infected persons excrete the organisms in their stool, and new victims acquire it by drinking contaminated water or eating contaminated food.

While a healthy person could survive these diseases, anyone whose resistance had been lowered through malnutrition, overwork, or a bout with another disease such as malaria was at risk of death. In addition, if diarrhea and vomiting were severe enough, the patient could succumb to dehydration. These diseases were present from the earliest times of English settlement. The first inhabitants of Jamestown reported widespread "flux." In 1669, New England saw an epidemic of "gripings, vomiting and flux, with a fever."[18]

One reason these diseases spread so easily was the ways in which colonists disposed of human waste. In rural communities and farms, each family had a privy or pit toilet behind the house. The facility was little more than a hole in the ground with a small shack built over it for privacy and shelter from rain and wind. When the hole was almost full, it was covered with earth, and a new hole was dug nearby. However, if the privy were far away or otherwise inconvenient, most people would simply relieve themselves where they were—in the fields, woods, or barn. At night chamber pots took the place of the privy and were emptied in the morning, often by just dumping them on the ground outside. In places with a high water table, the contents of the privy could easily seep into the well or other water supply, and the habit of relieving oneself on the ground created another potential source of contamination.

In the cities, higher population density made sanitation more difficult. Often two or three families shared one privy. In addition, garbage, dead animals, cow and horse manure, and other filth accumulated in the streets. Roving groups of pigs and dogs were welcomed as "garbage collectors." The few laws passed by city councils to deal with the problem probably only made the situation worse. For instance, a 1731 ordinance in New York City required each householder to sweep all the "dirt filth and soil" on their property into a heap which was to be "thrown into the River." In fact, householders were required to empty their chamber pots directly into the river; those who did not were subject to heavy fines.[19] This last ordinance may have kept the streets a little cleaner, but it did not do much for the water supply.

It is not surprising, then, that water-borne illness was a recurrent source of colonial epidemics. The mid-seventeenth century saw several waves of illness in New York and New England, all characterized by "gripings, vomitings and flux with a fever, which proved mortal to many." Boston saw an outbreak of "bloody flux" in 1676 that was especially deadly to children.[20] In the eighteenth century, epidemics were a common complaint in the Carolinas and other areas in the South, and some forms of intestinal illness became endemic in wide areas. Along with malaria, dysentery was a likely candidate for the seasoning illness of newly arrived European immigrants.

As is often the case, social disruption worsened the effects of disease. When Native Americans attacked the South Carolina countryside in 1715, refugees crowded into the city of Charleston, and an epidemic quickly followed. One inhabitant wrote that "it Pleased God of a flux of feaver July 13 in Charles-Town."[21] He noted that the illness killed at least as many persons as the war.

Cures for the flux were diverse. Some recommended frequent bleedings early in the disease; others suggested pills made of black pepper, turpentine, and flour. Butter mixed with beer and molasses was probably slightly more palatable. For the truly desperate, there was this remedy: "Take an Egge and Boyle it very hard, then pull off the Shell, and put it as hot as you can well endure into the fundament [anus] of the patient Grieved."[22]

The 1793 Philadelphia Yellow Fever Epidemic: Pestilence and Progress

Yellow fever had disappeared from British North America for 30 years, from 1763 until 1793. However in 1793, one of the worst epidemics of all time struck Philadelphia. The crisis it created made the outbreak one of the most significant events in the history of American medicine and public health.

In 1793, Philadelphia was the new nation's capital and a bustling center of commerce, with a population of 55,000 people. The summer that year was unusually hot and dry, but the nation's business went on as usual. In July, a ship arrived in the city carrying French refugees from the slave rebellion in Haiti. The Caribbean has a climate conducive to the life cycle of the yellow fever mosquito, and it seems likely that the bilge water of the refugee ship contained mosquito larvae. At any rate, the first case of the disease appeared shortly thereafter, even as more refugees continued to arrive. By August, it was clear that another epidemic was underway.

Almost immediately, residents began fleeing the city. Anyone who could afford to do so, or had relatives or friends outside the city limits, packed their belongings as quickly as they could and went. One in four white Philadelphians abandoned their homes; one in 10 African Americans left. In early September, President Washington and Congress dispersed to their homes, and the work of the federal government came to a halt.

The epidemic took on vast proportions. In September alone, there were 1,400 deaths. The hot weather continued through October, and people continued to succumb. By the time frosts and the first snow of the year had killed the mosquitoes at the end of November, somewhere between three and five thousand people had died of the disease. (Estimates vary because it is not clear whether all the deaths during the time of the epidemic were due to yellow fever or whether some were due to other causes.) In addition, the epidemic had lingering effects socially, scientifically, and in the realm of government policy.

Yellow Fever and African Americans

One of the first consequences was in race relations. There was a widespread belief that African Americans were less susceptible, if not immune, to yellow fever. In September, city officials approached the African American community, asking for their help during the crisis. Two African American ministers, Absolom Jones and Richard Allen, offered the services of their congregations. Jones and Allen felt that such an offer was their Christian duty and also hoped that this service would raise the status of African Americans in the city.

As one historian put it, the African American community "Assumed the most onerous, the most disgusting burdens of demoralized whites."[23] Volunteers drove patients to the city hospital, nursed the sick, checked on abandoned property and warned off looters, dug graves, and brought corpses to the graveyard. While performing these services, 198 African Americans died of yellow fever.

However, their efforts did not have the effect Jones and Allen had hoped. Matthew Carey, a prominent Philadelphia journalist, published his own account of the epidemic just weeks after it ended. In it, Carey accused the "vilest of the blacks" of exploiting the sick by charging outrageous rates for nursing care, and of "plundering the houses of the sick."[24] While Carey praised Jones and Allen for their offers, the message was clear: they had not prevented their congregants from taking criminal advantage of the epidemic and the suffering of white Philadelphians.

Jones and Allen responded with a pamphlet of their own. In it, they recounted the heroic work done by members of their community and noted that many of the volunteers would accept no pay. They described the unending work done by the volunteer nurses: "Alone, until the patient died, then called away to another scene of distress, and thus have been for a week or ten days left to do the best they could without sufficient rest."[25]

Jones and Allen used their pamphlet for another purpose as well: to galvanize the antislavery movement in Philadelphia and call for increased education, solidarity, and abolitionist activism among

African Americans. If the community's heroic service during the epidemic could be so easily dismissed and insulted, they argued, it was time for African Americans to demand and work for respect and autonomy. In this, Jones and Allen were successful. Throughout the nineteenth century, Philadelphia became a center of abolitionist activism, and its African American community was "known nationally ... for its high level of education and culture."[26] While the yellow fever epidemic was a terrible tragedy for all Philadelphians, it also was a trigger for some positive change.

Scientific and Medical Debate

As might be expected, the epidemic also engendered a crisis of confidence among the medical profession. The careful observations of the disease made by physicians seemed to undermine most of the medical theories of the time without suggesting any new solutions or hypotheses. As such, the epidemic demonstrated the limits of eighteenth-century medical theory as well as the surprising sophistication of eighteenth-century methods of clinical observation and experiment.

Physicians divided into two camps concerning the cause and treatment of yellow fever. One faction was led by the prominent physician (and Revolutionary leader) Benjamin Rush. Rush believed that yellow fever was a disease caused by overstimulation of the nerves and blood vessels by putrefying humors. The cure, therefore, was to weaken the overstimulated tissues with a regime of intense bleeding and purging. Under Rush's regime, as much as 80 percent of a patient's blood volume might be drained away, supplemented by massive doses of mercury-based purgatives.

A competing theory, supported by many of the French refugee doctors in Philadelphia, took the opposite view. Yellow fever was a disease of depleted and weakened blood vessels, requiring stimulants and tonics (such as quinine) to strengthen the system. Under this theory of the disease, bleeding was absolutely forbidden.

Both schools of thought had evidence to support their view. Rush and his followers noted that the disease caused a rapid pulse and respirations, and that autopsies revealed severe inflammation of the intestinal tract and blood vessels—all of which, in their view, pointed to overstimulation. Those in the other camp pointed to the slow pulse and coma of the late stages of the disease as evidence of generalized weakness. They also asserted that the intestinal inflammation Rush saw in autopsies was a result of Rush's treatment method rather than the disease itself. Both provided highly detailed documentation of their evidence.

The debate over yellow fever's cause and treatment demonstrated both the strengths and weaknesses of eighteenth-century medicine. While physicians of the time were skilled observers and record-keepers, and had fully accepted the scientific method of argument from observed evidence, neither had an accurate theory as to the cause of disease, and their treatments may well have done more harm than good. With yellow fever, the humoral theory of health and medicine had reached its limits. As one historian put it, "Any of [the physicians] may have been disappointed with the efficacy of the method he chose, but each was confident that he was doing the right thing for the right reason."[27]

Yellow Fever and City Government

In some ways, the most important and long-lasting effect of the epidemic was not medical but governmental. While the physicians debated the proper cause and treatment for the disease, in the end they accomplished little of lasting effect. On the other hand, the yellow fever epidemic prompted the Philadelphia government to accept responsibility for public health and helped lay the groundwork for modern public health reform in the nineteenth century.

In August of 1793, as it became clear that the epidemic constituted a serious crisis for the city, Mayor Matthew Clarkson convened a committee to organize care for the poor and improve sanitation. One of the first measures taken was to adopt measures to clean the houses of yellow fever victims. City employees scrubbed and swept the houses of the sick and fumigated them with smoke. Since it was widely believed that yellow fever was caused by the foul air or "miasma" given off by rotting garbage, city officials took steps to clean the city streets. Special carts were commissioned to remove both liquid and solid waste. The committee also organized other equipment to wash down the public sidewalks and control the dust that was also associated with disease. All of these measures were made permanent in January of 1794. These measures prompted the city council to look into long-term improvements to the city's water supply, which culminated in building a modern, steam-powered waterworks in the early nineteenth century.

The more immediate problem before the committee in the summer of 1793 was how to care for the sick. The city took over an abandoned mansion named Bush Hill, located just outside city limits. Bush Hill became a public hospital, staffed by volunteer physicians and nurses (many of the latter African Americans organized by Absolom Jones and Richard Allen). Other volunteers drove carts to transport patients to the hospital and carry corpses away for burial. The establishment of the hospital accomplished two goals: to provide care for yellow fever victims, and to isolate the sick and dying from the rest of the city.

Of course, none of these measures could have prevented or cured yellow fever. But their implementation made Philadelphia a healthier city overall, with fewer outbreaks of water-borne disease. They also signaled a new role for government in the modernizing city and the nation as a whole—when the "general welfare" of the American people included looking out for their health.

Before an understanding of the true causes of infectious disease, epidemics were an inevitable part of life in early America. However, the people of the time mounted the best response they could. Inoculation and public health measures ameliorated the effects of infectious disease and helped set the stage for modern medicine.

NOTES

1. Alfred Crosby, *The Columbian Exchange: Biological and Cultural Consequences of 1492.* Westport, CT: Greenwood Press, 1973, p. 56.

2. Quoted in Crosby, *The Columbian Exchange,* p. 41.

3. Ibid., pp. 40–41.

4. David S. Jones, "Virgin Soils Revisited," *The William and Mary Quarterly,* 60, no. 4 (October 2003), p. 703.

5. Crosby, *The Columbian Exchange,* pp. 24–29.

6. Jones, "Virgin Soils Revisited," pp. 731–732. Both David Jones and Alfred Crosby reject genetic vulnerability as an important factor, as does Gary Nash in his book *Red, White, and Black: The Peoples of Early North America.* Upper Saddle River, NJ: Prentice Hall, 2000.

7. Edmund S. Morgan, *American Slavery, American Freedom: The Ordeal of Colonial Virginia.* New York: W.W. Norton, 1975, pp. 160, 175.

8. Darrett B. Rutman and Anita H. Rutman, "Of Agues and Fevers: Malaria in the Early Chesapeake," *William and Mary Quarterly,* 3rd Series, 33, no. 1 (January 1976), p. 44.

9. Rutman and Rutman, "Of Agues and Fevers," pp. 50–60.

10. Quoted in John Duffy, *Epidemics in Colonial America.* Baton Rouge: Louisiana State University Press, 1953, p. 143.

11. Duffy, *Epidemics in Colonial America,* pp. 144–145.

12. Ibid., pp. 101–103.

13. Rebecca Tannenbaum, *The Healer's Calling: Women and Medicine in Early New England.* Ithaca, NY: Cornell University Press, 2002, pp. 119–120.

14. Elizabeth Fenn, *Pox Americana: The Great American Smallpox Epidemic of 1775-1782.* New York: Hill and Wang, 2001, p. 32.

15. Quoted in Fenn, *Pox Americana*, p. 36.

16. Quoted in Duffy, *Epidemics in Colonial America*, p. 29.

17. Letter from Abigail Adams to John Adams, 13–14 July 1776 [electronic edition]. *Adams Family Papers: An Electronic Archive.* Massachusetts Historical Society. http://www.masshist.org/digitaladams/.

18. Quoted in Duffy, *Colonial Epidemics*, p. 215.

19. Kathleen M. Brown, *Foul Bodies: Cleanliness in Early America.* New Haven, CT: Yale University Press, 2009, p. 124.

20. Quoted in Duffy, *Epidemics in Colonial America*, pp. 215–216.

21. Ibid., p. 219.

22. Ibid., p. 221.

23. John Harvey Powell, *Bring Out Your Dead: The Great Plague of Yellow Fever in Philadelphia in 1793.* New York: Arno Press, 1970, p. 98.

24. Quoted in Phillip Lapsansky, " 'Abigail, A Negress': The Role and Legacy of African Americans in the Yellow Fever Epidemic." In J. Worth Estes and Billy G. Smith (Eds.), *A Melancholy Scene of Devastation: The Public Response to the 1793 Philadelphia Yellow Fever Epidemic.* Philadelphia: Science History Publications, 1997, p. 61.

25. Quoted in Lapsansky, " 'Abigail, A Negress,' " p. 64.

26. Lapsansky, " 'Abigail, A Negress,' " p. 74.

27. J. Worth Estes, "Introduction: The Yellow Fever Syndrome and Its Treatment in Philadelphia: 1793." In J. Worth Estes and Billy G. Smith (Eds.), *A Melancholy Scene of Devastation*, p. 14.

CHAPTER 7

"Dangerous Trades" and Occupational Health

The world of work was a dangerous place in the Colonial era. Almost any trade—from farming to shoemaking—brought with it the risk of injury or illness. However, some occupations were more risky than others. Whalers, fishermen, and merchant sailors risked not just storms and pirates, but starvation and scurvy. Sex workers were vulnerable to disease and violence. Finally, slavery was an "occupation" that undermined the health of its victims as well as their dignity and freedom. These occupations are extreme examples of the dangers all workers faced in their daily lives.

THE MARITIME TRADES

Of all Colonial era jobs, working at sea was probably among the most dangerous. While all those who worked on ships shared some risks—storms and shipwreck most prominently—fishing, whaling, and merchant sailing each had unique dangers of its own.

Seafaring was for the most part work for young men. The physical demands required strength, agility, and health. Most sailors began their careers in their mid- to late teens. The average age of a sailor on an Atlantic merchant ship in the first half of the eighteenth century was 27.6, with only 9.1 percent over 40, and 2 percent over 50. Even captains—the oldest and most experienced members of the crew—were usually in their thirties.[1]

Merchant Ships

A merchant voyage in the transatlantic trade meant committing to long periods of work in an isolated environment with no means of walking out. Most trading voyages lasted six to nine months, and slaving voyages took longer—usually 10 months to a year. During this time, the crew saw no one but each other for weeks at a time, and discipline was at the absolute discretion of the captain. The crew was also completely dependent on the ship and its supplies for food, water, shelter, and medicine.

The work itself consisted of handling the cargo and steering and maintaining the ship. When the ship began its voyage, the sailors were responsible for loading cargo into the ship. Dockworkers also participated in this work, but stowing the cargo properly so that the ship was balanced was the responsibility of the crew. Sailors operated pulleys, tackles, and cargo hooks to load and arrange heavy crates, bales, and barrels of goods. When the ship came into port, the same process was carried out to unload the ship and take on the next load of cargo.

Once the ship was at sea, the nature of the work changed. Navigation was a specialized skill, but all sailors took turns at the helm, following the course charted by the captain or the helmsman. When not at the wheel, a ship's crew spent much of its time adjusting the sails and rigging. Much of this work required that sailors climb to the top of the masts. On ships that required a lookout, crew members took turns standing in the "crow's nest" at the top of a mast. While at sea, there was constant labor to maintain the ship, such as mending sails or coating ropes with hot tar to make them waterproof.

Each of these tasks carried its own risks. Loading enormously heavy containers of cargo often resulted in serious injury. For instance, a rolling barrel could crush a hand or foot, or a shifting crate could break a sailor's arm. A worker could be injured by the equipment itself. In addition, the work could result in a "rupture," or hernia, which could permanently end the career of a manual laborer. Once at sea, a sailor could fall "from the rigging, [be] washed overboard or [be] fatally struck by falling gear." A pot of boiling tar could tip over and cause severe burns.[2]

Even if all went well with these tasks, ships and sailors were at the mercy of the weather. When a storm struck, or when winds drove the ship against a shoal or submerged rocks, it was time for the crew to "work for our Lives." The crew scrambled to take down sails or even cut down masts to prevent high winds from capsizing the ship. If the ship began to take on water, it was time to man the pumps in an effort to avoid sinking. One voyager recorded his experience in a storm: as water began seeping into the ship's hold, he marked the waterline with a piece of chalk; if the water rose despite pumping, he knew the ship would be doomed. Luckily, the crew's efforts rid the ship of enough water to save their lives. Not all crews were so fortunate.[3]

The isolation and crowded conditions shipboard also meant that disease could spread quickly. Sailors died of typhus and other "fevers"; skin diseases and infected wounds were also common causes of death and debility. Disease was a particular problem for merchant sailors who worked in the slave trade. European Americans were especially vulnerable to the diseases endemic to Africa, such as malaria, yellow fever, and various other tropical diseases. Most sailors considered Africa "a very unhealthful place." The risk of disease was exacerbated by the common practice of waiting several months at the slave trading ports to acquire a full cargo. The longer a ship lingered, the more likely it was that the crew would fall sick. A popular verse of the time summed up the sailors' fears:

> Beware and take care
> Of the Bight of Benin;
> For one that comes out
> There are forty go in.[4]

If any kind of disease broke out on board, every crew member was likely to get sick, and even if the ship carried a surgeon or physician, some of the crew were likely to die. During one slaving voyage in 1714, sickness broke out among the Africans first. One hundred and twenty of the 360 Africans on board died; when the disease spread to the crew, eight of the 20 sailors died.[5]

One of the most feared diseases was scurvy. We know today that scurvy is caused by a vitamin C deficiency. Vitamin C is found in fresh fruit and vegetables; however, in the days before refrigeration, such foods would spoil quickly at sea. A sailor's diet was likely to consist of salt meat, "ship's biscuit," and oat porridge, with little or no fresh food. Scurvy causes bleeding at the gums and along the fingernails, swelling of the arms and legs, loose teeth, joint pain, and a lowered immune response. In extreme cases, scurvy can cause nerve damage and death. While several seventeenth- and eighteenth-century ship's surgeons had made the connection between scurvy and the lack of fresh food, it was often impractical to follow their advice.

Starvation and dehydration were also possibilities. If a ship was becalmed or delayed by storms, supplies could run out. Food could spoil or be washed overboard. Stored water could become foul from contaminated barrels. Captains rationed food and water carefully to avoid these problems.

Finally, there was the issue of ship's discipline. Captains had absolute power over the crew while at sea and the legal right to issue "correction" to unruly workers as they saw fit. The usual tool of this discipline was the "cat o'nine tails," a whip with nine lashes, but some captains beat sailors with ropes, clubs, or oars. Some captains were so brutal in their punishments that sailors were permanently injured or even killed. The death of Richard Baker in 1734 is a particularly gruesome example. Baker had been sick with a flux for some days and unable to work. The captain, James Blythe, suspected Baker of malingering and ordered him to go back to work. When Baker did not comply, Blythe first whipped Baker with the cat o'nine tails, then strapped him to a mast and forbade anyone to release him. Baker died four days later.[6]

A danger specific to the slave trade was the possibility of mutiny. Such uprisings were much feared among sailors, and some resorted to brutal measures to prevent them. When such measures did not work, the enslaved Africans often killed all or most of the crew.

Fishing and Whaling

Fishermen and whalers faced many of the same dangers as merchant sailors. However, these trades had additional perils of their own. Killing and processing whales brought risk of injury from harpoons, the whales themselves, or pots of boiling whale oil; fishing required sailing during the winter, when storms and shipwreck were more likely.

The eighteenth century saw the beginnings of the deep water whaling industry in New England. Whaling began as an industry similar to fishing: whalers took short trips, close to shore. However, as coastal whale populations declined, and demand for whale oil increased, American whalers began taking longer and longer voyages in search of deep sea species. Primary among these species was the sperm whale. Sperm whales provide high quality oil as well as products unique to their species: spermaceti, used for the most luxurious candles and lamps (it burns with minimal smoke and soot), and the even rarer ambergris, used in perfumes.

Deep sea whaling was a high risk, high payoff occupation. Whale oil was a high priced commodity, and even the lowest ranking sailors could make good money from their shares of a ship's profits.

However, the voyages were long and dangerous. Most young men put a limit on their time on whaling ships, retiring by their early thirties to pursue land-based businesses, which they often funded with profits from their whaling trips.

Whaling came with the usual dangers of sea voyages. The length of whaling ventures magnified these dangers. A ship that pursued whales to the coast of Africa could be gone for eight months to a year. While this was within the same range as some merchant voyages, one key difference is that most of a whaling voyage was spent at sea, rather than visiting ports. Time spent in the isolation of the open ocean meant more danger from storms, malnutrition, and accidents.

The work of hunting, killing, and processing whales created unique hazards as well. When the lookout spotted a pod of whales, the crew lowered small rowboats into the water to pursue and kill them. Rowers brought the whaleboat within range for the harpooner. Once a whale was speared, the rowers had to keep the whaleboat out of the way of the animal's struggle; often more than one harpoon was necessary to kill the whale. When the whale was dead, the rowers towed the carcass back to the ship for processing.

Rendering a whale for oil was an unpleasant, messy, and labor-intensive process. Crew members opened the whale's head to reach the spermaceti, which was ladled out first. Then the crew stripped the blubber from the rest of the carcass and hauled it onto the deck. While some workers were busy with this task, others set up enormous kettles to boil the blubber down for oil. Boiling down or "trying out" the blubber of a large whale could take several days. The boiling blubber created an enormous stench and left an oily, sooty residue on the deck of the ship.

None of these activities was without its own danger. Wounded whales could and did attack whaleboats and ships, as this account from 1752 relates: "She came at our boat, and furiously ran over us and oversat [overset] us. . . . a wonder and a mercy it was . . . that we all had our lives spared."[7] Sailors and harpooners could get tangled in harpoon lines and pulled overboard. Sharks often gathered at whaling sites, attracted by the blood in the water and the offal discarded during the butchering process; anyone who fell overboard was likely to be attacked. The fires used on the decks of ships were also hazards, which were exacerbated by the spilled oil that soaked the wooden decks. Finally, kettles of boiling oil could be upset by the motion of the ship, so serious burns were another occupational hazard.

Cod fishing in New England did not require the long voyages of whaling. Most fishing trips left and returned the same day, and most fishermen made only three trips per week (the rest of their time was spent salting and drying the fish for sale and shipment). If the catch was small, trips might extend to two days, but rarely longer since the fish could spoil if not processed quickly. Cod fishermen used hooks and lines rather than nets. Each crew member was responsible for baiting, hauling, and maintaining two lines.

The short trips protected fishermen from some of the dangers of seafaring. Scurvy and malnutrition were not an issue, for instance. Cod fishermen did not escape the hazards of the sea completely, however. Cod fishing took place year-round, meaning that many fishing trips took place in frigid weather. Since most fishing boats did not have a shelter for the crew, fishermen were exposed to cold winds, snow and sleet, and icy sea spray. Winter storms could blow up suddenly, putting the crew in further danger. One Maine fishing crew went out on a day in February 1645 and did not return. The boat was later found half full of water, with the three-man crew frozen to death. The following summer, a fishing boat capsized and sank in the same waters. While the air temperature was warm, the water was still very cold; while the crew survived the initial shipwreck by clinging to an oar, two of the three died of exposure before they could be rescued.[8]

FEMALE SEX WORKERS

While men dominated the maritime trades, some women's occupations were also especially hazardous. Sex work, or prostitution, was one of these trades. During the eighteenth century, port cities such as Philadelphia and New York City saw enormous growth in the sex trade. Most sex workers worked out of taverns or bawdy houses (brothels). Other women worked independently, or in loose confederation with other workers. The line between paid sex work and other kinds of illicit sex was not always clear; some unmarried or adulterous couples (especially interracial couples) used bawdy houses as a trysting places; some women traded sex for money only intermittently and worked in other jobs most of the time; and any woman found in a tavern might be labeled as a prostitute whether she engaged in sex work or not.

However, those who engaged in sex for pay were faced with particular occupational hazards. Venereal disease was one of the most prominent. During the 1760s, physicians' advertisements offering cures for sexually transmitted infection proliferated, suggesting that patients with these diseases were also quite common. Treatment for syphilis was unpleasant, even by standards of the time, involving enormous doses of mercury to the point of uncontrollable nausea, vomiting, "salivation," and tooth loss. As a result, many doctors advertised cures that avoided such side effects. One such advertisement promised "he will engage to cure it, from the slightest infection to the most virulent degree, without salivation, hindrance of business, or danger of impairing the most tender constitution, and cures a fresh infection in a few days." Another doctor promised that the medicine he sold worked "without the least inconveniencey, or imparting the secret to a bedfellow."[9]

Women for whom these cures did not work had other, albeit also unpleasant, options. Those who were destitute could enter the medical wards of almshouses where they were given food, shelter, and a modicum of medical treatment. Such institutions, however, often provided a dose of humiliation along with their charity. Records of Philadelphia almshouses describe clients as "that dirty little hussey" or "a worthless hussey."[10] By the early nineteenth century, almshouses began to refuse medical treatment to sex workers unless they named their "madams" and fellow prostitutes to the courts. Other institutions, the Magdelen homes, aimed their services at sheltering and reforming prostitutes. They did not, however, accept women showing obvious signs of sexually transmitted infections.

None of the eighteenth-century remedies for sexually transmitted infections were very effective. Syphilis, in particular, has an insidious course. The initial sore disappears, and many patients would then think themselves "cured." As modern medicine now knows, however, the infection remains. The disease organism attacks internal organs such as the brain, heart, and blood vessels. After many years of increasingly severe symptoms, the patient dies. Gonorrhea may show few or no early symptoms in women but can infect the uterus and fallopian tubes, and lead eventually to peritonitis, septic shock, and death.

Another danger of sex work for women was pregnancy and childbirth. While childbirth was dangerous for all women in this era, sexually transmitted infections and poverty raised the risk for sex workers. Impoverished women often entered an almshouse to give birth. These women were housed in the medical ward alongside other inmates with communicable diseases. Such conditions increased the likelihood that a woman would contract a deadly postpartum infection. Infants born under these circumstances were also at high risk: one in six infants born in Philadelphia almshouses died, usually within days of birth.[11]

Sex workers were also especially vulnerable to violence. Public women were considered fair game for several different kinds of violence. Bawdy houses were frequent targets of spontaneous vigilante attacks by outraged neighbors. Dissatisfied customers might attack a sex worker individually, or lead a mob against the tavern or house where she did business. Attacks on sex workers and bawdy houses sometimes came in waves, as each assault inspired others to do the same.

In 1793, a group of soldiers who felt they had been cheated at one establishment led a series of riots that attacked a group of bawdy houses. They first attacked the house where the alleged cheating had taken place, destroying furniture and household goods as well as chasing the employees into the street; they then descended on neighboring bawdy houses until the houses were "demolished, and their miserable inmates driven naked and houseless into the streets."[12] In another case, in which the owner of the house was suspected of kidnapping the daughter of a sea captain, a crowd of outraged neighbors attacked with the object of rescuing the young woman and tearing down the house. In both cases, the violence grew out of a long tradition of informal community justice. The attackers' object was punishment and public shaming of the "culprits."[13]

As time passed, however, the violence escalated and became more personal. By the early nineteenth century, community attacks on brothels had transformed into "sprees" of violence carried out by drunken young men. These incidents sometimes "evolved into scenes of sadistic terror" in the words of one historian. In one instance, three young men attacked one bawdy house and then turned their rage on its owner. They "knocked her down, beat her on the face and head so as to blind her entirely, and after having knocked her down, kicked her." The attackers also assaulted the woman's disabled son. In another incident, a man on a "spree" threw sulfuric acid in a young woman's face, leaving her severely burned. Sex workers made easy targets for young men looking for a fight or an outlet for violent impulses. Although many victims of this kind of violence reported the assaults and participated in the prosecution of the perpetrators, many others did not. The stigma of prostitution made them reluctant to seek help from official sources.[14]

ENSLAVED WORKERS

Slaves worked in the worst conditions, did the hardest work, and had the lowest living standards of all Colonial era workers. It is no surprise that slavery endangered the lives and health of its victims. In addition to the many health dangers of slavery discussed elsewhere in this volume, slaves were exposed to horrific conditions on the voyage from Africa to America and after they arrived were often put to work at the most dangerous jobs, such as mining. All of these conditions combined to create a health gap between Americans of African and European descent that persists to this day.

Like all sea voyages, the middle passage was dangerous to those who undertook it. While the captives held in the bellies of the ships shared many dangers with the crew, those dangers were exacerbated by enslavement. Most prominently, disease and malnutrition took a larger toll among the captives than the captors.

Epidemic disease was greatly feared by slave traders. Slave buyers did their best to buy only the healthiest captives. Traders inspected the mouths and teeth of potential slaves for tooth decay or other diseases; they forced captives to jump up and down to check their "wind" and general health; and they examined genitalia for signs of sexually transmitted infection and to ensure that the person's reproductive organs looked normal. In addition, a captive's clothing was confiscated before he or she boarded the ship to prevent the cloth from bringing disease or parasites into the hold. Captives were kept naked for the duration of the voyage.

Even so, epidemics could begin even before a ship left Africa since ships often lay in port for weeks waiting to acquire a full compliment of "cargo." One captain brought aboard a "fine" young man. Even though the ship's doctor warned that the man was showing early symptoms of smallpox, the captain ignored the warning. Ten captives died within a day of the young man's arrival, and soon after most of the people in the hold were sick.[15]

Once at sea, epidemic disease continued to be a risk. In the crowded and unsanitary conditions in a slave ship's hold, disease could develop and spread with alarming speed. Smallpox was especially deadly at sea for this reason. Ships could lose not just their captives but the crew as well. In one case, 170 of 216 persons on board a ship died of smallpox. Many slave ship captains were early adopters of inoculation for the disease, and they inoculated captives before leaving port. Other methods of cure included dietary changes and drinking "tar water," that is, water in which a small amount of tar had been dissolved. Some captains insisted that captives and crew alike drink tar water for the entire journey as a preventative.

Along with smallpox, flux or dysentery was most feared. Historians have noted that gastrointestinal diseases were the leading cause of death from disease on slave ships, and one eighteenth-century ship's surgeon noted that "You must observe, that when this Flux comes upon them [captives], they know they shall surely [die]." Ship's surgeons tried many remedies, including bleeding (which often meant restraining the unwilling "patient"), a bland diet, herbal purgatives (to drive out the bad humors), and mercury derivatives. Sick captives were sometimes (but not always) isolated from the others, which may have helped prevent further spread of the illness. Despite these attempts, the mortality rate remained high.[16]

Sexually transmitted infections were another cause for concern, especially among female captives. While a check for obvious symptoms was part of the presale inspection, many sexually transmitted infections show few initial symptoms in women. Some women entered late stages of disease while shipboard and thus came to the attention of the ship's doctor or captain. Ships' logs described various "swellings in the groin," "wart-like excrescences," and discharge of "watery, whitish fluid." Most women did not die of these diseases on the ship (although some did), but the suffering was tremendous. The common mention of sexually transmitted infection on slave ships also suggests that women were being sexually abused or raped.[17]

Enslaved Africans also suffered disproportionately from malnutrition during the Middle Passage. Like most shipboard diets, the captives' food was primarily salted meat or fish, combined with some sort of starch, such as biscuit or oatmeal. Yams were also a common slave ship staple since they were widely available in the African ports where the ships docked and bought supplies. (African yams are not the same as sweet potatoes; they are starchier and drier.) While all on board ate more or less the same diet, and suffered the consequences of scurvy and other vitamin deficiencies, the captives were often fed less food of lower quality. Most captains provided only two scanty meals per day. In many cases, this was a financial decision—the captains needed to make as much of a profit as possible from each voyage. Whatever the reason, semistarvation meant that captives were more vulnerable to any infectious disease that came on board.

One common cause of the dreaded "flux" among the captives was spoiled food. Insects and mold often infested the ships' food stores, and spoiled food was given to the captives rather than the crew. One ship's doctor noted that "one of the great causes of losing the slaves, comes from very bad food." Some captains did their best to keep food from spoiling by rotating it from the damp hold onto the deck, and making sure the storage areas were kept dry and well ventilated.[18]

Slaves, like all those at sea, were vulnerable to scurvy. Conditions on the ships for captives, however, exaggerated the suffering from the disease. Scurvy often causes swelling of the arms and legs; for those whose limbs were restricted by heavy chains, the pain must have been intense. Women who suffered hemorrhages from the genitals or anus would have been subjected to humiliating examinations and possibly harmful mercury treatments for what the captors assumed was venereal disease. Tooth loss would have made the crude diet even more inedible and exacerbated the effects of malnutrition.[19]

Those who survived the journey were then set to work in the sugar fields, tobacco plantations, and rice ponds of North America. However, there were some particularly dangerous jobs that were reserved for slaves. The early coal mining industry in eighteenth-century Virginia is a good example. Henry Heth operated the Black Heath mine, one of the earliest coal mines in the United States, which opened in 1788. From the beginning, the majority of the workers were enslaved. Some were owned by Heth himself, but as his business expanded, he began to hire slaves from other owners. Slaves worked in the pits and in support jobs such as blacksmithing, barrel making, and bricklaying. The work was both back-breaking and dangerous, and mine owners considered slaves the best and most efficient labor force. As one nineteenth-century mine owner commented, "Every day's experience confirms my opinion that it is next to impossible to prosecute my mining interest successfully with free labor. . . . No reliance whatever can be placed upon it. . . . I must have a negro force or give up my business."[20]

Rock falls were one danger. Heth's foreman reported to his boss that three hands were seriously injured when "a piece of coal fell from the roof"; one was able to return to work after a day's rest, but the other two would remain invalids for some time. In another incident, a miner was killed. One of Heth's continuing business expenses was compensating the owners of hired hands for injuries to their slaves.[21]

Mines were also subject to sudden floods. When miners dug deep into the water table, the shaft could flood with water with no warning. At the Black Heath mine, a shaft suddenly filled with water. Supervisors struggled to reach the workers trapped by the rising waters; two white overseers were rescued, but seven slaves drowned.

In coal mines, fire probably represented the greatest and most terrifying danger, and the Virginia mines had a particularly bad reputation. Coal seams often coincide with pockets of methane gas; when the gas is released, the smallest spark can cause an explosion and fire. Mine fires can continue for astoundingly long periods of time, fed by the seams of coal. One fire in the Black Heath mine began in 1788 and continued to burn for 30 years. (The burning sections were sealed off and mining continued.) Smoke and gas from mine fires can seep into usable sections, suffocating workers. At Black Heath, Heth's business partner entered a smoky mine shaft to determine if it could be reopened. Soon after, his escorts began to "stagger" under the effects of smoke. The inspection party barely made it out alive. Actual explosions resulted in high death tolls. One of the worst explosions in Black Heath mine killed 45 slaves and two white overseers, and blew most of the "internal works" of the mine "to atoms." Another worker was being lowered into the shaft on the "basket" when the explosion occurred; he fell clear of the fire but broke both arms and both legs.[22]

Even for slaves who were not put to work in mines, slavery carried dangers that did not apply to other kinds of work. Slaves faced malnutrition and physical and sexual abuse, with no means of redress. Some historians have argued that the institution of slavery set the stage for a disparity in health and longevity that continues to this day.

Slavery marked the beginnings of a segregated health system. White indentured servants lived in conditions similar to slaves during the terms of their contracts. They, however, had means of legal redress that slaves did not. Servants had the right to complain to a justice of the peace if their masters did not provide adequate food, clothing, and shelter, or if the "physical correction" doled out by the master crossed the line into abuse or injury. Servants also had the hope of serving out their time and becoming free laborers or even landholders. In addition, their white color and English background allowed them to assimilate quickly once released. Slaves, on the other hand, had no such recourse and had to tolerate poor conditions for their entire lives. Furthermore, some Colonial American hospitals segregated African American patients into "Negro wards," where conditions and care were below the already low standard set by the wards for whites. As one historian put it, "Black patients continued to occupy the least desirable locations . . . they were shunted into basements or attics."[23]

When an enslaved person fell ill, the care was substandard, even for an age of substandard health care. While slaves established their own health practices, when white physicians were called to attend to slaves, they brought their own racial assumptions with them. Physicians attempted cures based on their own beliefs about the "inferiority" of black bodies. As a result, care was different for slaves, and often second rate. All of these factors—segregated, inferior medical care; racialized assumptions about African American patients; and, after slavery, the institutionalized poverty of many African Americans—created a health system that did not serve the African American population. As a result, the ultimate "occupational hazard" of slavery might well be the legacy of ill health and high mortality that has followed it.[24]

While all Colonial era people lived with dangers from their work, certain trades had more dangers than others. This sampling has suggested the ways in which work could affect a person's health, whether that person was a deep sea whaler or an enslaved coal miner. The connections among work, health, and disease would not be recognized for many years.

NOTES

1. Marcus Rediker, *Between the Devil and the Deep Blue Sea: Merchant Seamen, Pirates, and the Anglo-American Maritime World*. New York: Cambridge University Press, 1987, p. 299.

2. Ibid., pp. 92–93.

3. Ibid., p. 94.

4. Ibid., pp. 46–47.

5. Ibid., p. 48.

6. Ibid., p. 219.

7. Daniel Vickers, "Nantucket Whalemen in the Deep-Sea Whale Fishery: The Changing Anatomy of an Early American Labor Force," *Journal of American History*, 72, no. 2 (1985), p. 279.

8. E. A. Churchill, "A Most Ordinary Lot of Men: The Fishermen at Richmond Island Maine in the Early Seventeenth Century," *New England Quarterly*, 57, no. 2 (1984), p. 188.

9. Quoted in Clare A. Lyons, *Sex among the Rabble: An Intimate History of Gender and Power in the Age of Revolution*. Chapel Hill: University of North Carolina Press, 2006, pp. 112–113.

10. Quoted in Lyons, *Sex among the Rabble*, pp. 260–262.

11. Ibid., p. 263.

12. Timothy A. Gilfoyle, "Strumpets and Misogynists: Brothel Riots and the Transformation of Prostitution in Antebellum New York City," *New York History*, 68, no. 1 (1987), p. 48.

13. Gilfoyle, "Misogynists and Strumpets," pp. 48–49.

14. Ibid., p. 53.

15. Sowande Mustakeem, "I Never Have Such a Sickly Ship Before: Diet, Disease, and Mortality in Eighteenth Century Atlantic Slaving Voyages," *Journal of African American History*, 93, no. 4 (2008), p. 479.

16. Mustakeem, "Such a Sickly Ship," p. 485.

17. Ibid., pp. 489–490.

18. Ibid., p. 482.

19. Ibid., pp. 483–484.

20. Quoted in Ronald L. Lewis, "The Darkest Abode of Man: Black Miners in the First Southern Coal Field: 1780–1865," *Virginia Magazine of History and Biography*, 87, no. 2 (1979), p. 196.

21. Ibid., p. 196.

22. Ibid., p. 197.

23. W. Michael Byrd and Linda A. Clayton, *An American Health Dilemma: A Medical History of African Americans and the Problem of Race*, Vol. 1. New York: Routledge, 2000, p. 200.

24. Byrd and Clayton, *An American Health Dilemma*, p. 194.

CHAPTER 8

Surgery, Dentistry, and Orthopedics

Surgery in the Colonial era was not the sophisticated, high technology practice of today. Surgeons were of low status and often had less training than physicians. Anatomical knowledge was just emerging (literally) from the dark ages, and surgical techniques were crude. Perhaps the most important contrast with modern surgery was the lack of both anesthesia and antisepsis. Operations were excruciating for the patient, and carried a serious risk of postoperative infection and death. As a result, surgeons almost never attempted to cure disorders of the abdomen and the chest, and focused their practices on bone setting, amputations, therapeutic bloodletting, and the cure of superficial lesions and skin diseases. Dentistry was a subfield of surgery, although some dentists were beginning to separate their practice into its own profession.

SCIENCE, SURGERY, AND ANATOMY IN SEVENTEENTH- AND EIGHTEENTH-CENTURY EUROPE

Surgery was a separate vocation from the practice of medicine, or physick. Since medieval times, surgeons (who worked with their hands) were categorized with artisans; physicians (who worked with their heads diagnosing and prescribing) were classed with gentlemen. As is still well known today, surgeons and barbers were once part of the same profession. A barber-surgeon could shave a man's beard and then perform a therapeutic bloodletting for the same customer, perhaps even using the same razor. Barber-surgeons often worked at the direction of physicians, following instructions and carrying out the messy manual labor of amputations and bloodletting. While surgery and barbering had become separate trades by the time of Colonial settlement in America, surgery was still viewed as a lesser art than physick until the eighteenth century.

Surgery began to modernize during the Renaissance. At this time, European students of anatomy, most prominently Andreas Vesalius, made great breakthroughs in understanding the structure of the human body. Vesalius's *De Humani Corpora Fabrica* (The Structure of the Human Body) became one of the foundation texts of modern medical science, and its remarkably accurate illustrations are sometimes still used in textbooks today. With this foundation, surgeons and other practitioners were able to develop new and more effective surgical techniques.

Most formally trained surgeons focused on learning as much about human anatomy as possible and using that anatomical knowledge to push the limits of what surgery could do. There were, however, serious disadvantages that stood in the way of progress. Of these, the most important was the lack of anesthesia. Surgeons had to be assisted by several strong men to hold the patient still while the surgeon cut. Surgeons had to work as quickly as possible to spare the patient, and everyone breathed a sigh of relief if the patient fainted from shock and pain. Today it is hard to imagine undergoing an operation without the benefit of painkilling drugs. It is not surprising that surgery was a treatment of last resort, when the ongoing pain of a disease or injury outweighed the terrible suffering of undergoing surgery.

Postoperative infection was another barrier to real surgical progress. Surgeons fully expected wounds to become infected after an operation, and many welcomed the appearance of pus in a wound as evidence of healing. A patient who survived the trauma of surgery was not out of the woods until he or she had also survived the inevitable wound infection afterward.

Within these limitations, individual surgeons did their best to improve their techniques during the seventeenth and eighteenth centuries. One of he most influential figures of the time was French surgeon Ambrose Paré. Paré did most of his work in the late sixteenth century, but his influence continued for the next two centuries. After apprenticing as a barber-surgeon, Paré joined the military, in which he spent most of his career and made his most important discoveries. One of his most important contributions was a method of controlling bleeding by ligating blood vessels. Until that time, surgeons stopped bleeding during amputations and other procedures by cauterizing the wound with a red-hot iron or boiling oil. The burn sealed off the blood vessels but created yet more trauma and pain for the patient. Paré instead tied off the cut vessels, which allowed for quicker healing. Paré also published his findings and broke new ground by writing in vernacular French rather than scholarly Latin. Doing so made his findings accessible to a wider field of practitioners.

Other important breakthroughs during the seventeenth century included a variety of techniques for setting broken bones in a hard cast rather than simply splinting them with wooden slats. Surgeons dipped bandages in a variety of materials that stiffened when dry, such as this recipe adapted by English surgeon William Cheselden from a local bonesetter: "Wrap [the limb] up in rags dipped in the whites of eggs and a little wheat flour mixed; this drying, grew stiff and kept the limb in a good posture . . . I think there is no way better than this in fractures, for it preserves the position of the limb." A cast allows less movement of the bones and thus facilitates better healing.[1]

In the eighteenth century, surgeons and physicians began a systematic exploration of technique that was driven by the emerging scientific method. Surgeons in England and Scotland in particular set out to systematize medical knowledge and to back up their hypotheses with observation and experiments. This surge in scientific inquiry combined with two other factors to make the eighteenth century a time of growth in surgical science. The first factor was a cultural shift toward social responsibility for the less fortunate. For the first time, the relief of human suffering seemed both possible and desirable. This new social impulse helped create the second factor that pushed surgery forward: the founding of medical schools, which included surgery as part of their curricula and which encouraged innovation among their faculty. While the most prestigious schools were European, the mid-eighteenth century saw the first North American medical school as well: The University of Pennsylvania medical school, founded in 1765. While these surgeon-scientists were still limited by the lack of anesthesia and germ theory, they did their best to improve their own knowledge and raise the status of their profession.

Many professor-surgeons made important discoveries in the physiology of the human body and the causes of common diseases. For instance, Percivall Pott of London was one of the first doctors to recognize a link between certain kinds of hazardous work and disease. In eighteenth-century London, small boys were often employed as chimney sweeps. They were forced to crawl naked into clogged chimneys; the soot became ground into their skin. These same boys often died of tumors on their skin, especially their genitals. Pott described this disease as "chimney sweep's cancer" and made the connection between exposure to soot and the deaths of the boys. Pott also contributed to surgical techniques such as a method of opening the skull to relieve pressure caused by internal bleeding.[2]

Perhaps the most important European figure in American medicine was John Hunter. Hunter studied with Percivall Pott in London and honed his technique as a military surgeon with the British Army during the Seven Years' War in France and Portugal. His excellent service brought him sufficient connections and reputation to set up as a successful surgeon in London and enough money to finance his own medical experiments. His contributions to science included papers on the structure of the placenta, a new technique for treating aneurysm in the femoral artery, and several pioneering experiments in transplantation and tissue grafting. In addition, Hunter supervised the training of a number of Americans who then returned to their homes as professors and scientists in their own right, including Phillip Syng Physick (sometimes called "The Father of American Surgery") and the obstetrician William Shippen. Both Shippen and Physick were faculty members of the University of Pennsylvania Medical School.

WHO WERE THE SURGEONS IN AMERICA?

There were many practitioners of surgery in Colonial America, ranging from the high ranking and well educated to part-time, informally trained practitioners who dabbled in other trades. These last represent the bottom of the profession's hierarchy. Most of these specialized in one procedure. One example is the practice of the tanner and leather-worker Daniel Ela, who lived and worked during the 1670s in Essex County, Massachusetts. Ela had a sideline cleaning and dressing wounds often, but not always, under the supervision of local physicians. In the 1760s, Mrs. Parker of Westborough, Massachusetts, practiced as a bonesetter. When someone was injured, she was called to splint and bandage the bone, using her homemade "apparatus" for holding the limb straight.

One step up from these part-time practitioners were the traveling surgeons and "cancer doctors." They kept to a regular route and schedule, appearing in a town every few weeks or months to offer their services. It is not clear how much training these itinerant practitioners had—some called themselves "doctor"; others simply advertised their services or provided testimonials from satisfied patients. One man, calling himself Dr. Sharp of London, advertised in the *Boston Gazette* of October 1720 that he was available to cure "cancered breasts, other cancerous or scrophulous tumors... King's evil, leprosy, scurvy, rheumatisms, and ulcers." Three months later, he placed a similar advertisement in the newspaper of Portsmouth, New Hampshire. Such traveling surgeons seemed to have performed a significant portion of the elective surgery in Colonial America. One study of newspaper advertisements between 1720 and 1825 found 31 traveling surgeons and 26 "cancer specialists" in New England and New York. In addition, the same study found 64 "surgeon-dentists" advertising their services, which represented as much as 90 percent of the dental profession of the time.[3]

The military was another career path for surgeons. Many men learned surgical skills while serving in the military, and newly trained surgeons gained experience treating wounded soldiers. Experience as a military surgeon was an important credential even in civilian practice. James Thacher was 21 and had just finished his apprenticeship when he joined the Continental Army in 1775. In his wartime journal he wrote, "Here is a fine field for professional improvement. Amputating limbs, trepanning fractured skulls, and dressing the most formidable wounds..." After leaving the army in 1783, Thacher practiced the rest of his life in Plymouth, Massachusetts, and published multiple articles on surgical techniques.[4]

By the end of the eighteenth century, surgery had gained significant prestige and was rapidly becoming part of the larger practice of medicine. Medical schools in Europe and North America were producing highly educated, scientifically inclined practitioners. Philadelphia was the center of medical advances in America, and many of this new kind of surgeon practiced there, such as Philip Syng Physick. He traveled to Edinburgh and London for his training but returned to Philadelphia, where he eventually became professor of surgery at the newly founded University of Pennsylvania medical school. He also had a long and successful practice among the elite families of the city.

While most practitioners who called themselves surgeons were of European descent, people of other cultures also practiced surgery. Native American peoples of what is now North Carolina used rattlesnake fangs as "scarifiers"—instruments to produce small cuts or scratches in the skin. The practice was at times cosmetic, producing elaborate patterns of scars or tattoos. At other times, scarification was medical, producing a counter-irritant effect that relieved the pain of larger injuries. Many cultures sutured wounds, using deer tendons, plant fibers, or human hair. Similarly, most peoples had methods to set and splint broken bones. The Ojibwa people of modern Michigan and Canada used cedar wood to make splints, and plastered broken bones with a poultice of wild ginger. Finally, archeological evidence indicates that the practice of trephination, or deliberate opening of the skull, was widespread in pre-Columbian America. Some skulls have several healed trephination scars, indicating that the patient had recovered fully from the operation.[5]

It is also worth noting that some Native American peoples seemed to have a concept of asepsis in surgery, long before Europeans developed their own germ theory. Native American practitioners often irrigated wounds or surgical sites with boiled water to cleanse the area. The Choctaws cleaned wounds with water boiled with medicinal roots explicitly to prevent gangrene.[6]

One of the earliest African Americans to be described as a healer by whites was a surgeon. The *Pennsylvania Gazette* ran a short article on an escaped slave named Simon who was able "to bleed and draw teeth."[7] Some white surgeons trained slaves to serve as their assistants, and some of these assistants went on to practice on their own. Of these, the most famous was James Durham. Durham was born a slave in Philadelphia, where he lived in the household of Dr. John Kearsley. Kearsley trained him as an assistant. Kearsley, a loyalist, was imprisoned during the Revolutionary War, and Durham passed into the hands of a British military surgeon, who continued Durham's training and taught him to assist during operations. Eventually, Durham was sold to yet another doctor, Robert Dow, who allowed Durham to purchase his freedom. Durham then went on to an independent career as a physician and surgeon. There were likely many more anonymous African Americans who learned surgical skills in this way, but their names and careers have been lost.[8]

TREATING TRAUMA

Even as science advanced, surgeons were restricted to treating only a limited number of illnesses and injuries. Surgeons spent most of their time treating traumatic injuries ranging from gunshot wounds to broken bones. A surgeon set bones, reduced dislocated joints, controlled bleeding, and provided appropriate dressings for wounds. In severe cases, the surgeon amputated injured limbs.

Bone setting was one of the oldest jobs of the surgeon. Hippocrates wrote of the difference in treatment between simple fractures (in which the skin is not broken) and compound fractures (in which the broken end of the bone protrudes through the skin). Medieval Anglo-Saxon medical writings describe the proper way to splint a broken leg. In the seventeenth and eighteenth centuries, surgeons of all levels of training set broken bones, and many lay practitioners were specialized bonesetters. While these practitioners represented a wide range of social rank, they clearly used similar methods and exchanged knowledge. As is mentioned earlier in this chapter, the English surgeon William Cheselden learned his method of making a cast from a local bonesetter. This sharing of knowledge did not stop formally educated surgeons from complaining about their less learned colleagues. One article in a medical journal condemned the "motley crew" of carpenters, blacksmiths, and "breeches makers" who set bones as a sideline.[9]

Once surgery became a respectable academic field, medical students began to study more sophisticated techniques for setting bones. One Philadelphia medical student wrote an analysis of several published papers on the topic and suggested his own method of dealing with simple fractures. He disagreed with authors who recommended setting limbs in a slightly flexed position and instead advocated keeping the limbs perfectly straight. He argued that a healed fracture was likely to result in some stiffness, and that a stiff, straight limb was more usable than a flexed one. Instead of a cast, the student suggested placing the fractured arm or leg on a pillow, then placing splints along the sides of the pillow and binding everything together with tight bandages. While we cannot know for sure if this student went on to use these methods in his later practice, his recommendations are consistent enough with other practices of the time to suggest that he did.[10]

If a bone was too badly broken—a complex compound fracture, for instance, or the immense damage caused by a direct hit by an artillery round—the only remedy was to amputate. Without such drastic treatment, the patient was almost certain to develop gangrene, and gangrene was a death sentence. Pieter Stuyvesant, Dutch military commander and governor of New Netherland took a small cannon ball in the right leg while fighting the Spanish in the Caribbean. His leg was amputated immediately. One of Stuyvesant's close friends composed a poem on the occasion: "What mad thunder ball comes roaring toward your leg/My dear Stuyvesant, and causes your collapse?/The right pillar that used to support your body/is that crushed and stricken off this way in one blow?"[11] Stuyvesant returned home to the Netherlands to recuperate and be fitted with a wooden prosthesis, although he eventually returned to a career in Colonial government.

In addition to broken bones, wounds and skin ulcers were common ailments treated by surgeons, beginning with dressing and cleansing the wound and moving on to more aggressive measures as needed. John Hartshorn, a 19-year-old apprentice surgeon in Boston in 1755, recorded his care of a Mrs. Tucker, who suffered from a deep, infected ulcer on her leg. Following the instructions of his preceptor, Dr. Silvester Gardiner, he visited her daily to change the dressing on her sore and reapply a medication of turpentine, egg yolk, and oil of roses. However, her condition worsened. A second ulcer appeared on the ankle of the affected leg, which "issued Ichor" (i.e., drained fluid). Hartshorn inserted plugs of medicated lint into the new wound, but with no effect. As the months dragged by, Hartshorn and Gardiner tried lancing the wound, burning it with lye, and applying multiple plasters and poultices. Nothing worked. New draining sinuses appeared, and the patient was growing weaker. There was nothing else to do but amputate. Hartshorn described their method:

> We sat her in a chair & put a Large Bowl of Sand under her, apply'd the Tourniquet with a Compress or two upon the arteries. I handed the instruments. Dr. Williams held the tourniquets, after binding a Tape around the Leg about 5 inches below the patella (knee cap) for a Guide to the Knife D.G. [Doctor Gardiner] began the Incision & divided quite thro the membrana Adiposa ... next the muscles were divided, then the Catlin [a special amputation knife] to divide the inter osseous muscles, then w'h the Saw The Leg was separated ...[12]

The patient made a complete recovery and even gave birth to a healthy baby 11 months after her surgery.

The context in which surgeons saw the most trauma was of course during military service. Ancient Greek vase paintings depict soldiers binding each other's wounds; medieval surgical textbooks often have as a frontispiece a "wound man" depicting various weapons and the injuries they inflict. The introduction of gunpowder and firearms brought about more complicated injuries, which were often contaminated by gunpowder residue, fragments of clothing, and the bullet itself. Ironically, warfare also creates opportunities for surgeons to perfect their technique and create new ways of treating trauma. New methods of controlling bleeding, transporting the injured, and amputating shattered limbs all came about from surgeons' experiences on the battlefield.

James Thacher, Revolutionary War surgeon, recorded his experiences in a diary. While Thacher did not invent new techniques, he did make note of the unusual injuries he treated as well as his methods for treating them. For instance, he was astonished to treat a "brave soldier" who survived a musket shot to the forehead. The bullet had not entered the skull, and when Thacher explored the wound with his probe, he found the bullet "spread entirely flat on the bone under the skin." Thacher then extracted the bullet with forceps, commenting, "It is fortunate . . . that his skull proved too thick for the ball to penetrate." Another case proved more complex. A soldier was wounded through his chest and lungs. When the man inhaled, air escaped from his wound. The inexperienced Thacher assisted as a more senior surgeon, William Eustis, opened the wound still further and ordered copious bloodletting. While bleeding a wounded patient seems contraindicated in modern times, it was logical given the physiological theory of the eighteenth century. Surgeons had long noted that bleeding from one part of the body slowed bleeding in another (as the blood supply dwindled, all bleeding slowed down); chest wounds often become inflamed, and bloodletting was the standard treatment for inflammation; and finally, bleeding was also the standard treatment for shortness of breath. Thacher followed Eustis's instructions to the letter. He made "free use of the lancet" and kept the patient on short rations. The patient made a full recovery.[13]

CUTTING FOR THE STONE

While trauma made up much of a surgeon's practice, there were other diseases that were commonly treated with surgery. One of these diseases was stone in the bladder, commonly called simply "the stone." Bladder stones are just that—accumulations of hardened minerals in the bladder. Symptoms include painful urination, abdominal pain, and blood in the urine. The pain these stones cause can be excruciating. In the worst cases, the stone blocks the urethra entirely, making normal passage of urine impossible.

In the seventeenth and eighteenth centuries, bladder stone was much more common than it is now, for reasons that are not entirely understood. In modern times, bladder stones are most often found in older men and are often correlated with prostate enlargement. However, during the Colonial era, bladder stone was a common ailment among small children—so common, in fact, that some old medical textbooks suggested bladder stone as a common cause of "colicky" babies. Many famous people, from the English diarist Samuel Pepys to Napoleon Bonaparte, suffered from bladder stones. Pepys's stone was the size of a tennis ball when it was removed! In North America, perhaps the most famous victim was Benjamin Franklin. Franklin began experiencing symptoms of the stone at the age of 78, and at first the symptoms were mild. He hoped to keep his condition under control by "abstemious living and gentle exercise," but five years later he wrote that he was "in constant and grievous pain." He considered surgery but died (of pneumonia) before he could make up his mind to have it done.[14]

Surgery for bladder stone, called "lithotomy" or "cutting for the stone," was one of the earliest operations that entered the abdominal cavity. Many of the itinerant surgeons in Colonial America specialized in this procedure. While the methods changed somewhat over time, the basic principle remained the same. The surgeon palpated the stone, either through the skin with the fingers or internally using an instrument called a "sound" inserted through the urethra. Once the stone was located, the surgeon made a cut in the perineum through to the bladder, opened the bladder where the stone was located, and removed the stone with forceps. The operator then irrigated the bladder with cold water to wash out any remaining fragments, tied off the blood vessels, and inserted plugs of lint soaked in water or olive oil to control any further bleeding.

This procedure was so common that one of the earliest American documents describing surgery describes cutting for the stone. Dr. Zabdiel Boylston of Boston placed an advertisement in the *Boston Gazette* describing his success in performing a lithotomy on a young boy "grievously afflicted with the Stone" in 1710. Boylston noted that the stone was "of considerable bigness" and that the operation had "perfectly Cured" the boy. He wrote that he had performed this operation on two other patients with equal success, and he offered his services to the public for lithotomy as well as "all other Operations in Surgery."[15]

The biggest innovation that took place during the Colonial period was a change in the location of the incision into the bladder. For many years, the accepted method was to cut along the midline of the perineum and enter the bladder from its center, but some surgeons noticed that this incision sometimes damaged the pelvic muscles and rendered the patient incontinent. In England, the prominent surgeon William Cheselden modified and popularized a French procedure that entered the bladder from the side rather than the middle, which had better results. By the 1730s, this method was most commonly used. Boston surgeon Silvester Gardiner (mentor of John Hartshorn, discussed earlier) had studied with Cheselden in London and brought his method to America. In 1741, Gardiner presented a paper to a local medical society describing his success with the lateral method. Like Boylston's 1710 patient, Gardiner's patient was a young child—a six-year-old boy named Joseph Baker. Gardiner took the opportunity to disparage his competitors, writing that "for want of Skill and Discretion in the

Operator" this surgery "too frequently kill[s] the patient in a few days or Weeks" or else leaves them with a constant leaking of urine, making for "an uncomfortable life." Joseph Baker was luckier. Gardiner noted that within four days, the boy's urine "began to trickle in the natural way" and that three weeks after the surgery, "the Boy [was] at Play about the House."[16] This method of removing bladder stones remained in use until the early twentieth century.

BREAST CANCER AND MASTECTOMY

Cancer was another disease treated surgically. Colonial era surgeons could treat only cancers that were easily detectable on the surface of the body, however, such as skin and breast tumors. Cancers of the internal organs were either un-diagnosable or too rooted in the abdomen or chest to be operable. Nor did physicians and surgeons distinguish between malignant and benign tumors. The term "cancer" was used to refer to both.

Mastectomies had been used to remove cancerous breasts since medieval times. Physicians did understand that surgery was not necessarily a cure. Many noted that tumors had a tendency to recur once removed, and that many patients would die within months of diagnosis, whether surgery was performed or not. By the eighteenth century, some European researchers began to realize that removing breast tumors while they were still small gave patients the best hope for survival. French surgeon Henri Le Dran noted that once a breast tumor had spread to the lymph nodes in the armpit, the prognosis was very grave. One of his contemporaries, Jean-Louis Petit, recommended removing the lymph nodes as well as the breast for this reason.

However, most patients understandably waited until every other option was exhausted before undergoing the intense pain of unanaesthetized surgery. Tumors were usually treated with poultices, medicines, blisters, bleeding, and cautery before the patient resorted to surgery, so most cancers were well advanced before they were removed. Lorenz Heister, a German doctor, described a patient he operated on in 1720 who had suffered from a breast tumor (probably benign) for 16 years before consenting to have it removed. The doctor described the tumor as "nearly as big again as her head" and noted that it weighed 12 pounds. The patient survived her surgery and lived for "several years afterwards."[17]

Colonial era surgeons developed techniques that completed the removal of the breast as quickly as possible. Most involved tying off the base of the breast to compress it as small as possible and cutting in a circle around the ligature. Some supplemented the ligature method by having an assistant hold the breast away from the body to ensure that the cut could be made without a pause. Heister noted in his case records that he was able to remove the enormous tumor from his patient "in a minute."[18]

In 1720, the same year Heister operated on his patient, Zabadiel Boylston of Boston placed an advertisement in the local newspaper to inform the public that he had performed a successful mastectomy in 1718. (He had done the same 10 years earlier to announce his skill at removing bladder stones.) While not as detailed as Heister's description of the procedure, the circumstances are similar. Boylston's patient, a Mrs. Winslow, "had been labouring under the dreadful distemper of a Cancer in her Left Breast for Several Years, and altho' the Cure was attempted by Sundry Doctors from time to time, to no effect." Mrs. Winslow finally came to Boylston when she was desperate: "Her Life was almost despair'd of by reason of its repeated bleedings, growth, and stench, and there seemed immediate hazard of Life." Boylston removed the breast and "with the Blessing of GOD on his Endeavours, she has obtained a perfect Cure." Boylston understood that cancer could recur and thus had "deferred the Publication" of the advertisement for two years "least it should have broke out again." Since the patient had survived that long, Boylston decided that the cure was indeed "perfect."[19]

DENTISTS AND DENTAL CARE

Nothing seems to have caused more day-to-day pain for the people of Colonial America than toothaches. The New England minister Cotton Mather called teeth "Fifty-Two Tormentors in thy Gums." (Mather was counting both baby teeth and permanent teeth.) Mather, being a strict and unforgiving Calvinist, implored his readers to remember humanity's sinful nature as a cause of dental pain: "Think; 'The Teeth wherein I Suffer so much Torture; How much have I sinned with them!" Mather lists a number of sins committed with the teeth, ranging from gluttony to telling lies (since the teeth play a role in speech). He also noted that toothaches, however painful, were but foretastes of the pains of hell. Cold comfort for those who suffered from cavities![20]

However, Mather also collected a number of purported cures and preventative methods for toothache, giving us a sense of dental care and home remedies for abscessed teeth. For preventative care, Mather recommended rinsing the teeth with cold water daily. While he stated that water alone would be enough, he also suggested rubbing the teeth with tobacco ashes first and then rinsing with clean water. If these methods failed, he had a number of remedies to suggest. Some were used well into the twentieth century, such as oil of cloves or oil of oregano to kill pain. He also described a way of creating a homemade dental filling using beeswax and ashes. Finally, even the pious Reverend Mather recorded some cures that seem to take their effectiveness from folk magic, such as applying the thighbone of a toad to the aching tooth. However, he ends his list of remedies by saying, "If there's nothing else to be done, Draw the Tooth!"[21]

There were a number of practitioners who would provide this service. Blacksmiths, general surgeons, and laypeople all extracted teeth. Just as there were lay bonesetters in many towns, there were also laypeople that called themselves tooth-drawers. Among the many traveling surgeons who plied their trade in early America were some who specialized in dentistry. All could pull teeth, and many had special tools to help them do so. One instrument, called a key, provided extra leverage so that the dentist could easily extract even stubborn teeth. The hooked end was attached to the tooth, and the operator turned the handle to pull the tooth out. Others used instruments shaped like pliers and relied on their own brute strength to get the job done. In both cases, the danger was that the process would severely damage the gums, or even that it would extract neighboring teeth accidently.

One of the most successful and well-known dentists of the Colonial period was John Greenwood, who became George Washington's favorite dentist. He began as a lay practitioner without formal education but ended as one of the most respected and skilled dentists of his time. Greenwood probably learned his skills from his father Isaac, who practiced as a dentist in Boston. In addition, Isaac Greenwood was a skilled artisan who made and sold mathematical instruments. John Greenwood was apprenticed to his uncle, a cabinetmaker, for two years, but left his apprenticeship at the age of fifteen to enlist as a fife player in the local militia in 1775. After the war, Greenwood settled in New York City, where he took up his father's trade as a maker of scientific and nautical instruments. When a local physician asked for his help in drawing a tooth, however, Greenwood set up as a full-time dentist. He put his artisanal skills to good use in making dentures as well as designing dental instruments, including one of the first dental drills.[22]

Most dentists sold their own dentifrices (substances for cleaning the teeth) and toothbrushes. Dentists of the eighteenth century were just as enthusiastic about tooth brushing and dental hygiene as today's dentists. John Greenwood wrote: "Take advice which is good, keep your teeth and gums clean, likewise your whole person. Cleanliness is a sure thing to PROMOTE HEALTH."[23]

If a decayed tooth was not too far gone, the dentist could file away the decayed spot rather than pulling the tooth. For those who had teeth pulled, it was a common practice to reimplant a person's tooth after it was extracted. The dentist extracted the tooth, cleaned the socket of pus and decay, and restored the tooth to the gum. Often, the tooth grew back into its place and gave less trouble than before; and most patients preferred to have their own teeth back rather than be fitted with dentures.

For those who could afford it, another alternative to dentures was to have a dental transplant. In eighteenth century London, some dentists accommodated their wealthy patients with this service. James Spence, one of the most prominent English practitioners of his time, paid poor young people with healthy teeth to have their front teeth extracted. He then immediately implanted the new tooth into the empty socket of a waiting client. John Greenwood performed this procedure as well, paying the donors from one to four guineas per tooth, a small fortune for the time. (There is no evidence, however, that he ever performed this service for George Washington.) While these transplants were very expensive, the implants did not always "take"—many patients found that their new teeth fell out again after a few weeks.

Finally, some dentists made dental crowns, which were used when the body of the tooth had decayed but the root was intact, or when a tooth had been worn down from repeated filing. A crown covered the remnants of the original tooth and allowed for a normal appearance and normal chewing. Crowns were made of gold, animal ivory, or human teeth and attached to a gold pin implanted in the root canal. If several adjoining teeth had to be crowned, the crowns were wired together for stability.

If none of this worked, there were always dentures. Eighteenth-century denture bases were made of natural materials (usually animal ivory or bone) and the best had human teeth riveted into them. In Europe, entrepreneurs could make quite a bit of money by scavenging battlefields for the teeth of dead soldiers and selling them to dentists. In early nineteenth-century England, dental patients sometimes asked specifically for "Waterloo teeth" (scavenged from casualties from the battle of Waterloo), which were widely believed to be the best. However, most of the human teeth used in dentures were stolen from city mortuaries or "resurrected" from potter's fields. For those too poor or too squeamish to have cadaver teeth in their dentures, dentists carved teeth out of animal bone or ivory.

Eighteenth-century dentures were extremely uncomfortable and impractical. Before the age of rubber and plastics, there was no way to mold dentures to fit an individual perfectly. The bone or ivory bases were stiff, ungainly, and had a tendency to slip, making them function adequately only as cosmetic devices—normal eating and chewing was difficult or impossible. Upper dentures were particularly difficult to keep in place. They were often fitted with springs attached to a lower denture or were anchored by metal frameworks to the lower teeth.

Another problem with dentures was hygiene. Dentures made of human or animal teeth were just as subject to decay as the wearer's natural teeth. As one eighteenth-century dentist noted, "The liability to discoloration, decay, and the expense of renewing are insurmountable objections to the use of human teeth on a base of bone." This same dentist noted the "contaminating putrid accumulation" of decay on dentures, to which he attributed bad breath and indigestion. By the early nineteenth century, porcelain dentures became available, which solved this problem. However, in many ways, Colonial era dentures were no better than the teeth they replaced.[24]

Perhaps the most famous set of dentures in American history belonged to George Washington. Washington had dental problems that were severe even by the standards of the time. Washington had his first tooth extracted at the age of 22, and many of his diary entries mention toothaches and inflamed gums. He bought his first toothbrush in 1772 from the military surgeon and dentist John Baker. However, the efforts were too little too late. When Washington took the oath of office in 1789, at the age of 57, he had only one natural tooth remaining—a lower left premolar.

Washington had many sets of dentures. However, despite popular belief, none of them was made of wood. His most elaborate set was made by John Greenwood on a base of hippopotamus ivory, with upper teeth carved from hippopotamus tusk as well. The teeth on the lower set were human teeth (including one of Washington's own), and solid gold springs held the set together. These were the dentures he wore while president. However, the pressure of wearing these false teeth loosened Washington's one remaining tooth and eventually caused it to fall out. The most famous portraits of Washington illustrate the swollen lips and puffy cheeks caused by his uncomfortable dentures and long history of dental disease.

Surgery in the Colonial era was extremely crude by modern standards. However, the history of surgery of this time illustrates the ingenious ways practitioners found to do the best they could with the knowledge they had. While they may not have had as much success as they would have liked, it does seem that Colonial surgeons and dentists managed to relieve at least as much suffering as they caused.

NOTES

1. Quoted in Harold Ellis (Ed.), *The Cambridge Illustrated History of Surgery*. Cambridge: Cambridge University Press, 2001, p. 42.

2. Ellis, *Cambridge Illustrated History of Surgery*, p. 56.

3. Peter Benes, "Itinerant Physicians, Healers, and Surgeon-Dentists in New England and New York: 1720–1825." In Peter Benes (Ed.), *Medicine and Healing: The Dublin Seminar for New England Folklife Annual Proceedings: 1990*. Boston: Boston University Press, 1992, pp. 96–97, quotation p. 96.

4. Quoted in A. Scott Earle (Ed.), *Surgery in America: From the Colonial Era to the Twentieth Century*. New York: Praeger, 1983, p. 46.

5. Virgil J. Vogel, *American Indian Medicine*. Norman: University of Oklahoma Press, 1970, pp. 191–194, 215.

6. Vogel, *American Indian Medicine*, p. 194.

7. W. Michael Byrd and Linda A. Clayton (Eds.), *An American Health Dilemma: A Medical History of African Americans and the Problem of Race: Beginnings to 1900*, Vol. 1. New York: Routledge, 2000, p. 240.

8. Charles E. Wynes, "Dr. James Durham, Mysterious Eighteenth-Century Black Physician: Man or Myth?" *Pennsylvania Magazine of History and Biography*, 103, no. 3 (July 1979) p. 328.

9. Quoted in Ellis, *Cambridge Illustrated History of Surgery*, pp. 151–152.

10. Oscar Reiss, *Medicine in Colonial America*. Lanham, MD: University Press of America, 2000, p. 432.

11. Quoted in Russell Shorto, *The Island at the Center of the World: The Epic Story of Dutch Manhattan and the Forgotten Colony that Shaped America*. New York: Doubleday, 2004, p. 153.

12. Quoted in Earle, *Surgery in America*, pp. 18–19.

13. Ibid., pp. 46, 48–49.

14. Quoted in Ellis, *Cambridge Illustrated History of Surgery*, p. 194.

15. Quoted in Earle, *Surgery in America*, p. 6.

16. Ibid., pp. 12–13.

17. Quoted in Ellis, *Cambridge Illustrated History of Surgery*, pp. 167–169.

18. Ibid., p. 168.

19. Quoted in Earle, *Surgery in America*, p. 8.

20. Cotton Mather, *The Angel of Bethesda*, edited with an introduction and notes by Gordon W. Jones. Barre, MA: Barre Publishers, 1972, pp. 62–63.

21. Mather, *Angel of Bethesda*, pp. 64–66, quotation p. 66.

22. David Krasner, "John Greenwood," *American National Biography Online*. Retrieved July 21, 2010 from http://www.anb.org/articles/12/1200350.html.

23. Quoted in Bernhard Weinberger, *The History of Dentistry*, Vol. 1. Birmingham, AL: Classics of Dentistry Library, 1981, p. 365.

24. Quoted in Christine Hillam (Ed.), *The Roots of Dentistry*. London: British Dental Association, 1990, p. 16.

CHAPTER 9

The Brain and Mental Disorders

Peoples of the Colonial era recognized mental illness, cognitive disability, and neurological problems. However, Colonial era cultures perceived these disorders as a combination of spiritual and physical imbalance. Anglo-American culture thought demonic possession, divine punishment, or a disease of the brain could cause mental disorders. African American and Native American cultures also believed demons or evil spirits could cause mental illness, and they incorporated mental and spiritual treatment into their cures for both mental and physical disease.

Unlike modern people, Colonial era people of European descent put disorders such as mental illness, epilepsy, and intellectual disability into one category. In their view, people with these disorders all lacked "reason" and could be showing a sign of sin or God's displeasure. Colonial ordinances providing for the care of mentally disabled people reflected this belief. Similarly, neurological disorders such as stroke and paralysis were categorized as having a religious as well as a physical component, and thus belonged in separate category of disease.

In European American culture, scientific changes during the eighteenth century caused a shift in perceptions of mental illness. Rather than a divine or spiritual affliction, physicians redefined mental illness as a physical illness that required physical treatment. By the mid-eighteenth century, doctors began treating people with mental illness in specialized hospital wards, setting the stage for the establishment of the first mental hospitals, or asylums, in the early nineteenth century.

UNDERSTANDINGS OF THE BRAIN IN EUROPEAN AMERICAN CULTURE

The function of the brain and spinal cord was a subject of dispute in the history of Western medicine. The "fathers" of European medicine, Hippocrates, Galen, and Aristotle, disagreed about whether the brain or the heart was the organ where thought and emotions were located. Medieval physicians split the difference, locating sensory processing and thought in the brain, and emotions in the heart.[1]

By the late sixteenth and early seventeenth centuries, most scholars agreed that the brain was the center of both cognitive and emotional functioning. Most writers, however, located brain function in the wrong parts of the brain: the pineal gland and the ventricles. The ventricles are three chambers in the brain filled with cerebrospinal fluid; the pineal is a small gland in one of the ventricles that produces the hormone melatonin. Early modern scientists posited that the ventricles were reservoirs of nervous fluid produced by the pineal that circulated through the nerves to conduct sensory impressions, movement, and emotions.

Sensory impressions were "collected" in the brain and processed there in the anterior ventricle. Sight, hearing, smell, and so on all came together in what natural philosophers called "common sense" (a use of the phrase very different from the way we use it today). Imagination and rational thought took place in the middle ventricle, and memory was located in the posterior. Sensory impressions from the common sense flowed into the other chambers and contributed to the processes that took place there.[2]

Many important questions remained, however. How did the brain perform these functions? And what was the role of spirit or soul in thought and reason? One of the most significant steps toward answering these questions was made by an English scholar named Thomas Willis. In 1664, Willis published a Latin treatise on the anatomy and physiology of the brain called *Cerebri Anatome*, or, in English, *The Anatomy of the Brain*. While the treatise was published under Willis's name, Willis noted in the preface that the book was a collaborative effort by himself and three other scientists. The book was based on careful dissections of both human and animal brains, and included detailed illustrations of the brains and spinal cords of human beings, oxen, horses, and sheep. Willis's work was immensely influential on scientific thinking. His book went through multiple editions, was translated into many European languages, and continued to be cited almost a century after its publication.

The book was one of the first to correctly locate the functions of the brain in the cerebrum, rather than the ventricles or pineal gland. Willis noted that the nerves were not hollow and thus could not circulate fluid. He also noted that their primary attachment was to the solid tissues of the brain, not the ventricles or other structures.[3]

When it came to the nature of the human mind, Willis established a middle ground between a mind that was purely spiritual and one that was purely physical. In this he differed from some of his contemporaries. Philosophers like Descartes and most theologians separated the mind (or soul) from the body. Eighteenth-century physicians would go in the other direction and conceive of the mind as a product of physical forces. Willis proposed that human beings possessed two "souls": a "Sensitive Soul" and a "Rational Soul." Both souls took nourishment from the body and had a physical presence there. The Sensitive Soul extended throughout the body and conveyed sensory information back to the brain. Both human beings and animals had Sensitive Souls. However, only humans had Rational Souls, which reside in the brain. The Rational Soul processed the impressions provided by the senses and analyzed them. Only the Rational Soul was capable of abstraction and reason, and only the Rational Soul survived death. The existence of these two distinct souls explained the unique nature of the human mind as well as the traits human beings share with animals. The two souls also explained the place of human beings in the cosmos "between angels and brutes." This balance between spiritual and physical explanation for the functions of the brain and nervous system would affect how Anglo-Americans viewed many disorders, including neurological disease and mental illness.[4]

NEUROLOGICAL DISEASE

People of Colonial America recognized several neurological disorders: stroke (or apoplexy), paralysis, and epilepsy (also known as the falling sickness, or just "fits").

Apoplexy (Stroke)

During the Colonial period, the malady we call stroke—sudden blockage of a cerebral blood vessel or bleeding into the brain—was called by its older name, "apoplexy." Apoplexy was believed to be a sudden "stroke" from God, in which an apparently healthy person would collapse and become paralyzed. In addition to the theological cause, physicians and writers suggested physical causes. For instance, some proposed that an excess of acid could coagulate the blood or puncture the cerebral veins, either one of which could throw "the patient into the arms of death, from whence rarely are any rescued without falling into a palsy." As this quotation suggests, Colonial era people recognized the seriousness of stroke. One medical text quotes Hippocrates on the topic: "To cure a violent apoplexy is impossible; to cure a slight one is not easy."[5]

Anglo Americans recognized two kinds of stroke: the "sanguine" and the "phlegmatic." Sanguine strokes were closer to modern medicine's definition of stroke—bleeding into the brain. However, in the humoral medicine paradigm, an excess of phlegm could also cause disease. Some strokes were caused by a "back up" of excessive phlegm into the brain.

For phlegmatic strokes, emetics and enemas were the treatment of choice. Another way of ridding the body of excess phlegm was to force the patient to sneeze by putting powdered herbs (such as rue) up the nose. Pouring herb-infused vinegar on a hot stone and breathing the fumes would have the same effect. Sanguine strokes required other remedies. Chief among them was bleeding and cupping, especially from the top of the head. Rubbing the soles of the feet with salt and vinegar was thought to draw excess blood away from the brain. Finally, cautery and blistering substances applied to the head were used for all kinds of strokes.[6]

Paralysis or Palsy

Colonial physicians and laypeople recognized that paralysis (or palsy) was a common result of a stroke. They also recognized that while paralysis could come about from many causes (including injury): "The Seat of this Disease, Every Body knows, is in the Nerves." Prayer was an important remedy for this malady, and ministers and medical writers alike cited the Biblical story of Jesus healing a paralyzed man. While the seat of paralysis may have been in the nerves, the ultimate cause was the sinful nature of human beings: "Our SAVIOUR several times, does mention unto Paralytics, their SINS as having brought their Maladies upon them."[7]

While the patient prayed for forgiveness and a miracle, doctors tried their best with physical remedies. Massage was a common technique to bring life back into paralyzed limbs. Massage was sometimes accompanied by applying irritating substances, such as nettles, to the affected part. Hot baths infused with herbs such as pennyroyal was another technique, as was rubbing the paralyzed limb with hot animal fat. Finally, one could try elaborate remedies such as mixing up a potion that included ingredients ranging from peony flowers to "powder of Humane Skull" and "oil of Foxes," and rubbing it on the spine while the patient held a decoction of (toxic) mistletoe in the mouth.[8]

Some European observers wrote that Native Americans rarely suffered from neurological disorders. Native Americans did not know "those health wasting diseases which are incident to other countries, as fevers ... convulsions, apoplexies ... or the like." Whatever the truth of this observation, Native Americans had many herbs in their pharmacopeias that were used to treat paralysis. It was also one of the few ailments for which some Native Americans, such as the Maricopas, used bloodletting. The Flambeau people had paralyzed patients inhale smoke from burning flowers of a plant called "pearly everlasting." Other plants used by different tribes included poison ivy, American senna, and wintergreen. Finally, some South American peoples used electric eels to give paralyzed persons mild shocks.[9]

Epilepsy

Epilepsy and other seizure disorders can be terrifying for onlookers. One eighteenth-century writer described a seizure this way: " ... a sudden Abolition of Sense, the Eyes distorted, the Mouth perhaps foaming, the Face with an Aspect full of Agony and Convulsive Motions of the Limbs." Many Anglo-Americans believed that seizures were a sign of demonic possession. As a result, people with epilepsy were feared and stigmatized.[10]

Colonial era physicians had a number of hypotheses about the origins of epilepsy. Thomas Willis, scholar of the brain, noted that convulsive disorders were "the most difficult to be unfolded" because "no marks at all of the morbific matter appear" at autopsy. Even a materialist like Willis admitted that he sometimes thought that attributing epilepsy to evil spirits might be justified. There were also several physical possibilities. Some proposed that either "fullness" or "emptiness" of the brain's ventricles could cause spasms of the meninges (the tissue that covers the brain). A "depraved" lymphatic humor might irritate the nerves. Other theories suggested that seizures were caused by "tainted" blood contaminating the brain.[11]

Women who suffered from seizures were sometimes diagnosed with hysteria rather than epilepsy. Hysteria originated in the womb, rather than the brain. "Foul" humors or vapors that originated in the uterus made their way into the rest of the body and caused a variety of symptoms, including seizures. Never-married women and widows were especially susceptible, since regular sexual intercourse and pregnancy both prevented the buildup of putrid humors in the womb. Pregnant women could also suffer from "fits of the mother" or "fits in childbed." These seizures were no doubt caused by eclampsia, a mysterious and sometimes fatal disorder of pregnancy characterized by swelling of the legs and face, and severe headaches as well as seizures. Hysteria and childbed seizures had their own remedies, such as parsnip seeds dissolved in wine, herbal plasters laid on the abdomen, or asafetida and mugwort taken with wine.

Treatments for other seizure disorders varied as much as theories of their origins. Immediately after a seizure, a physician might try to revive the patient with ammonia or other strong smelling substances held under the nose. There were also long-term treatments. Leeches were applied behind the ears to draw off tainted blood directly from the brain; bleeding from the foot might draw excessive blood out of the brain and into the rest of the body. One medicinal recipe suggested mixing together two gallons of ale, four ounces of peony roots, twelve ounces of raisins, and half a pound of peacock's dung. The difficulty of treating epilepsy led some physicians to try what sound like magical remedies, such as having the patient wear a belt made of wolf's skin or eat powdered human skull. Most physicians agreed, however, that if seizures had been present since childhood and continued into adulthood, "tis very hardly curable."[12]

Epilepsy was another disease that Europeans thought spared Native Americans. However, there were reports that Native American medicines could cure seizures. One anecdote tells of a French soldier who suddenly developed epilepsy. A local Native American woman gave him two balls of pulverized roots, saying that they would cure his disease. The soldier duly tried the remedy and never had another seizure. Unfortunately, the woman refused to disclose the name of the roots she had used.[13]

When an enslaved person suffered from seizures, the disease presented a special problem to the slave's owner. Because of the fear generated by the disease, a slave with epilepsy lost all value in the market. In addition, a person with uncontrolled seizures was unable to work. Many masters suspected slaves of faking symptoms to avoid work, which may have been true in some cases. An enslaved person might have feigned seizures to prevent sale away from family, to be exempted from an onerous task, or to evade punishment. A particularly striking case took place in nineteenth-century Virginia. A 15-year-old enslaved woman was convicted of arson and sentenced to hang; however, she avoided the death penalty when she developed epilepsy in jail. The court declared her mentally incompetent and commuted her sentence. While her master claimed she was malingering, he was forced to take her back into his home.[14]

Free white people with epilepsy who were unable to work presented a problem to Colonial society as well. If their families could not or would not support them, they became paupers. Many depended on "poor relief" from local governments. People with epilepsy who had no permanent homes often spent their lives in poor houses, classed with the mentally ill and the cognitively disabled as "non-compos mentis" (i.e., mentally incompetent).

INTELLECTUAL DISABILITY

European American cultures recognized a range of intellectual disability. Such disabilities could be permanent or temporary. They could be the result of natural or supernatural causes. The degree of social acceptance for the intellectually disabled varied, depending on how well they were able to work and care for themselves.

Some writers used the terms "idiot," "natural fool," or just "natural" to describe people born with cognitive disability. Scientists such as Thomas Willis looked for physical causes of intellectual disability by examining the brains of human cadavers. For instance, in his treatise on the anatomy of the brain, Willis included an illustration of the brain of a young man who "was foolish from birth." Willis noted that the brain showed an atrophy of the cerebral cortices, the area that Willis associated with rational thought.[15]

Willis also noted that "stupidity" could be acquired later in life. Alcohol and drugs such as opium could undermine the brain's function, but the condition could be cured if the patient gave up those vices. Physical disease could also damage the brain. Infants could be born normal but be damaged by high fevers or convulsions. Finally, Willis believed that cognitive disability could be inherited—either from disabled parents, or from parents who indulged in vices such as drunkenness or sexual excess.

Willis recommended that those with intellectual disabilities be given special education with the goal of teaching them "the use of reason in a little measure." Willis classed people "uncapable of all learning" with animals, however, since they lacked the rationality that defined human beings. Willis was not alone in this thinking. John Locke compared the severely mentally disabled to oysters since they could not "distinguish compare and abstract."[16]

Popular culture also questioned whether people with intellectual disabilities were entirely human. Parents suspected intellectually disabled children of being "changelings." A changeling was just that—a baby that had been secretly stolen and replaced with another. Some legends blamed fairies, pixies, or elves for the exchange, while others blamed the devil. In both cases, the "real" child was taken captive and changed for a pixie or a demon baby. Some Christians believed that a disabled child (whether the disability was physical or intellectual) was God's punishment for the parents' sins.

During most of the Colonial period, people with intellectual disabilities were classed with the mentally ill and people with epilepsy as mentally "incompetent." Many statutes designed to provide services or support for those unable to work were called "An Act for the Relief of Idiots and Distracted [mentally ill] Persons." The severely cognitively disabled presented a challenge to Colonial families and governments. If a person's family was unable to provide care, the government stepped in, either by paying another household to care for the person or by housing the person in a poorhouse, almshouse, or hospital.

MENTAL ILLNESS

Mental illness was a serious concern among Colonial Americans. How to care for, support, and cure the "distracted" or "mad" was a problem that all cultures faced. Each culture approached the problem in its own way.

Mental Illness in Native American Cultures

European missionaries to Native American societies recorded cases of "melancholy," "lunacy," and "demonic possession" among their flocks. Many of those afflicted (as well as their families and neighbors) described these illnesses as "soul loss" or "being lost to oneself." Souls could be lost after the violation of a taboo or through the intervention of a malevolent spirit. In other cases, the soul could wander off during sleep and not return. Some of the Huron people believed that French Catholic missionaries stole converts' souls. One missionary wrote that many Hurons believed that one traveling priest was on a journey to collect souls, "a box of full of which he wished to take along with him." Soul loss could result in physical as well as mental illness. In either case, the cure was the same: a healing shaman had to perform a ritual to return it to the body. Other cultures defined mental illness as being "out of balance" with the physical and spirit world, or the expression of an unfulfilled wish.[17]

However they defined the affliction, most peoples had curing rituals to heal the mentally ill. Among the Navajo, the cure was a weeklong ceremony called a "night chant," which was (as the name suggests) performed at night. A shaman, or "singer," painted a special image on the ground. The patient sat on a different portion of the image each night as the shaman invoked the spirits depicted there.[18]

Much of Native American medicine had a psychological or spiritual element as well as a physical one. Healers and patients alike sought cures for illness through dreams or visions. Some cultures, especially those of what is now the southwestern United States, used drugs such as peyote to induce those visions. Other cultures used jimson weed, another powerful hallucinogen.

Shamans also asked many questions of their patients. They asked about dreams, about desires, and about the violation of community values. Pressing a patient to confess to bad behavior or relate his deepest wishes was part of many healing ceremonies and may have helped those suffering from mental disorders as well. One anthropologist noted that all Navajo curing rituals have "a powerful appeal to the emotions" that adds to their effectiveness.[19]

Native Americans used mental methods to treat many disorders. The Penobscots cured hiccups by surprising the patient with an unexpected question. Potawatomi healers supplemented their medicines with songs that told the patient that he or she was getting better, as did the Meswakis. Many healing rituals involved the patient's family, or even the whole community, giving the message that the patient had the support of the whole group. Finally, the Seneca believed that no medicine had the power to heal unless the patient believed that it did. Faith, emotional support, and suggestion all played their part in the Native American treatment of disease.

Mental Illness in African American Culture

As was the case for Native Americans, African American concepts of mental health and mental illness overlapped with concepts of spirituality, magic, and witchcraft. Also like Native Americans, African Americans incorporated spiritual and mental healing into their treatments for physical as well as mental disorders.

African American healers brought many traditions with them from Africa. One belief that survived the transfer was the idea that all illnesses had a spiritual component and could be caused by a curse from either a malevolent spirit or human being. Mental illness in particular was thought to be the result of a curse. Healers (sometimes called "root doctors" or "conjurers") incorporated magical ritual into their treatments. All illness was highly personal to the patient—some action on the patient's part had helped to bring it on, even if that action was offending another person. Healers and patients alike used dreams and visions to find the root cause of their problems.

African American healers were able to curse as well as cure. Doing so gave slaves an outlet for anger, an emotion that could be severely punished by slave owners. If a master punished a slave unjustly, sold a relative, or otherwise mistreated a slave, magic and cursing offered an outlet for the victim's rage. In this sense, magical healing was both a psychological treatment and a form of mental resistance to slavery. One oral tradition transcribed in the 1930s described a "conjurer" who took revenge on a master who had murdered a fellow slave. The man cursed the planter's family with mental illness. The planter fell into a despair so deep that he died.[20]

African Americans who believed themselves to be cursed often exhibited symptoms of mental illness. Some, believing death to be inevitable, stopped eating and drinking, and died of starvation and dehydration; others crawled like animals and lost the ability to speak. The curses were clearly effective, whether one believes their power came from magic or from psychological manipulation.

Whites had their own views of mental health and illness in slaves. While little was written in the Colonial era on this topic, by the early nineteenth century, white doctors in the slave south had created a literature describing diseases they thought were specific to African Americans. These race-specific diseases included mental disorders. For instance, one plantation manual mentioned "Cachexia Africana," an affliction in which the patient compulsively eats dirt or ashes. This disease is now called "pica," and it sometimes results from nutritional deficiencies, which were common among slaves.[21]

Another physician, Samuel Cartwright, described two form of insanity he claimed were unique to "negroes." One he called "drapteomania," which he defined as the irrational desire of a slave to run away. For this disorder, the physician recommended kind treatment and good diet, but that was not the case for all the disorders he described. For instance, Cartwright described a mental illness he called "Dysaesthesia Aethiops." The main symptom of this "disease" was carelessness and clumsiness in work. Those who suffered from this disease broke tools, tore their clothing, and stole from their masters. The cure for

Dysaesthesia was punitive—hard physical labor (such as sawing wood), combined with beatings with a leather strap to "stimulate the skin." Interestingly, Cartwright noted that Dysaesthesia was more common among free blacks and slaves that "live like free negroes." Too much freedom, it seemed, was bad for their mental health. By redefining normal responses to the cruelty of the antebellum racial system as "diseases," such definitions of "mental illness" helped support the institution of slavery and the oppression of free blacks.[22]

Mental Illness in Anglo-American Culture

Understandings of mental illness in Anglo-American culture depended on both religious and physical explanations. In the early years of the Colonial period, the "distracted" were understood to be suffering from a physical illness that had supernatural origins. As was the case with cognitive disability, mental illness was not necessarily a permanent state; the symptoms could come and go, and God could decide at any time to cure the illness. As the eighteenth century went on, purely physical explanations became more dominant, although the moral element did not disappear completely.

Cotton Mather, who claimed expertise in both medicine and theology, commented that some persons were more susceptible to mental illness. He wrote that some people's bodies contain a "mass of blood . . . disordered with some fiery acid" that gives off "vapour." This mass of blood provides a "bed" where demons can live comfortably and shoot "fiery darts" into the patient's brain. While the patient had to resist the temptation to let the demon in, not everyone had the moral strength to do so. Mather distinguished between those who were completely possessed by demons and those tempted into madness by Satan and his minions. In possession, the demon took full control of the patient's body and voice; in madness, the "fiery darts" shot by demons caused a variety of symptoms, but the person remained in control of the body and the voice.[23]

God could also cause mental illness. Sometimes madness could be a punishment for grievous sin. For instance, a layman preached a sermon in which he attacked the clergy. For his sin of pride, "God smote him with a horrible madness." At other times, God might afflict someone with mental illness as a way of demonstrating his divine power, a test of faith for the afflicted, or for mysterious reasons of his own.[24]

Despite these moral explanations, the mentally ill were tolerated in their communities as long as they had means to support themselves and were not a burden on the town. Ministers and schoolteachers, for instance, were sometimes allowed to continue in their jobs as long as their symptoms did not include violence. A Maine minister called Joseph "Handkerchief" Moody acquired his nickname because of his habit of always wearing a handkerchief over his face. Moody said he felt himself unworthy of being in the company of other people. He continued to preach, however, handkerchief and all. Unfortunately, his symptoms worsened over time. He began turning his back to the congregation as well as wearing the handkerchief; and soon thereafter he was unable to speak in public at all. Even so, his congregation continued to employ him as their minister, hiring substitutes to preach sermons and allowing Moody to mime prayers during the service. Moody was still the town's minister when he died at the age of 53.[25]

Those unable to work presented a different problem. For the most part, they were cared for within the family. Those who were violent were often confined or chained to prevent them from harming others; those who were not violent were allowed more freedom but were often housed separately from the rest of the family. For instance, John Smith of Framingham, Massachusetts, build a small house for his mentally ill wife in the 1740s. From court records of the time, it seems that Mrs. Swift had a habit of wandering off, and Mr. Swift may have built the house as a way of keeping her safe. When she began making threats against the neighbors, however, the separate house became her prison.

If they had no family willing to care for and support them, mentally ill persons became public charges. A 1694 Massachusetts law addressed the problem of caring for the mentally ill (as well as those with cognitive disabilities). It obligated towns to "take care and make necessary effectual provisions for the relief, support and safety" of those who were unable to care for themselves. The town could confiscate any property the person owned, but after the money was gone, the support had to come out of town funds.[26]

Towns usually paid a local family to care for the mentally ill. Local records tell of towns supporting their "distracted persons" for many years, albeit grudgingly in many cases. Towns could also be adamant about refusing support to anyone who was not an official resident. Strangers were "warned out"—meaning that they were informed that the town would take no responsibility for supporting them. At times, "warning out" was more literal—the town of Cambridge, Massachusetts, forcibly escorted mentally ill nonresidents back to their hometowns.

In large towns and cities, "distracted" paupers sometimes outnumbered the families who were willing to take them in. In those cases, the mentally ill were housed with other paupers in the almshouse.

However, this system created problems of its own. Residents of the almshouse were expected to work to earn their keep, and many mentally ill or cognitively impaired residents were unable to do so. Furthermore, some non–mentally ill residents complained of being housed with "lunatics." Cities began housing the mentally ill separately, or even building discrete "madhouses" to shelter them. These facilities were custodial only, not to be confused with the medically oriented asylums created later.

While the mentally ill in early America were looked on as primarily a theological and economic problem, some physicians attempted physical cures. Cooling drinks were believed to damp down the troubled spirit. Herbal medicines were often used, including violent purgatives such as hellebore and other herbs such as St. John's Wort, which some modern researchers have claimed is an effective treatment for mild depression. Other treatments were more unusual, such as "living swallows, cut in two, and laid reeking hot unto the shaved head." In addition, bleeding and the application of leeches were often used for mental illness as they were for many other diseases.[27]

EIGHTEENTH CENTURY CHANGES

During the second half of the eighteenth century, ideas about mental illness began to change. Rather than conceiving of mental illness as a spiritual disorder exacerbated by physical disease, physicians began to classify mental illness as primarily physical in origin. Mental illness became a medical rather than a spiritual or religious problem. The treatment of the mentally ill changed accordingly. Ironically, reclassifying mental illness as a somatic disease led to less societal toleration for its victims. The public began to view mentally ill people as overwrought, potentially violent victims of their own passions, rather than sinners whose fate was part of the human condition. Medical treatment also meant that the mentally ill were isolated in hospitals rather than cared for in their communities.

The dominant American figure behind this paradigm shift was Philadelphia physician Benjamin Rush. Rush incorporated mental illness into his larger medical theory, which proposed that the vascular system was the root of all disease. Mental illness was caused by "morbid action" of the blood vessels in the brain. Rush compared mental disease to a "chronic fever; which affects the part of the brain which is the seat of the mind."[28]

However, Rush did not exclude moral considerations in the etiology of mental illness. The blood vessels could be inflamed or damaged by excessive passions, including sexual desire, grief, fear, personal ambition, or greed. In the larger culture, fears of social disorder were growing, and the mentally ill were terrifying symbols of what could happen when a person (or a nation) lost self-restraint. Rush made a connection between a societal obsession with becoming rich and an increase in cases of mental illness. Rush also voiced fears that religious revivals and the multiplication of religious sects would drive more people into madness.[29]

Rush's treatments for mental illness reflect both his somatic theory and his social concerns. Since he viewed mental illness as a form of hyperactivity, the first goal was to reduce the patient's agitation. Rush did this in several ways. The first objective of the treatment was to slow the pulse, which would reduce the "morbid tension" in the cerebral blood vessels. Copious heroic bleeding was therefore the most important part of the regimen. Patients were also kept on a "low" diet, meaning that their food was severely restricted. Both of these measures would slow bodily activity.

Weakening the body through bleeding and a restricted diet was only the first step, however. The passions that caused the somatic morbidity also had to be tamed. Rush used several techniques intended to further reduce the bodily activity and sensory overload that contributed to "excessive" emotion. One of the best known was his "restraining chair." The chair had fetters for the hands and feet, as well as belts around the waist and shoulders. The top of the chair was equipped with a wooden box that covered the patient's eyes and ears, and was stuffed with cloth to further dull sounds and light. Since patients were kept in the chair for days at a time, a bucket was attached to the seat for sanitation. Rush also designed a "gyrator," a horizontal board that spun in circles to produce dizziness and redirect circulation; and, when all else failed, Rush poured buckets of cold water on overwrought patients to literally "cool" their passions.

Finally, the doctor-patient relationship was crucial. Rush believed that the mentally ill had degenerated into an animal-like state through their loss of reason, and that the doctor had to dominate the patient through force of personality. He compared people with mental illness to wild beasts, and physicians to animal trainers. Doctors had to use a commanding stare when interacting with a patient: "He is for the most part easily terrified, or composed, by the eye of the man who possesses his reason."[30]

Other physicians adopted Rush's techniques, though not always with good results. For instance, when Mary Sewall of Augusta, Maine, ran away from home to join the Shaker religious sect, her father brought her home again and enlisted a local physician for advice. While the doctor did not record a diagnosis, it seems that her unusual religious beliefs were considered extreme enough to qualify as mental illness. The family soon acquired "a Chair, in which confined M," as well as a bed that featured a "lid to shut down." Mary spent 73 days in the restraining chair and bunk. She was also placed on a severely restricted diet. After three months, the family became alarmed at her physical condition, and increased her food—whereupon she became "wild, restive, and unmanageable" and was again confined to the chair and denied food. Unfortunately, the treatment proved worse than the disease—Mary Sewall died after six months of this regimen.[31]

Despite cases like this, Rush's ideas were accepted enough to become the basis for the treatment plan at the Pennsylvania Hospital, which established one of the first wards dedicated to the care and treatment of the mentally ill in 1751. The initial impetus behind the founding of the mental hospital was to confine the mentally ill, protect the public, and establish a place for the impoverished mentally ill to live besides the almshouse. The original legislative declaration authorizing funds for the hospital stated that the purpose of the mental ward was to protect the "Neighbors" of the mentally ill, who "are daily apprehensive of the Violence they may commit." The conditions in the hospital during the early years reflect this purpose. The patients were housed in barred cells. Some were chained to the wall. While the patients received some visits from physicians, little effort was made to treat or cure them.[32]

Rush was an attending physician there from 1783 to 1813. During his tenure, conditions improved somewhat. In addition to medical treatments described previously, Rush encouraged recreation and amusements for the patients, and retrained the staff in his methods. Rush encouraged the staff to refer to the patients as a "family" and treat them as children rather than criminals. Some of Rush's treatments were just as confining as the chains and bars of the previous era, however, and he, too, fell into the common habit of thinking of the mentally ill as bestial. Finally, neither Rush nor his staff could completely put a stop to the practice of allowing the public to "view the lunatics" as a kind of entertainment.

Other hospitals followed Pennsylvania's model. New York City proposed its own hospital with "wards or cells for the reception of lunatics" in 1771, although it was not built until after the Revolutionary War. In 1773, a freestanding mental hospital was built in Williamsburg, Virginia. After the Revolution, a mental hospital was founded in Maryland, and in 1818 McLean Asylum for the Insane (which still exists today under the name McLean Hospital) opened in Massachusetts.[33]

The spread of medical wards and hospitals for the mentally ill reflected the dominance of the medical paradigm, a view of mental illness that would continue through the nineteenth century and beyond. The mental hospitals of the nineteenth century continued to treat the bodies of the mentally ill. However, they soon incorporated an early form of psychotherapy called "moral treatment," first proposed by the French physician Philippe Pinel. Moral treatment required the physician to engage with the emotions of the patient through the physical environment and social interaction. Daily routine, work, and kind treatment were essential elements of the regimen.

While moral treatment was more humane than many other early treatments for mental illness, it did have the lasting effect of increasing the isolation of the mentally ill from the community. Moral treatment required that the patient be closely monitored and isolated from disturbing influences. In practice, this often meant that people with mental illnesses were incarcerated in mental hospitals for much of their lives. Despite the good intentions of its advocates, the medical model of mental illness meant that the mentally ill lost the relative freedom and the social toleration of the Colonial period.

NOTES

1. Nancy G. Siraisi, *Medieval and Early Renaissance Medicine: An Introduction to Knowledge and Practice*. Chicago: University of Chicago Press, 1990.

2. Robert L. Martensen, *The Brain Takes Shape: An Early History*. New York: Oxford University Press, 2004, p. 47.

3. Martensen, *The Brain Takes Shape*, pp. 75–91.

4. Ibid., p. 136.

5. Cotton Mather, *The Angel of Bethesda*, edited with an introduction and notes by Gordon W. Jones. Barre, MA: Barre Publishers, 1972, pp. 139–140.

6. Ibid., pp. 139–141.

7. Ibid., pp. 137–138.

8. Ibid., pp. 138–139.

9. Virgil J. Vogel, *American Indian Medicine*. Norman: University of Oklahoma Press, 1970, quotation pp. 149–150; other citations pp. 181–187, 203, 350, 394–396.

10. Mather, *The Angel of Bethesda*, pp. 141–142.

11. Quoted in Martensen, *The Brain Takes Shape*, pp. 141–143.

12. Mather, *The Angel of Bethesda*, p. 143.

13. Vogel, *American Indian Medicine*, p. 203.

14. Dea H. Boster, "An 'Epileptick' Bondswoman: Fits, Slavery, and Power in the Antebellum South," *Bulletin of the History of Medicine*, 83, no. 2 (Summer 2009), pp. 271–301.

15. Martensen, *The Brain Takes Shape*, p. 145.

16. Ibid., pp. 146, 148.

17. Vogel, *American Indian Medicine*, p. 20.

18. Lynn Gamwell and Nancy Tomes, *Madness in America: Cultural and Medical Perceptions of Mental Illness Before 1914*. Ithaca, NY: Cornell University Press, 1995, p. 13.

19. Vogel, *American Indian Medicine*, p. 189.

20. Gamwell and Tomes, *Madness in America*, p. 18.

21. Herbert C. Covey, *African American Slave Medicine: Herbal and Non-Herbal Treatments*. Lanham, MD: Rowman and Littlefield, 2007, p. 29.

22. Samuel A. Cartwright, "Report on the Diseases and Physical Peculiarities of the Negro Race." In John Harley Warner and Janet A. Tighe (Eds.), *Major Problems in the History of Medicine and Public Health*. New York: Houghton Mifflin, 2001, pp. 103–106.

23. Mary Ann Jimenez, *Changing Faces of Madness: Early American Attitudes and Treatment of the Insane*. Hanover, NH: University Press of New England, 1987, p. 12.

24. Ibid., p. 17.

25. Ibid., pp. 33–34.

26. Ibid., p. 51.

27. Mather, *The Angel of Bethesda*, p. 132.

28. Jimenez, *Faces of Madness*, p. 73.

29. Ibid., p. 73; Gamwell and Tomes, *Madness in America*, p. 20.

30. Gamwell and Tomes, *Madness in America*, p. 21.

31. Laurel Thatcher Ulrich, "Derangement in the Family: The Story of Mary Sewall: 1824–1825." In Peter Benes (Ed.), *Medicine and Healing: The Dublin Seminar for New England Folklife Annual Proceedings: 1990*. Boston: Boston University Press, 1992, pp. 169–170.

32. Gerald Grob, *The Mad Among Us: A History of the Care of America's Mentally Ill*. New York: Free Press, 1994, p. 19.

33. Ibid., p. 20.

CHAPTER 10

The Apothecary and His Pharmacopeia

Medicines, especially herbal medicines, were part of all healing traditions in Colonial America. As a result, exchanges of herbal remedies and knowledge among colonists, Native Americans, and African Americans were common. Native Americans used local plants as medicines, some of which are still part of natural healing practices today. African Americans incorporated European and North American plants into traditional African practices. Anglo-Americans brought their own healing traditions from home and were quick to adopt North American herbal medicines.

Of the three cultures, only Anglo-Americans separated pharmaceutical practice from general medical practice. In addition, the Anglo-American pharmacopeia incorporated far more mineral and chemically based drugs than Native American and African American traditions. Anglo-American apothecaries and drug merchants were part of a large international trade in medicines that sent North American plants to Europe (and beyond) and which imported drugs from around the world.

NATIVE AMERICAN TRADITIONS

Because religious ritual was so tightly tied together with healing practice, it is hard to define what constituted a "medicine" in Native American cultures. Shamans kept roots, leaves, and pollen in their medicine bundles along with animal bones or sacred stones. Practitioners also burned plant material (especially tobacco or sage) when they "smudged" their patients as part of a healing ritual. Water itself could be a "drug" when a healer recommended a ritual bath. Ingestion of medicine was just one use among many for healing substances.

Early European observers were especially struck by the wide variety of Native American herbal remedies. Native American healing traditions incorporated hundreds of plants. Each tribe used herbs native to its location and ecosystem, and used them according to their own belief and ritual. It is possible, however, to make broad classifications of Native American herbal remedies.

Astringents are medicines that reduce swelling or cause contraction of body tissues. Astringent drugs are used to stop bleeding, reduce diarrhea, or shrink hemorrhoids. Many plants used for this purpose contain large amounts of tannins, which are a natural astringent. Native American astringent drugs included hemlock, oak bark (especially high in tannins), bayberries, and wild geranium.

All Colonial era cultures had a wide variety of cathartics (laxatives). It seemed to be almost a universal belief that illness could be driven out by purging the bowels. Some Native American cultures believed that disease-causing spirits would leave the body if the patient were made sufficiently uncomfortable by strong laxatives. Europeans, who also believed that purging was crucial to curing, eagerly adopted many of these drugs.[1]

Two examples of cathartic plants native to North America were may apple and cascara sagrada. May apple is native to the east and southeastern regions of the continent, and was used by the Cherokee and the Delaware peoples (as well as others). The part of the plant most often used was the fruit or "apple," which appears in early summer. The Delaware used the fruit as food as well as medicine. In addition to the fruit, some peoples used the root as a purge; but many regarded the root as a poison. One European observer reported that a Native American woman used an overdose of the root to commit suicide.[2]

Cascara Sagrada is a tree native to the Pacific Northwest. The bark is used as a medicine—at one time "the most widely used cathartic on earth," which was used through the twentieth century in commercial laxatives. An indigenous oral tradition notes that the plant received its modern named when a Spanish missionary learned of its properties and christened it the "holy bark" for its great effectiveness. Its Spanish name remained the common name for the plant.[3]

Cathartics were often used in conjunction with vermifuges, drugs that kill or expel intestinal parasites. Parasites were common among Native Americans both before and after European contact, and most cultures had a variety of remedies. One of the most common was pink-root, also known as Indian Pink. The plant grows wild in woodlands throughout the eastern half of North America. European Americans adopted pinkroot into their own pharmacopeias; at one time the plant was nearly extinct because of overharvesting. In addition to pinkroot, indigenous peoples used the roots of wild plum and wild cherry trees. Another common vermifuge was the seed of Jerusalem oak, also known as "wormseed."[4]

Like cathartics, emetics (drugs that induce vomiting) were widely used by all early American cultures. In Native American societies, vomiting was sometimes used to expel "invading" objects or charms that a sorcerer had used to cause illness. One Jesuit missionary watched a Huron shaman use emetics to induce a woman to vomit "a coal as large as one's thumb." Several societies, including the tribes of the Iroquois peoples, used hellebore roots for this purpose. Hellebores grow in wet, swampy ground and produce a flower in the early spring. While it is a very effective emetic, it is poisonous in large doses. One missionary to the Onondaga people reported that a woman died after an overdose of "roots steeped in water."[5]

Drugs that reduce fever were called febrifuges. The most famous of the febrifuge drugs native to the Americas was the South American cinchona bark, which became one of the most widely traded drugs of the seventeenth and eighteenth centuries. North American plants, however, were also used for this purpose. The Cheyenne people used the leaves of a plant known as Indian breadroot (*psorlea argophylla*) to lower temperature; tribes on the eastern seaboard used plantain leaves as a poultice to soothe patients with fever. Boneset, a wildflower common from Nova Scotia to Florida, was used by many indigenous peoples and is still used by naturopathic practitioners today.[6]

NATIVE AMERICAN MEDICINES AND EUROPEANS

Many European settlers were eager to adopt Native American medicines. In the European medical paradigm, diseases arose from the local environment. It was therefore logical to look for cures for American diseases among American plants. Some settlers went so far as to claim that Native American cures were superior to those used by European physicians. Antoine LePage DuPratz, an eighteenth-century French plantation owner in Louisiana, preferred Native American practices to French. He wrote of a French man whose condition had been worsening under the care of a French doctor until he "made his escape, with as much agility as a criminal would from the hands of justice." The patient then went to a Natchez practitioner and was completely cured in eight days. DuPratz extolled the virtues of Natchez medicine, and recommended local plants, such as bearded creeper and ground ivy as cure-alls.[7]

European settlers readily adopted many Native American remedies, such as pinkroot and boneset. However, two North American plants, sassafras and Seneca snakeroot, became so highly esteemed that they became an important part of the international trade in medicines.

Sassafras is a small tree or shrub common throughout eastern North America. Its most distinguishing characteristic is its leaves: each plant bears leaves of three different shapes. The bark and leaves have a distinctive sweet smell. Native Americans throughout its range used sassafras bark, roots, and berries for a variety of ailments, including bruises, coughs, bladder pain, and eye disorders.[8]

Europeans adopted sassafras for these disorders and more. A tea made from its roots was widely used as a "blood purifier" and as a stimulant beverage similar to coffee. In addition, sassafras tea gained a reputation as a cure for syphilis—so much so that by the eighteenth century, some people were embarrassed to be seen drinking it. In Pennsylvania, sassafras oil was used to flavor beer, which became known as "root beer." When the soft drink version of root beer became popular, sassafras oil remained a key ingredient. Sassafras was included in the first cargo of North American goods exported to England. By 1770, sassafras exports rose to 77 tons.[9]

Seneca snakeroot did not quite rise to the same popularity as sassafras, but it was popular enough to become an important trade item. As its name suggests, Seneca snakeroot was used by the Seneca people as a cure for snakebite (as well as colds, coughs, and other respiratory ailments). Its name derives as well from the snake-like shape of the root.

Anglo-Americans praised the plant as a cure for many diseases. John Tennet of Virginia, author of a popular home medical guide, recommended it as a cure for pleurisy (infection of the lining of the chest cavity). His published letter to an English doctor made the plant extremely popular in England. Other physicians used it as a febrifuge and anti-inflammatory drug. One writer, advocating snakeroot as a cure for gout, was so enthusiastic that he wrote that it had "enabled Cripples to throw away their crutches and walk several Miles." Like pinkroot, Seneca snakeroot became so popular as a medicine that the wild plant came close to extinction in much of its range.[10]

AFRICAN AMERICAN TRADITIONS

Herbal practice was crucial among African and African American healers. In African American culture, "herb doctors" were in a distinct category from "conjurers" and magical healers, although all used plants in their practices. Herb doctors were less likely to use religious or magical ritual in their cures and more likely to rely solely on the healing properties of plants (as well as some non-plant medicines). Like most traditional healers, herb doctors learned their craft from parents, grandparents, or other elders in an informal apprenticeship. Older practitioners taught younger ones to identify, harvest, preserve, and process medicinal plants and substances.

African practitioners believed that plants and the forest where they grew were imbued with spiritual power. Deities "owned" certain plants and filled them with their own attributes. As African Americans became Christianized, healers attributed the power of plants to the power of the Christian deity.

There were only a few African plants that were commonly grown in the American south. Most were food plants, such as black-eyed peas and sesame, but some had additional uses as medicines. Okra, for instance, was usually grown as a vegetable, but some healers used its leaves as a poultice. Other plants were explicitly medicinal. Senna, a plant native to North Africa, was used by both Europeans and Africans as a laxative. In Jamaica, a plant known as "Surinam poison" (but native to Africa) was used for skin ailments.[11]

However, North American and European plants were more common in the African American pharmacopeia. African American healers often used non-African plants in traditionally African ways. For instance, medicinal plants were not just ingested but worn in charms and infused in baths. Perhaps the most common plant worn as a charm was asafetida. Although the plant is native to south Asia, it had been used in European medicine since medieval times. Asafetida resin has a strong, unpleasant smell—so unpleasant that one of its other names is "devil's dung." Many African American parents hung bags of asafetida around their children's necks to ward off illness. If asafetida was not available, bags of garlic or other strong smelling substances were used in the same way. Other "medicines" that were carried or worn rather than swallowed included potatoes carried to prevent rheumatism, buckeyes (horse chestnuts) carried to ward off stomach cramps, or bags of camphor worn on the chest to cure colds and pneumonia. Medicinal plants were also placed in the doorways and corners of houses to ward off illness.[12]

One class of drug used more by African Americans than other cultures was "bitters." Although bitters were used in European medicine as well, bitter medicines had a special place in African American practice. In European practice, bitters were used as a tonic to strengthen the body. African Americans used bitter medicines for the same purpose but also to "purify" the blood. The bitter taste itself was believed to be medicinal. Two plants used as bitters in African American practice were balmony and bittersweet nightshade. Both were used as a medicine for any kind of serious illness. One ex-slave interviewed in the early twentieth century remembered: "When de slaves git sick dey would gets de bitterest weeds or bark and makes a tea outen it." Another remembered that any illness was treated with "de bitterest medicine."[13]

Like practitioners in both European and Native American cultures, African American herbalists used cathartics and emetics. One of the most popular laxatives was castor oil. Like bitters, castor oil was a panacea. Some ex-slaves remembered being dosed with castor oil as children for any illness, regardless of symptoms. Lobelia (also known as "pukeweed") found its way into the African American pharmacopeia as an emetic, although it was more commonly used in European American medicine. Other medicines, such as boneset tea, were classified as diaphoretics, or "sweats." Sweating was believed to drive toxins or putrid matter from the body. Boneset was also esteemed for its bitter taste.

AFRICAN AMERICAN EXCHANGES OF KNOWLEDGE

African Americans exchanged knowledge of medicines with whites and Native Americans. As we have seen, many native North American plants made their way into African American healing traditions. Some of this knowledge may have passed when African Americans and Native Americans were enslaved side by side early in the Colonial period. Some Native American peoples offered refuge to runaway slaves and encouraged intermarriage, another practice that led to cultural exchange. In addition to the plants mentioned previously, the African American pharmacopeia included such common North American plants as pinkroot, snakeroot, and the ever-popular sassafras.

White slaveholders sometimes trained slaves in European medical traditions, and employed slaves as medicinal gardeners and gatherers of plants. This gave the gardeners and gatherers knowledge that they could pass on to their children and other slaves. White mistresses often cared for sick slaves and prepared medicines for them. One African

American herbal practitioner learned one of her remedies for coughs from her mistress, and passed the recipe to her descendents.[14]

Whites also adapted remedies developed by African Americans. Some were so highly valued that their inventors won their freedom. In 1729, the Virginia government freed a slave named Papan in exchange for his recipe for a syphilis cure. Twenty years later, officials in South Carolina offered a similar deal to Caesar for his cure for snakebite and poisoning. Caesar's recipe found its way into published home health guides that remained in print throughout the antebellum period. Finally, South Carolina freed another slave, Sampson, in 1755 for an herbal snakebite remedy made of polypody, snakeroot, avens root, and rum. Sampson's medicine was so highly esteemed that he won not just his freedom but an annual salary for the rest of his life.[15]

ANGLO-AMERICAN APOTHECARIES AND MEDICINES

Classification of Medicines

Anglo-American physicians and apothecaries classified drugs according to their actions. In the dominant medical theory of the time, illness was caused by imbalance in the body, most often by excess or "putrid" bodily fluids or humors. Medicines were designed to expel these humors. Others were put into different categories, such as those that killed pain or strengthened tissues. In addition, drugs, especially herbs, were sorted by their degree of "temperature" and "moisture." A medicine, like an illness, could be hot or cold, wet or dry.

Dr. James Thacher, Continental Army surgeon and prominent civilian practitioner, published a summary of the many different types of drugs in the American pharmacopeia. Although this summary was aimed at educated physicians, Thacher's classification applied to the ways laypeople thought about medicines as well. A long section of Thacher's classification described what he called "local stimulants," all of which expelled or discharged material from different parts of the body. In addition to cathartics and emetics, Thacher listed diuretics, which produced urine; sialogogues, which caused a patient to salivate; and diaphoretics, which encouraged sweating. "Epispastics" were used to raise fluid-filled blisters on the skin.[16]

Thacher added a few more categories of drug that treated symptoms directly. Narcotics killed pain and calmed the patient, antispasmodics soothed cramps and colic, antihelmetics, or vermifuges, killed internal parasites. Finally, there were those medicines such as tonics and bitters that strengthened the body "by increasing the force of circulation, animal heat, secretions, digestion, and muscular action." Most drugs, whether made from homegrown plants or exotic imported minerals fell into one of these categories.[17]

Herbalists often added another category to their descriptions of medicinal plants. One of the most widely read herbalists was the English writer Nicholas Culpeper. His *Pharmacopoeia Londinensis or the London Dispensatory* was the second medical book to be printed in British North America; his other popular work, *The English Physician*, went through multiple American editions as well. Families passed down annotated copies of Culpeper's works as precious guides to home remedies. Culpeper classified each plant according to its degree of moisture and heat. In the humoral medicine paradigm, cold, moist diseases had to be treated with hot, dry medicines. Culpeper also recommended plants for each body part, depending on which planet "ruled" the herb according to astrologers.

Home Remedies

Making medicines was not a skill reserved for apothecaries. Most Anglo-Americans, especially women, knew how to prepare remedies for common ailments. Growing, preserving, and preparing medicinal herbs was a skill girls learned as part of their training for their adult role as housewives. Women grew medicinal plants in their kitchen gardens alongside vegetables and culinary herbs.

Many of these plants were imported from Europe. One commonly grown herb was chamomile, a small plant with apple-scented flowers used for stomachaches and insomnia. Other common "physick garden" plants included angelica, used as both a flavoring for food and as a tonic and rhubarb, used as both a fruit and as a cathartic. The Reverend Cotton Mather of Boston recommended that every household grow medicinal plants, including sage, rue, saffron, garlic, licorice, and elderberries. As a supplement to gardening, women gathered wild North American plants in the fields and woods.[18]

In addition to growing medicinal plants, girls and women preserved and prepared them. Plants could be dried, pickled in vinegar, or preserved in brandy. Medicines could be made by infusing herbs into tea, distilling them into concentrated essences, or blending them with beeswax or lard to make a salve. Published housekeeping guides included instructions for all of these processes. They were such a part of being a good housewife that one book published in England had as its title *The Accomplish't Lady's Delight in Preserving, Physick, Beautifying and Cookery*. "Physick" was as much a part of a woman's role as cooking.[19]

Home remedies were often quite sophisticated. The Brigham family of Massachusetts kept a notebook of its family medical recipes, giving us a window into home medical practice. The notebook was passed through four generations, covering the mid-seventeenth to the mid-eighteenth centuries. Many of its recipes are made from garden plants, such as an ointment for "piles" made of "8 handfulls" of sage mixed with lard and butter. However, some of the other recipes contain exotic ingredients such as sandalwood and gold leaf. Here the line between home remedies and those prepared and purchased at an apothecary shop was blurred. Many ordinary people without formal medical training felt confident enough to know which illnesses required these ingredients as well as how to prepare and administer them.[20]

Apothecaries and Their Shops

Defining "apothecary" in Colonial America can be difficult. Many physicians prepared medicines and kept apothecary shops; many shop-keepers who sold medicines also performed medical services such as bleeding or diagnosis. Unlike England, which regulated the practices of physicians, surgeons, and apothecaries, the American colonies had few legal restrictions on medical and pharmaceutical practice.

Most of those who called themselves apothecaries trained for their field as apprentices, although a few attended college. Those with higher levels of education were more likely to practice medicine as well as dispense drugs. Adding to this mix of training and skill were groups of merchants who specialized in the medicine trade. Those who sold drugs wholesale were usually called "druggists" rather than apothecaries, but some had retail shops in addition to their wholesale operations.[21]

Most physicians prepared and sold medicines as part of their practices. One historian has noted that many Colonial era apothecaries might better be called "dispensing physicians" because of their role as practitioners. Many apprentices who studied with physicians were specifically trained in "pharmacy" as well as surgery and medicine. However, as time passed, some distinctions began to emerge. A 1736 Virginia law setting limits on medical fees distinguished between physicians and "any apothecary making up the prescription of another." This differentiation foreshadows the modern definition of a pharmacist—someone who is an expert on the uses of drugs and the making of medicines but only dispenses them at the direction of a clinical practitioner.[22]

Apothecary shops sold a wide variety of goods. One Boston advertisement from 1721 includes "all sorts of Fruit and Spice, Ginger" as well as "snuff ... perfum'd or plain" and "Painters Colors." There was also a wide variety of medical equipment and medicines. This shop sold patent medicines, such as "The Royal Honey Water ... good against Deafness, and to make the Hair grow," as well as "Lockyear's pills." Customers could also purchase lancets, surgical instruments, and urine bottles. Other apothecaries were more specialized in their goods, catering specifically to physicians rather than the general public. A 1685 account book kept by Boston apothecary William Davis noted that he had filled orders for antinomy oxide, "ungenteum diampholyx" (white lead and belladonna), and red mercuric oxide.[23]

In addition to goods for sale, apothecary shops contained equipment for compounding and storing medicines. The most widespread tool was the mortar and pestle, used for grinding and mixing medicinal substances. The mortar and pestle was so common that it became a universal symbol of the apothecary's trade—so much so that many apothecaries used a painting of a mortar as a sign on their shops. Second only to the mortar and pestle in familiarity was the apothecary jar—a ceramic storage container labeled or color coded for its contents. Apothecaries also used copper stills to distill and condense "spirits, waters and oils." Pills were made in "pill rollers" that ensured that pills were of uniform size and dosage. Finally, most shops were equipped with elaborate scales and weights for measuring ingredients and weighing out portions of medicines to be sold.[24]

Patent Medicines

In addition to home remedies and physicians' prescriptions, Colonial era people had access to a wide variety of patent medicines. Apothecaries sold medicines imported from England and created their own. While some physicians deplored these remedies as "quackery," they remained extremely popular through the Colonial era and beyond.

Early English patents on medicines were granted directly by the king. In 1687, James II granted a patent to a physician named Thomas Weir for a product called "Anderson's Pills." Later Parliament refined the patent law, and a spate of new applications for patented compound medicines ensued. "Bateman's Pectoral Drops" were among the first patented under the new law, in 1726. Patent medicines usually kept their ingredients secret, but it seems clear that most contained a variety of vegetable compounds suspended in alcohol.[25]

Most patent medicines made extravagant claims. One of the most popular was a concoction called "Daffy's Elixir." Daffy's Elixir was invented about 1650 by Reverend Thomas Daffy, a clergyman who had lost his post and turned to medicine to support himself. After Thomas Daffy passed away, his kinsman Anthony Daffy took over its manufacture. It was Anthony rather than Thomas who made the medicine a worldwide success. Anthony wrote a pamphlet calling the formula "the choice drink of health" and promising that it cured "gout, the stone, colic . . . scurvy, dropsy, rickets, consumption and 'languishing' and 'melancholy.' " Daffy's elixir was widely advertised by American apothecary shops through the seventeenth and eighteenth centuries, and was still being sold in 1824.[26]

Other medicines made similar claims to be panaceas. One patent medicine advertised by a Virginia apothecary in 1766 purported to cure "scurvy, itch, leprosy and all other disorders of the skin." Another, to "remove all kinds of fits, lowness of spirits, giddiness, headaches, melancholy, and all hysterick . . . afflictions." An analysis of the ingredients of patent medicines done by the Philadelphia College of Pharmacy in 1824 suggests some reasons for the popularity of these remedies. Many, such as Hooper's Female Pills and Anderson's Scots Pills, were primarily made up of laxatives. Purging the bowels was widely believed to be the first step in curing any illness. Others, such as Bateman's Drops and Godfrey's Cordial, had an even better reason for their effectiveness—their main ingredient was opium, which was almost sure to make the patient feel better, no matter how temporary the effect. The addictive quality of the drug no doubt brought many repeat customers.[27]

American apothecaries often created their own versions of these popular medicines. Some they sold under their own names, others were blatant copies of the secret formulas of well-known brands. Account books and other records show American apothecaries ordering empty bottles marked "Daffy's Elixir" or with other names, presumably to fill with their own formulation.[28]

Pharmacy and Materia Medica in Elite Medical Practice

Physicians classified, compounded, and prescribed drugs according to the medical theories of the time. Many shared the Galenic humoral paradigm of illness and medicine, which was the basis not just for academic medicine but much popular practice as well. However, other theorists, such as Paracelsus, influenced the prescriptions of Colonial era physicians.

The purpose of a Galenic prescription was to restore humoral balance in the body. The organizing principle was to prepare a medicine that would embody qualities in opposition to the predominant humor in a patient. A "cold and moist" ailment like an upper respiratory infection would be treated with a "hot and dry" medicine. Galenic remedies were usually made up of many ingredients so that each could reinforce the others. Most remedies in the Galenic style were botanically based.[29]

Paracelsus, a Swiss physician, chemist, and philosopher born in 1493, had a strong influence among seventeenth- and eighteenth-century physicians. Unlike Galen, Paracelsus believed that the key to understanding human health was understanding the chemistry of the body. Disease was not caused by imbalances in bodily fluids but by malfunctioning chemical reactions. Paracelsian drugs were often "pure" or distilled minerals and metals rather than herbs. American physicians in the Paracelsian tradition prescribed sulfur, lead, mercury, and other substances to their patients.[30]

Two drugs crossed theoretical lines: cinchona bark (also called "Jesuit's bark" and "Peruvian bark") and opium. Both were widely used by physicians of all orientations. Cinchona bark comes from a tree native to the Andes and was first introduced to Europeans in the early seventeenth century by a Spanish monk. It contains quinine, a substance that inhibits the growth of the malaria parasite. It was quickly adopted in southern Europe as a cure for malaria, and by extension, for all fevers. It took some years for Protestant England to accept the use of this "Catholic" drug, but it soon became a widely prescribed medicine for all febrile diseases. As one historian noted, "The Peruvian Bark was used in more different preparations than any other agent except, perhaps, opium." Opium had been known in Europe since the days of the ancient Greeks. It is derived from the sap of the poppy plant, and has a strong effect as a sedative and painkiller. American physicians used opium (and its derivatives such as laudanum) for these purposes, as well as to control vomiting and diarrhea.[31]

In practice, most physicians recommended a wide variety of both botanic and mineral-based drugs. A study of the practices of four eighteenth-century Massachusetts physicians reveals that they prescribed over one hundred different drugs. These drugs included chemicals and minerals such as sulfur, nitric acid, antinomy and mercury salts; imported botanics such as myrrh, opium, and cinchona bark; and local plants such as snakeroot and sassafras. While each practitioner had been educated in different theories of medicine, it is clear that their practices took on a pragmatic rather than a theoretical orientation.[32]

It was perhaps this eclectic attitude toward prescribing that led elite physicians such as Dr. John Morgan to call for the separation of pharmacy and medicine in the eighteenth century. Morgan had been educated at the prestigious University of Edinburgh, was appointed as the apothecary to the Pennsylvania hospital in 1756, and was one of the founding professors of the Medical College of Pennsylvania. Morgan made a strong call for apothecaries to be members of a separate profession: "We must regret that the very different employment of physician, surgeon, and apothecary should be promiscuously followed by any one man: they certainly require different talents." Morgan argued that many physicians left the compounding of medicines to their apprentices. He felt that patients would benefit if trained professionals were in charge of all aspects of pharmacy: "Is not a man educated in the profession to be trusted in preference to one who is only learning the business?"[33]

Morgan's suggestions were not well received. Many physicians took a large portion of their incomes from selling medicines or even running apothecary shops—they did not want this lucrative business to go elsewhere. As one Philadelphia doctor wrote of his colleagues in 1784, "Their greatest profit arises from the private dispensation of remedies; to which end each physician has a select stock of drugs." The separation of pharmacy from medicine would have to wait.[34]

The International Trade in Medicines

Drugs and medicines were an important part of international trade. American medicinal plants such as sassafras went to Europe; opium, cinchona, and other resins and chemicals came to American ports from around the world. Apothecaries and merchants thrived on this complex global trade.

Most traders to the Americas were relatively small scale. They collected cargo from larger traders in London and then either resold them or traded them for American goods. One successful drug merchant, Joseph Cruttenden, supplied most of the goods to Boston's apothecary shops in the early eighteenth century. He took on cargo that included cinchona bark, opium, the Asian resin gamboge, and many patent medicines. He traded some of his goods for sugar in the West Indies and then went on to New England. There he sold the rest of his medicines and some of the sugar, and reloaded his ships with furs, turpentine, and lumber from New England before returning to London.[35]

Individual apothecaries placed orders with wholesalers to supply their shops. These orders reflect the global reach of the medicine trade.

The apothecary Thomas Wharton of Williamsburg placed an order with his supplier that included cinnamon (from Asia), aloes (from the West Indies), galbanum (from the Middle East), chamomile (from Europe), and Peruvian bark (from South America). While he may not have been thinking of himself as the center of global trade, Wharton had a piece of every corner of the world right there in his shop.[36]

Pharmaceutical practice was a microcosm of intellectual, cultural, and economic exchange. The cultures of North America exchanged medicines with each other, and the global medicine trade brought their knowledge around the world, as well as brought the world to them. The experience of illness and the desire to heal were things all the world's peoples shared.

NOTES

1. Virgil J. Vogel, *American Indian Medicine*. Norman: University of Oklahoma Press, 1970, p. 33.

2. Ibid., pp. 334–335.

3. Ibid., p. 289.

4. Ibid., pp. 175–176; 348–349.

5. Ibid., p. 173.

6. Ibid., pp. 174–175.

7. "LePage DuPratz, a French Observer in Louisiana, Reports on Natchez Nation Healing Practices: 1720–1728." In John Harley Warner and Janet A. Tighe (Eds.), *Major Problems in the History of American Medicine and Public Health*. New York: Houghton Mifflin, 2001, pp. 28–30; quotation p. 29.

8. Vogel, *American Indian Medicine*, p. 365.

9. George E. Gifford, "Botanic Remedies in Colonial Massachusetts: 1620–1820." In *Medicine in Colonial Massachusetts: 1620–1820: A Conference Held 25 and 26 May 1978 by the Colonial Society of Massachusetts*. Boston: The Colonial Society of Massachusetts, 1980, p. 270.

10. Vogel, *American Indian Medicine*, p. 371.

11. Sharla M. Fett, *Working Cures: Healing, Health, and Power on Southern Slave Plantations*. Chapel Hill: University of North Carolina Press, 2002, p. 63.

12. Herbert C. Covey, *African American Slave Medicine: Herbal and Non-Herbal Treatments*. New York: Rowman and Littlefield, 2007, pp. 73–124.

13. Covey, *African American Slave Medicine*, pp. 82–83.

14. Fett, *Working Cures*, pp. 65–67.

15. Ibid., p. 64.

16. J. Worth Estes, "Therapeutic Practice in Colonial New England." In *Medicine in Colonial Massachusetts*, pp. 365–366.

17. Estes, "Therapeutic Practice," p. 365.

18. Cotton Mather, *The Angel of Bethesda*, edited with an introduction and notes by Gordon W. Jones. Barre, MA: Barre Publishers, 1972, pp. 263–265.

19. Rebecca J. Tannenbaum, *The Healer's Calling: Women and Medicine in Early New England*. Ithaca, NY: Cornell University Press, 2002, pp. 23–30; quotation p. 30.

20. Ibid., p. 7.

21. Norman Gevitz, " 'Pray Let the Medicines Be Good': The New England Apothecary in the Seventeenth and Early Eighteenth Centuries," *Pharmacy in History* 42 (1999), p. 88.

22. Ibid.,p. 88; Harold B. Gill, Jr., *The Apothecary in Colonial Virginia*. Charlottesville: University Press of Virginia, 1972, pp. 25–26.

23. Gill, *The Apothecary in Colonial Virginia*, pp. 30–31; Gevitz, " 'Pray Let the Medicines Be Good,' " p. 93.

24. Gill, *The Apothecary in Colonial Virginia*, pp. 67–71.

25. George B. Griffenhagen and James Harvey Young, "Old English Patent Medicines in America," *Pharmacy in History* 34 (1992), pp. 201–202.

26. Ibid., p. 205.

27. Gill, *The Apothecary in Colonial Virginia*, p. 45; Griffenhagen and Young, "Old English Patent Medicines," p. 219.

28. Gill, *The Apothecary in Colonial Virginia*, p. 46.

29. Tannenbaum, *The Healer's Calling* pp. 4–5.

30. Gevitz, " 'Pray Let the Medicines Be Good,' " p. 92; Tannenbaum, *The Healer's Calling*, p. 5.

31. Estes, "Therapeutic Practice," pp. 337, 347.

32. Ibid., pp. 330–334.

33. Gill, *The Apothecary in Colonial Virginia*, pp. 27–28.

34. Ibid., p. 29.

35. I. K. Steele, "A London Trader and the Atlantic Empire: Joseph Cruttenden, Apothecary: 1710–1717," *William and Mary Quarterly*, Third Series, 34 (1977), pp. 282–297.

36. Gill, *The Apothecary in Colonial Virginia*, p. 71.

CHAPTER 11

War and Health

Warfare has a profound effect on human health. Soldiers are wounded and killed in battle; civilians are often victimized by military action; war leads to social disruption, famine, and disease. In early America, war had all of these effects. Somewhat surprisingly, the most important health effects of war occurred off the battlefield.

Colonial era wars almost always coincided with outbreaks of infectious disease. More soldiers died of disease than battlefield injuries. Troop movements and fleeing refugees helped spread disease among civilian population. In addition, soldiers were subject to diseases because of their living conditions. Crowding and poor sanitation contributed to military deaths. There is some evidence that military leaders took advantage of these conditions to practice a crude form of "biological warfare." While the evidence for this practice is not definitive, it is worth examining.

The eighteenth century saw the beginnings of organized medical care for soldiers as well as the beginnings of sanitation and hygiene as a military concern. George Washington introduced reforms in both these areas during the American Revolution. In doing so, he set the stage for the modernization of health care in the American military.

COLONIAL ERA WARFARE AND WEAPONS

Europeans and Native Americans used different kinds of weapons and tactics. After contact, each culture adapted some of the techniques of the other. Each culture had to learn how to cope with new kinds of battlefield injuries.

Early English settlers brought swords, pikes, and armor to America, but these proved impractical in the heavily wooded landscape of the American east coast. Firearms soon became the weapon of choice. Seventeenth- and eighteenth-century muskets had limited range and accuracy. In European-style battles, groups of soldiers fired massive, unaimed volleys in unison to compensate for the lack of precision in their weapons. By the time of the Revolution, a new innovation—the rifle—enabled soldiers to fire from longer distances and with greater accuracy, but rifles were reserved for snipers, and the flintlock musket remained the standard issue weapon.

Artillery pieces supplemented the smaller guns. Cannons were used both on ships and on land. Artillery fired two kinds of ammunition: grapeshot, small balls the size of grapes, which was used against human beings; and the more familiar cannon ball, which was used against ships, forts, and other structures.

European tactics included mass musket blasts, cannon fire, and cavalry charges. These tactics assumed that battles would be fought in the open, with opposing soldiers facing each other across clearly drawn battle lines. They were based on deploying large armies arrayed in formation, with clear lines of command.

Before European contact, Native Americans used clubs, hatchets, knives, spears, and bows for warfare. Native American archers were extremely accurate with their bows, much more so than a European soldier with a musket. Bows had their own disadvantages, however. They did not have as great a range as firearms and lost accuracy under windy conditions.

Native American warfare was very different from European warfare. Wars between Native American tribes were often fought as a series of raids by small groups rather than the pitched battles between large armies common in Europe. The goals of warfare were also different. Rather than wars of conquest and domination, many Native American wars were often focused on revenge for an insult or to compensate for the death of a relative by taking captives from another tribe. Even in cultures in which larger scale warfare was common, such as the Iroquois, war was not marked by the mass casualties often seen in Europe.

After European contact, however, the weapons, tactics, and purpose of war changed for both cultures. Native Americans were quick to adopt guns for both hunting and war. Muskets and gunpowder became highly favored "currency" in the fur trade and other exchanges between Europeans and Native Americans. On the Great Plains, Native Americans quickly became skilled with horses, and "cavalry" became an important part of their military tactics. Europeans, on the other hand, soon saw the usefulness of Native American custom of small raiding parties that could strike quickly and then escape. American militias found these techniques especially valuable when fighting the larger, better equipped British Army during the American Revolutionary War.

For both cultures, the purpose and "rules" of war changed drastically, especially when Europeans and Native Americans fought each other. In both cases, battle became more violent, and attacks on noncombatants more commonplace. Perhaps the best Colonial era example of this escalation of violence occurred during Metacom's War, also known as King Philip's War, fought in New England during 1675 and 1676. While its causes were multiple, Metacom's War represented a coordinated attempt by a coalition of Native Americans to drive out the English who were an increasing threat to their land and culture.

The war was one of the deadliest fought on American soil. As one historian put it, "In proportion to population, King Philip's War inflicted greater casualties upon the people than any other war in our history." One in 10 English men of military age died in the conflict, with deaths totaling 2,500. Mortality among Native Americans is estimated at 5,000, and thousands more were captured and sold into slavery.[1]

The war was marked by atrocities and massacres. Ironically, both sides adapted Native American tactics of stealth attacks and "guerilla warfare." Raids on villages and settlements were typical, as was the slaughter of women and children. In "The Great Swamp Fight," an attack on a Narragansett village by the English in December of 1675, English soldiers first set fire to the houses. Most of the inhabitants were women and children, hidden in the swamp for safety. As the occupants fled, the soldiers shot them. Those still inside the houses burned to death. Native American raids on English towns followed a similar pattern. The February 1675 raid on Lancaster, Massachusetts, became one of the most famous of the war after the publication of Mary Rowlandson's narrative of the attack and her subsequent captivity. The raiders killed the adult men and infants, and took the children and women captive.

TREATING BATTLEFIELD INJURIES

Colonial era practitioners did their best to deal with the injuries that resulted from warfare. Both European American and Native American cultures had medical techniques specific to battlefield injuries such as gunshot and arrow wounds.

Native American Techniques

European observers were impressed with Native Americans' skill at treating wounds made by both arrowheads and bullets. Typically, Native American practitioners treated wounds with dressings made from eggs, honey, or tree resin mixed with medicinal herbs. Some of the ingredients, such as honey or turpentine, may have had an antiseptic effect, which would have hastened healing. Practitioners also performed surgical procedures. In New Spain, some practitioners extracted bullets from wounds with a knife; if the bullet was too deep to remove easily, practitioners used plant material to open the wound further: "They introduce a piece of the slippery elm bark as far into the wound as is practicable, which is suffered to remain, till the sought for object is obtained."[2]

Another common method was for a practitioner literally to suck the wound until the bleeding stopped and the bullet or arrowhead was removed. One explorer watched a Flathead woman treat an arrow wound this way: she "sucked the wound perfectly dry, so that it appeared as white as chalk; and then she bound it up with a piece of dry buck-skin as soft as woolen cloth, and by this treatment the wound began to heal and soon closed up."[3]

Other Native American methods dealt with slashing or lacerating wounds, such as those made by knives or hatchets. Many cultures, including the Mohegans and the Apaches, used spider webs to stop bleeding. Others used puffball spores as a styptic for the same purpose. Other materials used to stem bleeding included sumac berries and "buzzard's down." For large gaping wounds, the Kalapooyahs of the Pacific Northwest laid green leaves across the wound and pulled the edges of the skin together with thin splints of pine bark.[4]

European American Techniques

Military medicine had a long tradition in Europe. Beginning with the sixteenth-century French surgeon Ambroise Paré, military surgeons had been at the forefront of the modernization of surgical techniques. Surgeons in the seventeenth- and eighteenth-century North American wars had access to the works of Paré as well as more recent works by Richard Wiseman who served with the Royalist army during the English Civil War and John Hunter, who trained many eighteenth-century American surgeons.

One of the first problems battlefield surgeons had to confront was the transportation of the wounded. There was no organized ambulance corps to move the wounded from the battlefield to the field hospital. If a wounded man was lucky, a friend might help him make his way to an aid station. In most cases, however, the wounded were left unattended until the battle was over, which could be as long as several days. Such neglect raised the mortality rate from wounds considerably. Shock, blood loss, and dehydration could change a survivable wound into a mortal one. In addition, soldiers lying helpless on the ground were often finished off by the enemy. A retreating army might also simply abandon its wounded, especially those who were too weak to travel. When the British troops retreated from the Battle of Lexington and Concord, they left behind nine wounded.[5]

Casualties were retrieved from the field in a slapdash manner. Officers might be slung across their own horses for transport. The more badly off were loaded onto horse-drawn carts or litters. Soldiers improvised stretchers from blankets and poles to carry their comrades. The less seriously injured often limped off the field on their own or with the support of another soldier.

Once a wounded soldier reached a field hospital, the surgeons took over. There were a variety of surgical and medical techniques to deal with the different kinds of wounds made by seventeenth- and eighteenth-century weapons. In addition to penetrating gunshot wounds, soldiers suffered from limbs shattered by artillery fire, slashes and punctures made by bayonets, and burns from "backfiring" gunpowder in muskets or cannons.

How a gunshot wound was treated depended on its location. Wounds to the extremities were the most survivable but still required attention. The first step was to stop the bleeding with tourniquets, pressure bandages, or ligatures. Surgeons then "explored" the wound to locate the bullet. Doing so often required additional incisions to widen the field of view. If the surgeon could locate the musket ball, he removed it—using his fingers, forceps, or a surgical spoon to dig the bullet out. The surgeon then packed the wound with absorbent lint and covered it with bandages. If bones had been broken as well, the limb was immobilized and placed in a splint.

Some severe wounds required that a limb be amputated, but surgeons differed on when amputation was necessary. Compound fractures, broken bones that protrude through the skin, were a common result of bullet wounds. Some surgeons recommended that limbs with compound fractures be amputated immediately; others, such as the influential John Hunter, preferred a wait and see approach. The main danger of a compound fracture was infection and gangrene. The shattered bones and ragged wounds of a compound fracture made both more likely. Most authorities agreed that any wound that damaged a joint or the head of a bone required amputation of the limb.[6]

It is no surprise that surgeons were reluctant to amputate. Doing so rendered the patient permanently disabled and visibly maimed. Being an amputee also made most kinds of civilian work impossible. A farmer needed all his limbs; an artisan needed both hands. Amputating a limb would often condemn a patient to a life of poverty as well as disability. Knowing this, some patients refused amputation and preferred to chance death from gangrene in the hope that the wound would eventually heal.

When amputations were performed, surgeons tried to operate rapidly. There was no anesthesia of any kind, and surgeons wanted to spare the patient as much pain as possible. Some operators claimed to be able to amputate a leg in 30 seconds. After the surgery, surgeons stopped the bleeding with ligatures for large vessels or cautery for small vessels and covered the stump with a cloth cap.

Wounds in other areas of the body required different treatment. Patients who had been shot in the head required surgery to relieve the pressure on the brain. Both seventeenth- and eighteenth-century surgeons used the ancient technique of trephination, in which holes were drilled in the skull and pieces of bone removed. One dramatic example of this surgery occurred during the Revolutionary War, when a soldier was brought in with his skull cracked and dented. Some doctors felt that treating the injury would be useless and only add to the patient's suffering, but one surgeon, Dr. Drowne, decided to attempt a trephination. He removed the damaged bone and put a silver coin in its place. According to Dr. Drowne, the man recovered completely and lived for another 30 years.[7]

Most wounds of the chest and abdomen were considered fatal, especially wounds to the heart. However, surgeons often attempted to treat some of these injuries, with occasional success. Wounds to the intestines were carefully stitched back together. Wounded lungs were treated with therapeutic bleeding to reduce inflammation and "redirect" blood away from the wound. In either case, surgeons did their best to remove dead or damaged tissue before dressing and treating the wound. After the suturing and dressing, both patient and doctor waited, watched, and hoped for the best.[8]

In addition to wounds, soldiers often came to the field hospital with burns. Burns were usually treated with different kinds of poultices and dressings. A simple dressing of spirit of wine was used on minor burns, but deep burns that involved the muscle required more elaborate treatment. The first poultices were "digestives" used to encourage dead tissue to slough away; these were followed with soothing dressings of animal fat or vegetable oil mixed with medicinal herbs. Some practitioners treated burns with bandages soaked in tea; variations on this technique were used until the twentieth century. As is still the case today, however, burns that covered large areas of the body usually resulted in overwhelming infection and death.[9]

Postoperative Care

Since there was no concept of antisepsis in this period, wound infection was almost inevitable. In fact, the appearance of pus in a wound was thought to be a sign of healing. Pus was also believed to drive harmful humors out of the wound. Surgeons understood that too much inflammation and putrefaction was dangerous, however, and used methods to avoid and minimize these symptoms.

Patients were almost always subjected to therapeutic bleeding, even if the wound had already caused a loss of blood. Inflammation in a wound was thought to be the result of "excessive" or "putrid" blood in the body; it was thus logical to bleed patients to avoid inflammation. Other preventative measures included keeping the patient on a "low" or sparse diet and a gentle purging of the bowels for the same reason. In addition, wounds were dressed with various "cooling" substances to keep the "hot" inflammatory blood away from the injury. Doctors often soaked bandages in wine or turpentine, which would have had the added advantage of providing some actual protection against infection although the physicians of the time would not have understood their antiseptic effect. Finally, patients were often dosed with opium and cinchona bark during their convalescence. Both were thought to strengthen the body and prevent fevers.

Opium and the "bark" were also used to prevent tetanus, another common aftereffect of wounds. Cinchona bark was the "wonder drug" of the early modern era. It contains quinine, which is an effective drug against malaria. As a result, seventeenth- and eighteenth-century physicians prescribed it to prevent and treat any kind of febrile disease. Opium, of course, is still used as a painkiller and sedative. Navy physicians routinely soaked bandages in opium as an antitetanus measure; the respected physician Benjamin Rush claimed to cure cases of tetanus by giving the patient two to three ounces of cinchona daily and "blistering" the patient's back with mercury.[10]

INFECTIOUS DISEASE DURING WARTIME

The greatest danger to both soldiers and civilians in time of war was not battlefield wounds but epidemic disease. One estimate states that during the American Revolution, 90 percent of deaths in the Continental Army and 84 percent of British deaths were due to disease. Military officials understood that keeping soldiers healthy was a priority, but it was not always possible.[11]

Soldiers lived under conditions that made them especially vulnerable to disease. They were subjected to great physical and emotional stress, and they lived in close quarters with inadequate sanitation and hygiene. Military muster brought soldiers from a wide area to one place, where one sick soldier could infect all of his messmates. In addition, soldiers were a highly mobile population. As they marched from place to place, microbes came with them and often spread to the civilian population.

Scabies or "The Itch"

Scabies is a skin condition caused by a microscopic mite that burrows under the skin. The main symptoms are a rash, small, pimple-like lesions, and intense, sometimes unbearable itching. The mites spread easily with close contact and can live for a short time in clothes or bedding. Scabies was common among seventeenth- and eighteenth-century soldiers. While it is not fatal, overzealous scratching can lead to skin ulcers and bacterial infection. In addition, the constant, unremitting itching can take a severe toll on morale and mental health.

The scabies mite found an ideal environment in military camps and hospitals. Most soldiers had one set of clothes and one blanket or bedroll, which they rarely if ever washed. Opportunities to bathe one's body were just as rare. Even medical facilities did not have the resources to provide fresh bedding for patients. During the Seven Years' War, a soldier who fell ill complained that he woke in his sickbed covered in lice; scabies mites were likely bedfellows as well.[12]

One British Army surgeon estimated that "the itch" was responsible for more hospitalizations during the Seven Years War than any other disease. An ointment made of sulfur and lard was the usual treatment and was probably somewhat effective. Sulfur for medicine was sometimes in short supply, however, since it was also a key ingredient in gunpowder. Some soldiers approached their comrades in artillery units to acquire sulfur to cure their itching.[13]

There were two recorded deaths from scabies at the Valley Forge encampment in the winter of 1777 and 1778. Both seem to be the result of men driven to desperation by constant itching. One soldier stole a pot of mercury ointment usually used for venereal disease and covered his entire body with it. He died the next day. Another tried a less exotic approach—he drank a quart of rum, perhaps with the thought of getting drunk enough to numb his skin. He died of alcohol poisoning.[14]

Typhus: "Military Fever" or "Camp Fever"

Typhus is another disease of close quarters and poor hygiene. The two organisms that cause it are carried by rat fleas (the "endemic" form of the organism) and human body lice (the "epidemic" form). While the symptoms of the two varieties vary somewhat, both forms are characterized by high fever, joint and muscle pain, and a mottled pink or red rash that begins on the torso and spreads to cover the entire body. Death rates for the epidemic, louse-borne form can be as high as 60 percent.

Typhus was associated with situations where human beings were exposed to rats, lice, and fleas. Like the scabies mite, the body louse passed easily from person to person by skin contact or unwashed clothes or bedding. Also known as "jail fever" and "ship fever," two Colonial era names for typhus reflect its association with the military: "camp fever" and "military fever." One historian has called it the "scourge of European armies." Typhus came relatively late to North America; the first recorded outbreak occurred during the Seven Years War when "spotted fever" spread among British and American soldiers in western New York. Shortly thereafter, a similar epidemic emerged in Rhode Island.[15]

Some of the worst American outbreaks occurred in military hospitals. Lice flourished in the unwashed clothes and bedding of sick and wounded soldiers. Lack of laundry facilities meant that new patients could easily become infested when they were put into an unwashed bed. The Seven Years War soldier whose encounter with lice was mentioned above tried to clean his bedding by ironing his blanket with a hot "tailor's goose"; when he did so, the blanket "turned red as blood" with the bodies of crushed insects.[16]

Typhus struck again during the Revolutionary War. In the winter of 1777, over seven hundred sick and wounded Continental soldiers were transported to a military hospital in Bethlehem, Pennsylvania. The building commandeered for the hospital could hold only four hundred comfortably, and it soon became unbearably crowded. Despite the conditions, patients kept coming. By the end of the winter, five hundred soldiers, or about a third of the patients, had died of typhus. Many of the hospital staff also succumbed: ten of the eleven surgeons developed the disease, as did two of the three stewards, and every orderly and nurse.[17]

American physicians of the time made the connection among typhus, poor hygiene, and crowding. Benjamin Rush believed that typhus resulted from the "bad air" created by the fumes from unwashed human bodies accumulating in an unventilated space. Rush recommended that military casualties be billeted on private homes rather than crowded together in hospitals, and that soldiers be required to wash their clothes and bodies regularly. If typhus occurred, he suggested treating it with tartar emetic, cinchona bark, and purges.[18]

Dysentery

Another common disease that plagued military encampments was dysentery, or the "flux." Dysentery is a collective name for several different diseases with similar symptoms: severe diarrhea, vomiting, fever, and dehydration. Like typhus, it is a disease associated with crowded conditions and lack of sanitation. In the case of dysentery, the germs are spread by human waste and a contaminated water supply.

Conditions in military camps were a perfect set up for the spread of this kind of disease. Tens of thousands of men might be packed into an area not much bigger than a small village. In some cases, the population density of military camps exceeded those of cities of the same area. Soldiers were reluctant to use latrines and often simply went to the edge of the camp to relieve themselves. The intense crowding and inadequate sanitation resulted in a disease environment that "assumed a nightmarish quality, more and more resembling life in rank and pestilential slums." Death rates from disease in army camps during the Seven Years War were as much as four times higher than for civilians in the same period.[19]

There were severe outbreaks of dysentery among American troops in Boston in 1775 and in New Jersey and Pennsylvania in 1777. Military physicians made the connection between crowding and the "flux." One doctor, Ebenezer Beardsley, noted that dysentery broke out in one group of soldiers who had been housed in the basement of one house in New York. Beardsley hypothesized that the dank air of the basement combined with the exhaled breath of so many soldiers to create a "miasma" that caused the disease. His hypothesis seemed to be proven when the soldiers recovered after being moved to better quarters with more space. Sanitation and crowding would be a continuing problem for Colonial era armies. It was not until sanitary and disciplinary reforms were put in place during the American Revolution discussed later in this chapter that these conditions began to change.[20]

Smallpox

While typhus and dysentery primarily attacked soldiers, smallpox was not so discriminating. Both the Seven Years War and the American Revolutionary War were accompanied by outbreaks of smallpox that spread to civilian populations as well. The outbreak that began in 1775 was particularly virulent. It lasted until 1783 and spread across the entire continent. Native Americans and Spanish and French settlers that had no involvement with the American Revolution sickened and died from an epidemic that was originally spread by marching armies thousands of miles away.

Smallpox in the Seven Years' War

Smallpox broke out soon after the commencement of hostilities in the Seven Years' War. While it is difficult to pinpoint the exact time and place the epidemic began, it seems likely that the first cases were among Native Americans in New France. As Native American populations migrated to safety in French missions, or as Native American diplomats met with French officers to negotiate alliances, a newly arrived, immune European passed the virus to a vulnerable Native American. By the fall of 1755 and through the winter of 1756, smallpox devastated Native Americans and nonimmune French and English populations. One group of Native American warriors allied with the French lost one third of their number to the disease.[21]

The epidemic affected the course of the war, especially for the French who were depending on Native American allies to supplement their numbers. Native Americans began withdrawing their support from the French war effort and moving to smallpox-free areas to wait out the epidemic. When news came that the epidemic was fading away, they renewed their support and sent warriors once again. As the war progressed, Native American participation waxed and waned with the spread of the virus. When smallpox was present, they withdrew; when it was absent, they joined their French allies once again. One historian has argued that it was smallpox, not likelihood of French victory, that was the key factor in Native American military and diplomatic decisions during the war.[22]

Anglo-Americans were also vulnerable to smallpox. Unlike Europe, the American colonies had no pool of immune adults. American soldiers serving with the British army fell ill and died at rates close to those of Native Americans. One American government official was appalled at the "havoc" wreaked by disease on American troops and noted: "In the beginning of the late war many perished by the sword, but much more by the diseases incidental to the campaign." Mortality rates among Anglo-American soldiers meant that military life "was routinely riskier than ... during the worst epidemics in New England's history."[23]

When soldiers returned home, they brought smallpox with them. Epidemics erupted in Boston, Philadelphia, Charleston, and other major cities between 1759 and 1762. From the cities, the disease spread into the countryside. Civilians were aware that war had brought the illness into their communities: "During the late war, the smallpox was brought into divers towns, in this and other colonies, by the return of our soldiers employed in his majesty's service." The American Revolution would follow the same pattern.[24]

The Smallpox Pandemic of 1775–1783

The American Revolutionary War and the great smallpox epidemic began at almost the same time. A few cases had been reported in Massachusetts in February of 1774, at the time when Parliament was passing the notorious Coercive Acts that would trigger hostilities in the colonies. By December of that year, the disease had spread to Boston. By the time the first shots of the war were fired in April of 1775, the epidemic was well established.

The Epidemic in Boston   Eighteenth-century Boston sat on a peninsula, accessible only by a narrow strip of land called "the neck." In 1775, the British Navy had blockaded the harbor; American troops, fearing an invasion, blockaded the neck against further incursions. The inhabitants of Boston found themselves trapped on a smallpox-infested island. One citizen noted that by July, there were "ten to thirty funerals a day." As was the case in the Seven Years' War, native-born Anglo-Americans were much more vulnerable to the disease than their British-born counterparts.[25]

Smallpox was not just a potential humanitarian disaster, it threatened America's military readiness as well. As thousands of young men mustered to fight, the potential for smallpox to devastate

America's army grew. George Washington saw the problem almost immediately. He first considered a mass inoculation campaign but dismissed it as impractical. He would later change his mind. He issued orders to prevent refugees from Boston from coming into contact with troops and arranged to quarantine any soldier who fell sick.[26]

The Invasion of Canada   Washington's strategy for smallpox containment worked temporarily. Smallpox would break out again, however, and with more virulence, during the campaign for Quebec. In the winter of 1775 and 1776, over a thousand Continental troops arrived at Quebec City in the hopes of capturing the "fourteenth colony" of Canada. After a disastrous attack on the city in December, the remaining troops sat down for a long siege. Unfortunately, the exhausted, starving, and frigid troops proved the perfect victims for the smallpox virus.

There had been sporadic cases of smallpox in Quebec before the siege; but it erupted with new ferocity after the battle on December 31. American soldiers taken prisoner were some of the first to succumb. One private described the terrible suffering among his fellow prisoners:

> Our flesh seemed a mass of corruption. At the same time we were covered with vermin. When we were a little recovered, we were moved back to our former prison without any cleansing or changing of our apparel. Our clothing was stiff with corrupted matter.[27]

Meanwhile, the soldiers outside the city walls were faring no better. Cases of smallpox increased with each month. By February, two hundred soldiers had fallen ill; by April, seven hundred, which was half of the remaining forces.[28]

As conditions deteriorated, soldiers who were physically able to do so began deserting and heading home. Those who remained stuck it out until May, when British reinforcements arrived to defend the city. The Americans fled in panic toward the American-held city of Montreal, leaving their sick behind. As the Americans marched through the Canadian wilderness, more and more troops fell by the wayside. As the American soldiers moved, so did the virus. The epidemic inexorably spread south and west. By July of 1776, John Adams was moved to write to his wife: "The small Pox! The small Pox! What shall we do with it?" It was clear to Adams and his colleagues in the provisional government that smallpox was weakening the military and devastating the civilian population.[29]

Smallpox and African American Soldiers

Some of the first African Americans to fight in the American Revolution did so on the side of the British. In November 1775, the loyalist governor of Virginia, Lord Dunmore, issued a proclamation offering freedom to any slave or indentured servant who was willing to fight with "His Majesty's Troops." Dunmore's intention was to undermine the economy of the south and weaken the rebellion, but many bound laborers saw the declaration as a unique opportunity for freedom. Somewhere between six and eight hundred African Americans jumped at the chance to escape slavery and joined Dunmore's "Ethiopian Regiment." The members of this regiment marched into battle with banners on their chests reading "Liberty to Slaves."[30]

Smallpox, however, would prove a terrible obstacle to their hopes. Dunmore stationed his new troops on ships in the Chesapeake Bay, from which he launched hit and run attacks on plantations and stores of military supplies. Smallpox soon broke out on the crowded ships, and Dunmore abandoned the ships and set up camp on a small island.

The African American troops were particularly affected by the disease, perhaps because they were kept segregated from the white soldiers. By July of 1776, only three hundred members of the Ethiopian Regiment survived, and those were still weakened by their ordeal. Dunmore wrote: "Had it not been for this horrid disorder, I should have had two thousand blacks; with whom I should have had no doubt of penetrating into the heart of this colony."[31]

Dunmore abandoned the island on July 9, 1776, taking his sickly troops with him. Virginia militia arrived in the former camp in triumph, only to encounter a horrifying scene. Many dying soldiers had been left behind to fend for themselves, and heaps of bodies remained unburied. After the taking of the island, smallpox began to spread among Virginia militiamen as well. By April of 1777, the disease had spread inland to Leesburg and Mount Vernon, where Martha Washington did her best to care for the plantation slaves and servants.[32]

War had made a perfect environment for the spread of epidemic disease. Vulnerable people gathered together in large numbers. When troops marched or refugees fled, the virus went with them. As one historian put it, "People were traveling about as never before, meeting, dispersing, and regrouping, silently exchanging pathogens at every turn."[33]

Meanwhile, smallpox had also appeared in Mexico City in 1779 and spread from there throughout Spanish-held territories. Traveling missionaries carried it to their Native American flocks. French fur traders brought smallpox with them from infected trading posts in the east. Loyalist British traders fled the fighting in Quebec and Hudson Bay, but they did not escape disease. As these traders met with Native American populations who had not previously been exposed to small-pox, the epidemic spread. By the early nineteenth century, European adventurers on the Pacific coast reported that when they encountered indigenous peoples there, many were marked or blinded by the pox. The disruptions of war on the Atlantic seaboard had made the small-pox epidemic a truly continental phenomenon.

GERM WARFARE?

There have long been suggestions that some military officials deliber-ately spread disease as a weapon of war. While this contention remains controversial among historians, there is enough documentation to make it a strong possibility. Smallpox was often the alleged "biological weapon" of choice during the Colonial period.

Native Americans had long suspected Europeans of deliberately infecting them with smallpox. This oral tradition from the Ottawa peo-ple tells one such story dating from the time of the Seven Years War. The British gave the Ottawa a gift in a tin box, with strict instructions not to open it until they reached their home territory:

> After they reached home, they opened the box; but behold, there was another tin box inside, smaller ... They kept on this way until they came to a very small box, which was not more than an inch long; and when they opened the last one they found nothing but mouldy particles in this last little box ... Pretty soon burst out a terrible sickness among them.[34]

The box had contained smallpox scabs, which incited an epidemic among the Ottawa. There is no doubt in the teller's mind that the dis-ease had been "sent by the British people, who actuated through hatred, and expressly to kill off the Ottawas and Chippewas because they were friends of the French Government."[35]

It is possible that Native Americans also used disease in warfare. During Queen Anne's War 1702 to 1713, a French observer reported that Iroquois sabotaged a British camp by contaminating its water supply with raw animal skins and other filth. An epidemic soon ravaged the camp. The French reporter estimated casualties at over a thousand.[36]

Perhaps the most notorious and best substantiated instance of the use of disease as a weapon took place in 1763, when General Jeffrey Amherst approved a plan to send infected blankets to the tribes of

Native Americans attacking British soldiers at Fort Pitt. When delegates from the allied tribes came to negotiate a surrender of the fort, British officers sent them home with gifts—food, liquor, and the infamous blankets. One commander wrote to Amherst of this act, "I hope it will have the desired effect." Soon after, smallpox broke out among the Native Americans. While it is true that smallpox was already spreading in the area, the timing of the outbreak and the letters exchanged between Amherst and his subordinates strongly suggest that the epidemic was planned.[37]

Native Americans were not the only targets of this kind of attack. In 1757, British officials accused the French of deliberately returning smallpox-infected prisoners to them in 1757 to spread the infection among the British. Similarly, American soldiers wondered if General Dunmore had purposely abandoned sick African American soldiers so that smallpox would spread to the Virginia troops who found them: "Was it done to communicate it to the People here on shore?" speculated one American official. Such speculation was not limited to Virginia. Similar accusations cropped up during the Revolutionary era smallpox outbreaks in Boston and Quebec.[38]

There is not sufficient evidence to prove these accusations definitively. In all cases, the accusers were at war with the accused, and had strong motives to paint the other side as villainous. During most of these wars, smallpox had already been spreading, and new eruptions of the disease might have occurred without human intervention. The number of accusations, however, backed up with evidence of increasing outbreaks, is highly suggestive that, at least in some instances, armies tried to undermine the health and morale of their enemies by deliberately spreading disease.

MILITARY HYGIENE, PHYSICIANS, AND HOSPITALS

The Seven Years' War and the American Revolutionary War saw the first attempts at organizing formal military procedures for camp sanitation and the care of the sick and wounded. Most were based on European models. Before the eighteenth century, most Colonial era wars were fought close to the soldiers' home ground by small, locally organized militias. The issue of establishing sanitary practices in military camps and organizing centralized hospitals did not arise. When large-scale wars broke out in North America, however, a need arose for standardized procedures under a central authority.

Camp Health and Hygiene

The Seven Years' War

Military manuals of the eighteenth century included diagrams of the ideal military camp. Enlisted men set up their tents in neat rows, organized by platoon. Company officers lived in their own enclave a small distance away, and the colonel or other commander presided over it all in glorious solitude. Kitchens were kept at a distance to minimize the annoyance from smoke and garbage heaps. Latrines were at least 50 yards from the camp boundary. British soldiers brought to America to fight against the French did their best to follow this plan.

Camps of American provincial soldiers lacked even a semblance of this ideal order. Cooking fires, garbage dumps, and latrines were scattered among the living quarters. As a result, the camps were filthy even by the standards of the time. One appalled British officer wrote of an American encampment: "The camp nastier than anything I could conceive. Their necessary houses, kitchens, graves, and places for slaughtering cattle, all mixed through the encampment." American and British alike commented on the almost unbearable odors of military camps.[39]

Commanders made efforts throughout the war to impose sanitation measures, with mixed success. American officers issued standing orders that all soldiers should wash their shirts once a week and their hands and faces daily. It seems, however, that these orders were often ignored. One soldier recalled washing his clothes only twice during his year of service.[40]

The most difficult task was getting the soldiers to use latrines. Officers forbade troops from relieving themselves anywhere but in the "necessary houses." However, like the rules about washing, these orders were routinely disregarded. One military chaplain described the grounds around his camp this way: "The land here is not tilled, but it is excellently manured."[41]

The American Revolution

When George Washington arrived in Cambridge, Massachusetts, to take command of the Continental Army in 1775, he was warned that his soldiers had no concept of camp hygiene or sanitation: "The Youth in the Army are not possess'd of the absolute Necessity of Cleanliness in their Dress, and Lodging ... and strict Temperance to preserve them from Diseases frequently prevailing in Camps," said Massachusetts officials. It was clear that if the men were left to their own devices, camp conditions similar to those of the Seven Years War would prevail.[42]

Washington took immediate action. Personal cleanliness and the use of latrines were the first priorities. Washington had several concerns. The first was disease. Smallpox was already spreading in Boston, and Washington's experience during the Seven Years War meant that he had seen the disastrous results of unsanitary camps. Perhaps more important, Washington wanted to instill military "virtue" in his soldiers. A virtuous soldier was brave, honorable, patriotic—and clean.[43]

Washington ordered that each company designate a "color man" to supervise cleanliness in the camp. The color man and his underlings were to dig and maintain latrines and collect and dispose of garbage. Soldiers were to use only designated latrines and garbage dumps. However, as in the earlier war, these rules were difficult to enforce. As late as 1781, Washington had to threaten to arrest officers who allowed "Offal and other offensive matter" to linger by the camps. Other commanders had to back up the sanitary rules with increasingly harsh penalties. One New Jersey officer became so frustrated that his men were "easing themselves about the Baracks yard or fence" that he made it a court martial offense.[44]

Personal cleanliness was also at issue. Washington's initial orders included instructions that soldiers wash their hands and faces, shave, and comb their hair every day. In addition, troops were encouraged to keep their clothes clean: "Nothing adds to the appearance of a man than Dress and proper Degree of Cleanliness," said one Massachusetts commander.[45] Keeping clothes clean was particularly difficult. Many troops had only one set of clothes, which they wore until they fell to pieces. Spare uniforms were hard to come by, and commanders had to beg quartermasters for adequate clothing for their men. In addition, opportunities to do laundry were rare. The army did use some of its funds to pay women to wash soldiers' clothes.[46]

Despite these obstacles, the sanitary measures did their work. While many camps suffered from poor sanitation during the years of fighting, by the end of the war, conditions had improved. Washington commented during his last encampment that "there was never any filth or trash to be seen on the parade nor any thing offensive to the sight or smell." While it had taken years, Washington had finally established sanitary discipline in the military.[47]

Washington's Inoculation Campaign

Another of Washington's innovations was to begin a systematic campaign of smallpox inoculation for soldiers. On February 5, 1777, he issued an order requiring that all new recruits be inoculated. Such a campaign was a military necessity. Washington could see that small-pox had already weakened his army; without an inoculation campaign, the Americans would not have an army at all. Even though a freshly inoculated soldier would be both contagious and out of commission for a time while he recovered from the procedure, Washington saw no other way to keep his troops healthy. "Inoculate your men as fast as they are enlisted," he wrote.[48]

Inoculation hospitals were set up in Virginia, Maryland, New Jersey, Pennsylvania, New York, and Connecticut. As fresh recruits arrived, regimental surgeons questioned them closely about their history with smallpox and examined their bodies for telltale pockmarks. Any soldier who had not already had the disease was sent for inoculation.

The program was an overall success. Thousands of recruits were ino-culated, with an acceptably low rate of complications and deaths. The policy continued with some revisions in procedure throughout the war. The epidemic slowed among soldiers, but kept its foothold among Anglo-American civilians, African-Americans, and Native Americans.

Physicians and Hospitals

Another of Washington's military reforms was to establish a central-ized medical department for the army. Previous military health care had been provided by civilian regimental surgeons in a haphazard way; the new department centralized hospital administration and standardized the staffing of hospitals. While the medical department was plagued by corruption and scandal, its establishment laid the groundwork for the emergence of a modern military medical service.

Personnel and Equipment

During seventeenth- and early eighteenth-century wars, surgeons attached to local militia units were local practitioners who may or may not have had military experience. During the Seven Years' War, some of these surgeons had the opportunity to train with the more pro-fessionalized British surgeons and to see the workings of the medical department of a professional standing army. Several of these veterans, such as John Morgan of Pennsylvania, were able to use that experience to help create the medical department of the Continental Army.

The first official hospital was established in 1775 to serve an army that then numbered 20,000 men. The law established staffing levels for the hospital: one director, four surgeons, one apothecary,

20 surgeons' mates, and "1 nurse to every 10 sick." Regimental surgeons and surgeons' mates were appointed by regimental commanders, although their ultimate responsibility was to the civilian director general of the hospital. As the army expanded, this staffing level remained stable, although the subsequent orders provided for more layers of centralized administration.[49]

Physicians and surgeons were to be issued tools and medicine chests. The regimental surgeon took charge of the supplies and their distribution. The standard list of drugs included cinchona bark and opium, as well as calomel (a mercury compound), rhubarb and jalap purgatives, tartar emetic, olive oil and beeswax for treating burns and making salves, and an unidentified substance called "blistering ointment." Surgical tools included three sets of amputation and trephination tools, scalpels, lancets, splints, and bolts of muslin for making bandages. The regimental surgeon was responsible for ordering and buying supplies, and reporting on their use and distribution to the director of the medical service.[50]

Army hospitals represented an opportunity for women to work in the war effort. Nurses and matrons were hired from the local female population or from the "camp followers" that accompanied the troops. Nurses were not the medical professionals they would later become. They rarely, if ever, performed direct patient care such as changing bandages. Instead, their duties focused on housekeeping and hygiene: sweeping floors, emptying chamber pots, and doing laundry. Matrons supervised the nursing staff, much as they did in civilian hospitals. In addition to the local women, soldiers were sometimes designated to do hospital duty.[51]

Organizing the Hospitals

Washington saw the need for a centralized hospital system early in the war. It took some years, however, before a workable model for administering the system came into being. From the beginning, the chain of command was never clear. Regimental surgeons were military personnel, loyal to their military commanders, while the directors of the hospitals and many of the other employees such as nurses were civilians. In addition, the original enabling legislation did not spell out a specific way of funding the hospitals or providing oversight.

As a result, the early years of the medical department were chaotic at best. Hospitals struggled for supplies and funding, and conflicts between military and civilian personnel meant that problems were difficult to resolve. In addition, the hospital department had trouble finding a reliable director. Scandals broke out with each administration. The first director, Benjamin Church, was caught passing sensitive information to the British. The next, John Morgan, quarreled incessantly with his subordinates until Congress dismissed him from his post. The third, William Shippen, was arrested and tried for embezzling funds and appropriating supplies for his own use. Although he was acquitted, he was forced to resign in disgrace. Meanwhile, the hospitals and the sick and wounded they cared for muddled through as best they could, dealing with supply shortages and delayed wages on their own.[52]

By the end of the war, however, the situation had improved. The final director of the hospital department, John Cochran, managed to negotiate the many obstacles in his way without scandal. He presided over 50 military hospitals in three districts, each with its own director and staff. The entrance of the French on the American side had brought a new source of supplies and funds. Even though infectious disease and less than ideal conditions continued to take their toll, Washington was able to write in 1782 that the military hospitals were providing "humane treatment and comfortable accommodations."[53] The foundation for a modern, large-scale military medical service was in place.

Wars encompassed a number of health issues. Whether wound care, epidemic disease, or the organization of health care, war had a profound effect on human health.

NOTES

1. Quotation from David Hawke, *The Colonial Experience*. New York: Macmillan, 1966, p. 252; Statistics from Caroline Frank, "War." In John Demos (Ed.), *American Centuries: The Ideas, Issues, and Values that Shaped U.S. History: Vol. 2, The Seventeenth Century*. New York: Facts on File, 2011.

2. Virgil J. Vogel, *American Indian Medicine*. Norman: University of Oklahoma Press, 1970, p. 228.

3. Ibid., p. 228.

4. Ibid., pp. 225, 231.

5. Philip Cash, *Medical Men at the Siege of Boston: April 1775–April 1776*. Philadelphia: The American Philosophical Society, 1973, pp. 20–21.

6. Mary C. Gillett, *The Army Medical Department: 1775–1818*. Washington, DC: Center of Military History, United States Army, 1981, p. 18.

7. Oscar Reiss, *Medicine and the American Revolution: How Diseases and Their Treatments Affected the Colonial Army*. Jefferson, NC: McFarland and Company, 1998, pp. 34–35.

8. Gillett, *The Army Medical Department*, p. 16; Reiss, *Medicine and the American Revolution*, p. 31.

9. Reiss, *Medicine and the American Revolution*, p. 32.

10. Gillett, *The Army Medical Department*, p. 17.

11. Ibid., p. 3.

12. Fred Anderson, *A People's Army: Massachusetts Soldiers and Society in the Seven Years War* Chapel Hill: University of North Carolina Press, 1984, p. 106.

13. Gillett, *The Army Medical Department*, p. 6; Reiss, *Medicine and the American Revolution*, p. 199.

14. Reiss, *Medicine and the American Revolution*, pp. 199–200.

15. John Duffy, *Epidemics in Colonial America*. Baton Rouge: Louisiana State University Press, 1953, p. 231.

16. Anderson, *A People's Army*, p. 106.

17. Reiss, *Medicine and the American Revolution*, pp. 187–188.

18. Ibid., p. 188.

19. Anderson, *A People's Army*, pp. 98, 101.

20. Reiss, *Medicine and the American Revolution*, pp. 178–179.

21. D. Peter MacLeod, "Microbes and Muskets: Smallpox and the Participation of Amerindian Allies of New France in the Seven Years War," *Ethnohistory*, 39 (1992), pp. 46–47.

22. MacLeod, "Microbes and Muskets," p. 54.

23. Anderson, *A People's Army*, pp. 99, 101.

24. Duffy, *Epidemics*, p. 63.

25. Elizabeth A. Fenn, *Pox Americana: The Great Smallpox Epidemic of 1775–82*. New York: Hill and Wang, 2001, p. 47.

26. Fenn, *Pox Americana*, pp. 48–50.

27. Reiss, *Medicine and the American Revolution*, p. 94.

28. Ibid., pp. 93–95.

29. Fenn, *Pox Americana*, p. 79.

30. Ibid., pp. 55–57.

31. Ibid., pp. 58–59.

32. Ibid., pp. 60–62.

33. Ibid., p. 62.

34. "Andrew Blackbird of the Ottawa Nation Records a Story from Indian Oral Tradition about the Decimation of his People by Smallpox in the Early 1760's." In John Harley Warner and Janet A. Tighe (Eds.), *Major Problems in the History of American Medicine and Public Health*. New York: Houghton Miffilin, 2001, p. 40.

35. Ibid.

36. Elizabeth A. Fenn, "Biological Warfare in Eighteenth Century North America: Beyond Jeffery Amherst," *Journal of American History*, 86 (2000), p. 1565.

37. Ibid., p. 1554.

38. Ibid., pp. 1567–1571.

39. Anderson, *A People's Army*, p. 95.

40. Ibid., pp. 96–97.

41. Ibid., p. 98.

42. Holly A. Mayer, *Belonging to the Army: Camp Followers and Community During the American Revolution*. Columbia: University of South Carolina Press, 1996, p. 63.

43. Kathleen M. Brown, *Foul Bodies: Cleanliness in Early America*. New Haven, CT: Yale University Press, 2009, p. 161.

44. Mayer, *Belonging to the Army*, p. 64.

45. Brown, *Foul Bodies*, p. 165.

46. Mayer, *Belonging to the Army*, p. 141.

47. Ibid., p. 68.

48. Fenn, *Pox Americana*, p. 94.

49. Gillett, *The Army Medical Department*, p. 200.

50. Ibid., pp. 6–7.

51. Mayer, *Belonging to the Army*, pp. 219–223.

52. Gillett, *The Army Medical Department*, pp. 22–49.

53. Ibid., p. 128.

CHAPTER 12

Institutional Facilities

Most health care in early America took place in the patient's home. Hospitals and other institutions played only a minor role in medicine until the late nineteenth century. The institutions that did exist were designed for the urban poor. During the earliest years of settlement, almshouses functioned as shelters for the elderly, chronically ill, and disabled as well as orphaned children and the homeless. By the end of the eighteenth century, New York and Philadelphia had established hospitals in the modern sense—institutions designed specifically to care for the sick and injured. However, even these hospitals were meant exclusively for the impoverished.

The establishment of hospitals represented a first step in the creation of modern medicine. In addition to providing care for the "sick poor," they also served as educational institutions. Medical students worked in hospitals to gain important clinical experience, establishing an educational tradition that continues to the present day. This function of the hospital set the stage for the exploitation of the poor as "clinical material" for medical students and researchers.

ALMSHOUSES

Almshouses were the first institutions to provide medical care for the poor. Most were located in port cities. Elected officials called "overseers of the poor" administered almshouses along with other forms of "poor relief." These institutions sheltered people with nowhere else to go, including many who needed medical care.

The almshouse system originated with the English Poor Law of 1601. This law, one of the first and most comprehensive laws for relief of the poor, set up a system of aid administered in England by the local parishes. In America, the town or city replaced the parish as the main administrative unit. Residents paid a special tax to support their impoverished neighbors. Almshouses provided shelter for the poor inhabitants of each parish. Only those who could prove residency were allowed in each local almshouse; others were sent back to their home parish or town. Overseers distributed the tax money and administered the almshouse.

Almshouse Residents

Poor people usually tried every alternative they could think of before entering an almshouse. Some turned to neighbors and family for help; some indentured their children to other families so that the children would have food and shelter; some turned to crime. If none of these strategies worked, the needy could apply to the overseers for "outrelief"— that is, they could ask the authorities to provide them with food, fuel, clothing, or cash but continue to live in their own houses. This system was by far the most common form of public aid during the Colonial period. Many chronically ill people who were unable to support themselves survived with outrelief provided by local authorities. Those too sick, elderly, or disabled to care for themselves were sometimes placed in the homes of other families, with money for their care going directly to the head of their new household. In other cases, the authorities placed a paid nurse or companion in the home of the patient.

Entering the almshouse was the last resort for the most desperate. Residents of the almshouse were required to work as much as their physical condition allowed in order to "earn their keep." Administrators grilled prospective clients on every aspect of their lives, separated families, and imposed harsh discipline on the inmates.

Many of these conditions reflect the suspicion and contempt almshouse officials had for their clients. The almshouse system was established in England in part to contain the "wandering poor" and "sturdy beggars" who disrupted town life. Many of the well to do believed that the poor had brought their condition on themselves through drink, laziness, or sexual excess. As a result, the almshouse had an atmosphere of

punishment as well as support. In some cases, this punishment was literal. In the Philadelphia Almshouse, unruly residents could be placed
in a special "punishment cell," placed on a bread and water diet, or
doused repeatedly with cold water.[1] It should come as no surprise that
"many individuals forewent assistance for long periods rather than
endure the prisonlike atmosphere of the almshouse."[2]

Those who did apply for help were often in desperate straits. The
overseers of the Philadelphia Almshouse reported to the *Pennsylvania
Gazette* that many of those seeking aid were "naked, helpless and ema-
ciated with Poverty and Disease to such a Degree, that some have died
in a few Days after their Admission." Another note in the records
described a man who was so weak from starvation that he had to be
carried to the almshouse in a cart.[3]

Medical Care in the Almshouse

Illness and injury were legitimate reasons for being unable to work, and
thus many almshouse clients were classified as sick or disabled. The
records of the Philadelphia Almshouse reveal that in 1800, 5.7 percent
of those admitted were "old," 43.1 percent were "sick," 10.2 percent
had a venereal disease, 4.8 percent had a mental illness, and 13.7 percent
of the women were pregnant. There is some evidence that at least a few
of these inmates were malingering. Almshouse administrators noted that
complaints such as "sore legs" became epidemic in the late fall and had
miraculous cure rates as soon as the weather warmed up in the spring.[4]

For those who had real illnesses, however, the care at the almshouse
was minimal. The sick were housed in large medical wards. Patients
were required to share their beds. Bed linens were seldom, if ever, laun-
dered. One minister who visited the medical wards in the New York
almshouse described "bodies stowed in beds as thick as they could
lie." The smell of sickness and unwashed bodies was so strong that
the minister felt moved to "vomition," despite the attempts of the staff
to dispel the odor by scrubbing the floors with vinegar. In one ward,
the body of a deceased patient remained in its bed for an entire day
before being removed. The food provided to inmates was minimal
and unappetizing. In the Charlestown, South Carolina, almshouse, the
diet was so inadequate that there were periodic outbreaks of scurvy
among the residents. While physicians visited almshouses to tend the
sick, their visits were infrequent and sporadic. Most of the medical care
and nursing was in the hands of the residents themselves.[5]

Pregnant Women

Childbirth was one of the most common medical events on the alms-house wards. Women who were pregnant out of wedlock often came to the almshouse to give birth. Like most almshouse residents, these women were at the end of their resources. The fathers of illegitimate babies were legally obligated to support their children, meaning that most pregnant women had some means of support. If the father was destitute or had fled the town, however, a poor woman might have no choice but to accept almshouse relief.

Typically, a woman entered an almshouse late in her pregnancy. For instance, Priscilla McPherson entered the Philadelphia almshouse only two weeks before she gave birth to her daughter. After the baby was born, McPherson stayed in the almshouse for two months while she recovered from childbirth; when she obtained a post as a "nurse" (probably as a wet nurse), she and her child were discharged. Another woman, Mary Perkins, arrived a month before she went into labor; her baby survived only one day. Just 11 days after giving birth, she too was discharged, having found work as a wet nurse.[6]

Pregnant African American women were in a special bind when they entered an almshouse even if they were not enslaved. In Philadelphia, for instance, slavery was abolished shortly after the Revolution. A pro-vision of the abolition law, however, stated that African American chil-dren could be indentured until the age of 28. As a result, many free blacks avoided giving birth in the almshouse for fear their children would be taken from them and effectively re-enslaved. One recently emancipated woman, Sylvia Clow, entered the Philadelphia almshouse a few months short of her due date. Her mother convinced the alms-house officials to release Clow, telling them that she would provide shelter for her daughter. It is likely that Clow and her mother made this arrangement to ensure that Clow could retain custody of her child.[7]

Pregnant women in the almshouse were attended by midwives. Many almshouse midwives were also inmates, and some almshouses actually paid skilled residents for their medical services. Mary Franklin was granted a salary at the New Castle County, Pennsylvania, almshouse for her care of the sick and the pregnant. Other almshouses hired local women to deliver babies as part of their outrelief program: poor women with medical skills were paid to work in the almshouse as an alternative to entering as a resident.[8] This system meant that the skill level of alms-house midwives was unreliable. While some of the women were no doubt fine practitioners, others had little experience or skill. The mortal-ity rate for infants born in almshouses reflects this erratic level of care as well as the poor health of their mothers. One in six babies born in the Philadelphia Almshouse died.[9]

Disease and Its Treatment at the Almshouse

Sexually transmitted disease was one of the few that merited its own category in the almshouse records. Having such a disease was undeniable evidence of immorality, and the patients were treated accordingly. The Charleston almshouse assumed that all women with sexually transmitted diseases were prostitutes and contrary to the mission of the almshouse charged them fees for treatment. If the women were unable to pay, the overseers attempted to track down their "employers" and dun them for payment. In New York, many of the physicians attached to the almshouse refused to treat those with venereal disease. Philadelphia almshouse workers described women with sexually transmitted diseases as "worthless" and "dirty." Almshouses remained the only institutions that would take in those with syphilis or gonorrhea. The first American hospitals refused to take patients with sexually transmitted diseases, and even institutions designed to shelter and "reform" sex workers, the Magdelen Homes, refused admission to anyone with symptoms.[10]

As for those whom the almshouse records categorized merely as "sick," they probably represented a wide range of the many diseases that afflicted the urban poor in early America. Urban mortality records list causes of death that include yellow fever, smallpox, cholera and other infectious disease, as well as accidents and childbirth. In addition to these specific conditions, many poor people died of what was described as "decay" or "mortification." These terms seem to have described a general deterioration of health. Possible modern diagnoses of "decay" might include tuberculosis, vitamin deficiencies, or starvation. Few of the poor lived long enough to have a cause of death listed as "old age"—this category describes less than one percent of the deaths of the poor.[11]

Almshouses and the Elderly

For those who lived long enough, almshouses served as homes for the aged. As was the case for most residents, the almshouse was a last resort. Most of the frail elderly lived with family members or accepted outrelief. In fact, many almshouse overseers rejected elderly applicants if age was their only "qualification." For instance, one elderly woman whose only means of support was begging at the city market was rejected by the almshouse overseers. As her situation deteriorated, she began "cursing and abusing those who refuse her charity." This new approach still did not earn her a place—instead, she ended up in the city jail. The overseers did admit some elderly residents, however. One 85-year-old man had supported himself for seven years by scavenging and reselling rags. When he became "feeble and unable to contribute to his support by that or any other way of employment" he entered the almshouse.[12]

Some of the elderly who spent their last years in the almshouse had fallen from a higher status. The same minister who was so appalled by the conditions at the New York Almshouse was equally shocked to find an elderly fellow minister living in the squalor of the medical ward. Patients such as this one had to bear the shame of having nowhere else to turn, despite their previous life as respectable citizens. Ending up in the almshouse "meant their abandonment by family, by employers, even by congregations if they were churchgoers."[13]

Almshouses and the Disabled

People too disabled to work entered the almshouse when no family member could care for them. This was particularly true of disabled men. In 1751, half of the men in the Philadelphia almshouse were permanently disabled. Most had a severe, permanent disability such as blindness or paralysis. For instance, a man named Robert Maxfield was accepted because he had "a disorder in his Legg by which he is rendered unable to gett a subsistence." Interestingly, women were more likely to be accepted if they simply claimed poverty, especially if their husbands had deserted them. Such differences reflect gendered beliefs about work. Women could become "deserving" of aid if they had no man to support them; men were expected to support themselves unless physically unable to do so.[14]

Mental illness and developmental disability were also reasons for a person to become a resident of the almshouse. Unlike persons with other disabilities, residents with mental or cognitive disorders came from all walks of life. Even the affluent sometimes abandoned family members with these disabilities and left them for the town to support. Other residents of the almshouse complained about having to live in proximity with "lunatics" and "idiots."

Almshouses and People of Color

With some exceptions such as Sybil Clow, discussed previously, most almshouse residents were white. Native Americans were unlikely to be official "residents" of the port cities where almshouses were located and were thus ineligible for aid. The exceptions were Native Americans who were servants or slaves of white families. If a Native American servant became disabled, his or her employer might apply to the overseers for aid on the servant's behalf. Most local authorities supplied the employer with outrelief to support the servant. Such was the case with a Rhode Island woman named Tent Anthony who "was taken with a numb palsey fit" a stroke while working in the household of Josiah Arnold. The stroke left her paralyzed on one side and unable to work. The overseers arranged to pay for Anthony's care. African slaves were another special case. The assumption was that slaveholders would be responsible for their care, and enslaved workers were rarely residents in the almshouse or recipients of outrelief. As populations of urban free blacks grew during the eighteenth century, however, more African Americans needed the services of the almshouse. As a result, overseers of the poor and later, the administrators of the early hospitals began establishing segregated wards.[15]

THE FIRST AMERICAN HOSPITALS

There were few institutions in early America that met the modern definition of "hospital." These were not centers of technical sophistication where the worst illnesses and injuries came to be cured. Procedures such as surgery and childbirth took place for the most part in the patient's home. Instead, hospitals were adjuncts to other institutions with larger charitable or religious missions. Some hospitals were part of religious missions to the Native Americans especially in New Spain; in Anglo-America, as we have seen, almshouses, the predecessors of hospitals, were primarily designed for the care of the poor rather than the specific care of the sick.

By the mid-eighteenth century, however, the first Anglo-American freestanding hospital was founded in Philadelphia. The Pennsylvania Hospital was conceived as an alternative to the almshouse wards for the truly "worthy" poor and had admission standards designed to exclude undesirable patients. In addition, the urban hospitals in British North America were conceived as educational institutions for young physicians—first as a place where apprentices might practice their skills, and later as adjuncts to newly founded medical schools.

Medical Missionaries and Hospitals in New Spain and New France

Spanish Franciscans and French Jesuits both incorporated medicine into their religious missions. Trained nuns, priests, and laypeople provided medical care to both Native Americans and fellow Europeans. In some cases, medical missionaries incorporated indigenous medicines into their practices; in others, European style medicine served as a tool of cultural and religious assimilation.

New Spain

The Spanish saw hospitals as part of their religious mission. In Spain, religious orders had founded hospitals along well-traveled roads to provide food, shelter, religious services, and medical care to religious pilgrims. The first Spanish hospitals in the Americas followed this tradition. The Spanish hospitals resembled the almshouses in England and British North America in that their primary purpose was to shelter the poor. The Spanish also conceived of hospitals as "a tool to convert Indians to Christianity."[16]

Spanish missionaries took quick note of the religious aspects of Native American medicine. At some missions, Spanish priests encouraged potential converts to come to the mission for medical care in order to demonstrate the healing power of the Christian god. In early New Mexico, for instance, priests seeking to Christianize the Pueblo Indians "impersonated medicine men." In one case, a missionary who had trained as a surgeon invited a wounded war chief to the mission to be cured. The missionary's surgery proved successful, and the chief accepted baptism. In another case, a group of Hopi medicine men challenged a missionary to cure a young boy of blindness. The priest did so according to his account by simply placing a cross on the boy's eyes. At other times, the Spanish use of medicine as a religious symbol was more coercive. In the New Mexico settlements, Spanish missionaries attempted to bind the Pueblos more closely to their mission by killing local medicine men and forbidding indigenous medical practices. Soon, the mission became the only source of medical care.[17]

As the Spanish established cities in their colonies, they also established institutions that focused specifically on medical care. Such hospitals were open to both Europeans and Native Americans, and were usually located next to the church. The first of these hospitals was founded in 1521 in Mexico City. Like other European-style hospitals, its mission was to care for the "sick poor." However, it excluded from care those suffering from highly contagious or stigmatized diseases like leprosy or syphilis. By 1555, Colonial administrators decided to establish special hospitals exclusively for the Native American population. The first of these was also established in Mexico City and was supported by increasing the tribute demanded from local tribes.[18]

Some Spanish American hospitals grew out of more altruistic motives. In 1531, a Colonial official named Vasco de Quiroga set out to ameliorate the abuses of Native Americans he saw around him, and set up a group of Native American settlements centered around a hospital, school, and church. The project was successful in its educational and religious goals, but the health care did not stop the steep decline in the Native American population.[19]

Whether the care provided was philanthropic or coercive, the Spanish were very successful in establishing a hospital system. By 1600, New Spain had 128 hospitals spread throughout its territory.

New France

Hospitals in New France were funded by the government and staffed by Roman Catholic nuns of several "nursing orders." French hospitals were of two types: one that specialized in the care of the seriously ill, and one more like an almshouse that sheltered the poor, disabled, and chronically ill. The earliest hospitals in New France the first founded in 1639 were of the first kind. Unlike Spanish hospitals, the French institutions cared primarily for French settlers and soldiers. Care at the hospitals had a good reputation. The nursing sisters were highly regarded both by their patients and their sponsors. As a result, the French hospitals escaped the stigma and fear which characterized institutional care elsewhere: "It is customary in this country for everybody to let themselves be taken [to the hospital] when sick—the powerful, the rich, and all the clergy."[20]

While Native Americans were not often patients in French hospitals, French missionaries made a point of providing medical care to their potential flocks. Nuns in Quebec wrote their sponsors in France to request a variety of medicines, including myrrh, chamomile, and opium. Similarly, French missionaries in Illinois wrote for "ointments, plasters, alum" as well as a "syringe." In addition, the French were open to incorporating indigenous remedies into their pharmacopeia. Father Louis Hennepin, who worked among the Illinois and Miami tribes, was deeply impressed with local cures for "agues" and snakebite.[21]

Hospitals in British North America

The first hospitals in British North America emerged out of the almshouse tradition. The first three Anglo-American hospitals—The Pennsylvania Hospital which opened in 1752, the New York Hospital, which was chartered in 1771 and opened in 1791, and the Massachusetts General

Hospital, which opened in 1821—all had a mission to serve the poor. For the middle class and wealthy, the hospital carried as much of a stigma as the almshouse. Entering any institution for medical care implied that the patient had no family, no community, and no resources. Institutional care would also force the affluent to mingle with the poor and "immoral." In addition, both the hospital and almshouse were feared: "Hospitals were regarded with fear, and rightly so. They were dangerous places; when sick, people were safer at home."[22] Even the poor avoided the hospital when any other alternative was available.

Anglo-American hospitals were based on an English model. Rather than being funded by local taxes like almshouses, private or "voluntary" hospitals were funded by private donors called "subscribers". In England, physicians volunteered their services to support these local charities. When the founders of the Pennsylvania hospital were considering their project, they looked closely at the structure of successful voluntary hospitals in England.[23]

The motives for founding American hospitals also followed English precedent. As one historian put it, "The founding of the Pennsylvania hospital as well as the founding of many provincial hospitals was a logical outgrowth [of a] lack of faith in the established methods of dealing with poverty." Poor rates seemed too high, and almshouses ineffective in transforming the poor into productive members of society. The hospital was a way of further dividing the poor into "deserving" and "undeserving," and ensuring that the deserving received better services: "the main impulse grew out of a desire to help ... those poor who showed a decent respect for the 'work ethic.' "[24]

Admissions Standards at Anglo-American Hospitals

Anglo-American hospitals were established as an alternative to the almshouse for the "respectable" poor. They would provide medical care in a purely medical setting, free of charge. In addition, hospitals originally set out to take only "curable" cases. The hospital was to be a place where patients came, were cured, and were discharged healthy. The terminally ill, those with contagious disease, and those with sexually transmitted diseases were specifically excluded. "Contagious" disease in this context included influenza, smallpox, typhus, and dysentery. Victims of these diseases were turned away as a danger to other patients and as probably incurable. Venereal disease was both communicable and a sign of immorality. Finally, chronic diseases with the exception of mental illness were also excluded as incurable.

As a result, most hospital admissions consisted of those injured in accidents, pregnant women who needed a safe place to deliver their babies, and the "semi-chronic" cases the doctors felt they could cure. Typical of this population was one middle-aged woman who had been admitted for "rheumatism." In addition, she complained of "weakness in the breast, great palpitation of the heart . . . want of appetite and costiveness." After a few weeks of rest, she was discharged "much improved."[25]

Perhaps more important, hospital patients had to prove that they "deserved" care. Patients were not admitted to the hospital unless they came with a reference from either a board member or "subscriber." Subscribers were allowed a certain number of recommendations per year, depending on how much money they donated. For instance, in New York, a subscriber who contributed $5 per year could recommend two patients; a $50 donor had unlimited privileges. In other cases, a donor would sponsor a particular bed; the donor then had the right to approve or reject the occupant of "his" bed.[26]

A patient had to prove moral worth. As one historian put it, "Membership in a particular church, long service to a particular family, an appropriate demeanor—all served to separate the worthy sheep from the . . . goats."[27] A typical recommendation for hospital admission looked much like this one:

> I have known Mrs. Milne since four or five years; and she is well known to Mrs. Jackson, my sister Mrs. Henry . . . and to many other ladies. I believe we can all testify that she is deserving, industrious, and respectable.[28]

When it came to admitting "respectable" patients, pregnant women presented a particular problem. If a woman was married and living with her husband, she was not likely to be so desperate as to need the hospital; however, single pregnant women were by definition "not respectable." Some hospitals would admit unmarried pregnant women only if they were pregnant for the first time. After that, they were on their own, or destined for the almshouse. The New York Hospital eventually closed its maternity ward for fear the presence of unmarried mothers would drive other patients away: "Worthy females would suffer want and even hazard life, before subjecting themselves to such association."[29]

African American patients presented another dilemma for the administrators. Even if they met the other criteria for admission, administrators feared that their mere presence would stigmatize the hospital. Segregated wards were the rule almost from the beginning. At the Pennsylvania Hospital, black patients were housed in a separate building. In addition, the owners of slaves treated at the hospital were charged a higher rate for their care than other paying patients. At the New York hospital, some doctors refused to even enter the ward for black patients.[30]

There was one exception to these stringent admission rules. If patients could pay, exceptions could be made to accommodate them. Thus, the Pennsylvania Hospital admitted contagious cases for a rate of $4 a week; those with sexually transmitted diseases or alcoholism for $5 a week. "Incurables," such as those suffering from cancer, would also be admitted as paying patients.[31]

The hospital did not replace the almshouse. Given the restrictions on hospital admissions, the almshouse was still a necessary institution. The patients rejected by the hospital usually found themselves on the medical wards of almshouses. In fact, as the hospital system evolved during the nineteenth century, many almshouses became public hospitals. Bellevue Hospital, for instance, emerged from the New York Almshouse. The stigma and squalor of the almshouse, however, remained with these hospitals for many years and contributed to the image of the hospital as "a house of death."[32]

The Hospital and Medical Education

In addition to supplementing the almshouse as a refuge for the sick and poor, the early hospitals also served as centers of clinical education for young physicians. Eighteenth-century American physicians trained in Europe wanted to establish a similar system of medical training at home; they also wanted to raise the status of the American medical profession. American medical students could receive a European-style education without the physical dangers of an ocean voyage or the moral danger of life in the metropolises of Edinburgh or London. Established physicians could use their public service at a hospital and their status as a medical professor to attract important paying patients.[33]

A hospital would provide a supply of patients who could not protest being treated by students or apprentices. Medical students would have a chance to develop their skills, and attending physicians would have a chance to pursue new techniques. As one of the founding trustees of the Massachusetts General Hospital put it, access to hospital patients would ensure that "those physicians to whom necessity compels us to entrust the lives of our wives and children, do not witness patients for the first time in our chambers nor apply their first remedies to those whose health is so precious to us."[34] The poor would receive free care, the medical profession would improve, and the health of the general public would benefit.

The Pennsylvania Hospital

The Pennsylvania Hospital in Philadelphia was the first hospital in British North America, and for 40 years it was the only institution of its kind in the United States. Its administrative structure served as a model for the American hospital system and is the best-documented example of the ways in which early American hospitals contributed to the development of American medical education. Finally, the story of the Pennsylvania Hospital illustrates the ways in which hospitals and other institutions were affected by the Revolutionary War.

The driving force behind the founding of the Pennsylvania Hospital was Dr. Thomas Bond. Bond had been educated in Europe and had trained at hospitals in London and Paris. Upon his return to Philadelphia, he was appointed port inspector for contagious diseases, a post that exposed him to the needs of Philadelphia's poor and which sparked his interest in public health.

Bond was a good friend of Benjamin Franklin. Franklin and Bond served together on a number of civic and scientific organizations, including the Library Company of Philadelphia and the American Philosophical Society. In 1750, Bond proposed establishing a hospital in Philadelphia "for the reception and cure of poor sick persons."[35] However, his efforts were unsuccessful until he convinced Franklin to support the project and join the fundraising appeal. Franklin wrote a proposal for a hospital that Bond presented to the Pennsylvania Assembly. In 1751, the Assembly granted a charter and 2,000 pounds for the hospital contingent upon Bond raising a matching amount in private funds. The hospital accepted its first patient in February of 1752, with Franklin as secretary of the board of managers and Bond as head of the medical staff. In addition to Bond, two other physicians joined the staff: Thomas Bond's brother, Phineas Bond, and Lloyd Zachary. As was the practice in English hospitals, the three physicians served without pay.

Administrative Structure

The hospital included several other permanent staff in addition to the physicians. Unlike the physicians, these employees were paid a salary.

The board of managers followed English precedent in staffing the hospital with a matron, a steward, and an apothecary. One of the first hired was the hospital matron. The post of matron was one of particular responsibility. The matron was in charge of buying supplies and keeping the hospital's accounts. Matrons hired and supervised other female staff members such as maids and nurses. The first matron was a pious widow who took the job in order to support her two children; after she remarried and resigned, matrons were often hired as part of a husband-wife team of steward and matron.[36]

Stewards enforced the rules of the hospital and had special responsibilities for the care of mentally ill patients. The job description of the first steward at the Pennsylvania Hospital was to "take care of the lunaticks, to use his endeavors to oblidge the patients to observe the rules of the House . . . to keep the garden lotts in order and diverse other services now mentioned to him."[37] The steward also supervised the "Cell Keepers" whose job was specifically to control any mentally ill patient who became violent.

The best-paid and most prestigious post was that of apothecary. The apothecary bought, prepared, and sometimes administered medicines at the direction of the medical staff. Some of the early apothecaries had medical training as well. The apothecary often worked directly with medical students and apprentices as part of the hospital's educational mission. Unlike the staff physicians, the apothecary lived at the hospital. As a result, the apothecary often took on an informal responsibility as a resident physician as well as a pharmacist.[38]

The Pennsylvania Hospital and Medical Education

The Pennsylvania Hospital participated in medical education from the time of its founding. In the early years, students apprenticed to staff physicians had the privilege of attending hospital patients. Soon other apprentices asked for similar access. Demand grew to the point where the hospital administrators decided to charge a fee to all apprentices not working directly with staff physicians. Until 1762, however, allowing apprentices to work on the wards was the extent of formal education at the hospital. In that year, a donor gave the hospital a set of anatomical drawings on the condition that they be used to illustrate a set of anatomical lectures by William Shippen. These lectures eventually were incorporated into the curriculum at the Medical College of Philadelphia.

Lectures and clinical practice were not the only educational facilities incorporated into the hospital. In 1752, the hospital opened an anatomical museum, and in 1762, a medical library. The museum began with a donation of a human skeleton; the skeleton was soon joined by another, as well as a set of preserved specimens of muscles and arteries. Students were charged a small fee to study the museum materials.

The library also had modest beginnings. It began with the donation of a single book on pharmacology. The donation inspired the board of managers to begin collecting books for a library, funded by the fees paid by medical students and apprentices. By the time of the Revolution, the library filled an entire room in the hospital, and was so heavily used that the managers had to restrict library privileges to hospital physicians and medical students.[39]

The Pennsylvania Hospital and the Revolution

The Revolutionary War created a financial and administrative crisis for the Pennsylvania Hospital. The facility was commandeered by the military—first by the Continental Army, then by the British, and then by the Continentals once again. Income from both paying patients and donors all but disappeared.

The hospital board did its best to keep the hospital open. When food became scarce, they increased the size of the hospital gardens and purchased two cows to provide milk. They rented out some facilities to military physicians. They laid off some staff, and even considered firing the steward and matron to cut costs. Finally, the board begged the Pennsylvania Assembly for a grant; the Assembly authorized the money, but as a loan.

In the meantime, the war had divided the board. Some loyalist members were arrested and exiled from the city. Even after they returned, bad feeling remained, and the board had trouble agreeing on policy or making decisions. Several devout, pacifist Quaker members objected to any military use of the hospital and its facilities, thus alienating some donors and members of the Assembly.[40]

Financial and administrative problems meant that conditions in the hospital deteriorated. The building itself was badly in need of repair. Broken windows meant that the wards were frigid. The basement, which housed the mentally ill, had no source of heat, and there was not enough money to provide blankets. There were chronic shortages of drugs as well as food.

As a result, the number of patients dropped. By the end of the war, the population of civilian patients was cut in half. More disturbingly to the hospital's managers, the severe financial crisis engendered by the war meant that the hospital could no longer take more than a handful of nonpaying patients. The original mission of caring for the "sick poor" seemed in danger. The only patient population that did not decline was the mentally ill. Many of these patients came from affluent families who continued to pay for their care.

The end of the war came just in time. The board was reconstituted, and the members put aside their previous differences. While donations did not rebound to prewar levels, the hospital was able to raise enough money to return to its previous charitable mission. By 1801, there was even enough money to construct a new building with a fashionable central dome and marble pillars. As the new century opened, the hospital was once again "a monument to the social concerns of … Philadelphia."[41] The two new hospitals that opened in New York and Boston took the Pennsylvania Hospital as an inspiration and a model they emulated in their early years.

Hospitals in early America were "premodern" institutions. They grew not from a desire to create a center of innovative medical care but as charitable institutions for the poor. It would take efforts by physicians and advances in medical science to create the modern hospital as a center of medical excellence, an effort it would take most of the next century to achieve.

NOTES

1. Charles E. Rosenberg, *The Care of Strangers: The Rise of America's Hospital System*. New York: Basic Books, 1987, pp. 17, 36.

2. Billy G. Smith, *The "Lower Sort": Philadelphia's Laboring People: 1750–1800*. Ithaca, NY: Cornell University Press, 1990, p. 167.

3. Ibid., pp. 169–170.

4. Ibid., p. 168.

5. Rosenberg, *The Care of Strangers*, pp. 16, 32.

6. Clare A. Lyons, *Sex Among the Rabble: An Intimate History of Gender and Power in the Age of Revolution: Philadelphia 1730–1830*. Chapel Hill: University of North Carolina Press, 2006, p. 263.

7. Lyons, *Sex Among the Rabble*, p. 265.

8. Monique Borque, "Poor Relief 'Without Violating the Rights of Humanity': Almshouse Administration in the Philadelphia Region: 1790–1860." In Billy G. Smith (Ed.), *Down and Out in Early America*. University Park: Pennsylvania State University Press, 2004, p. 205.

9. Lyons, *Sex Among the Rabble*, p. 263.

10. Rosenberg, *The Care of Strangers*, p. 40; Lyons, *Sex Among the Rabble*, pp. 260–262.

11. Simon Newman, "Dead Bodies: Poverty and Death in Early National Philadelphia." In Smith (Ed.), *Down and Out in Early America*, p. 55.

12. Smith, *The "Lower Sort,"* p. 170.

13. Rosenberg, *The Care of Strangers*, p. 16.

14. Karin Wulf, "Gender and the Political Economy of Poor Relief in Colonial Philadelphia." In Smith (Ed.), *Down and Out in Early America*, pp. 170–171.

15. Ruth Wallis Herndon, "Who Died an Expense to This Town: Poor Relief in Eighteenth Century Rhode Island." In Smith (Ed.), *Down and Out in Early America*, pp. 141–142.

16. Guenter B. Risse, "Medicine in New Spain." In Ronald L. Numbers (Ed.), *Medicine in the New World: New Spain, New France, and New England*. Knoxville, University of Tennessee Press, 1987, p. 37.

17. Ramon A. Gutierrez, *When Jesus Came, The Corn Mothers Went Away: Marriage, Sexuality and Power in New Mexico: 1500–1846*. Stanford: Stanford University Press, 1991, pp. 56–57.

18. Risse, "Medicine in New Spain," pp. 38–39.

19. Ibid., pp. 40–41.

20. Toby Gelfand, "Medicine in New France." In Numbers (Ed.), *Medicine in the New World*, p. 87.

21. Virgil J. Vogel, *American Indian Medicine*. Norman: University of Oklahoma Press, 1970, pp. 87–88, 91.

22. Paul Starr, *The Social Transformation of American Medicine*. New York: Basic Books, 1982, p. 72.

23. William H. Williams, *America's First Hospital: The Pennsylvania Hospital: 1751–1841*. Wayne, PA: Haverford House Publishers, 1976, pp. 8–9.

24. Ibid., pp. 11, 14.

25. Rosenberg, *The Care of Strangers*, p. 26.

26. Ibid., pp. 24–25.

27. Ibid., p. 24.

28. Ibid., p. 25.

29. Ibid., p. 23.

30. Williams, *America's First Hospital*, pp. 59–60; Rosenberg, *The Care of Strangers* p. 40.

31. Rosenberg, *The Care of Strangers*, p. 23.

32. Starr, *The Social Transformation of American Medicine*, pp. 150–151.

33. Rosenberg, *The Care of Strangers*, p. 20.

34. Ibid., p. 21.

35. Williams, *America's First Hospital*, p. 3.

36. Ibid., pp. 52–53.

37. Ibid., p. 53.

38. Ibid., pp. 48–52.

39. Ibid., p. 47–48.

40. Ibid., pp. 73–76.

41. Ibid., p. 103.

CHAPTER 13

Disease, Healing, and the Arts

Images of health, wellness, and disease permeated artistic expression and popular culture during the Colonial period, even in unexpected places. The poet Anne Bradstreet used the body and its ills as a metaphor for the human condition, and wrote of the emotional experience of her own illnesses. Ministers such as Cotton Mather wrote as much about disease as they did about sin. Popular books such as almanacs were filled with health advice and images of the human body. Those who kept diaries wrote extensively of their own health and that of their families and friends, even when they did not record other events in their lives.

For Native Americans and African Americans, visual art, song, and poetry were an important part of the healing process. The sand paintings and healing songs used by Native American shamans were works of art as well as healing tools, as were the healing amulets of African Americans.

ALMANACS AND POPULAR PRINT

If an Anglo-American household was literate, it usually owned a Bible; and if it could afford only one other printed book, it owned an almanac. One historian has estimated that one out of three families bought an almanac each year. These little books were an integral part of popular culture, read by thousands. An almanac had many uses. It was a calendar. It was an astronomical guide, indicating the phase of the moon and the positions of the planets over the course of the year, and many included astrological predictions as well. American almanacs noted important historical dates, such as the date of the king's accession. Many almanacs also published comic poems and jokes. But perhaps the almanac's most important use was as a home health guide. Every Colonial almanac recorded a range of medical information and health advice.[1]

When a reader opened a typical almanac, one of the first pages was sure to include a curious illustration: the "man of signs," "the anatomy," or "the zodiac man." The image depicted a human being, usually male, surrounded by the symbols of the zodiacal constellations Aries, Taurus, etc.. Lines or arrows connected each constellation with the part of the body it "governed." Aries governed the head, Taurus the neck, Gemini the arms, and so on, down to Pisces, which governed the feet. Sometimes almanac authors included an explanatory poem in addition to the illustration:

> The Ram possesseth head and face,
> The neck the Bull commands . . .
> To Capricorn we give the knees
> The legs unto Aquarius
> Now none but Pisces wants a share
> To Him we give the feet,
> Then Aries head and face again
> And so make both ends meet.[2]

Odd as it may appear to modern readers, the man of signs was a crucial part of home health care. One of the most important uses of the illustration was as a guide to propitious moments to perform therapeutic bleeding. When the moon passed through the sign of the zodiac that governed each body part, blood was drawn to that part; thus, it was dangerous to bleed from that area at that time, since the patient might lose more blood than the practitioner intended.

This was not the only use of the anatomy. It also offered a guide as to when to use or make different kinds of medicines. One almanac publisher offered the following mnemonic in 1694:

> With Electuaries, the Moon in Cancer.
> With Pills the Moon in Pisces
> Good to Take Vomit, the Moon Being in Taurus . . .
> To stop Fluxes and Rheums, the Moon being in

Taurus, Virgo, or Capricorn
To Cut the Hair of the Head or Beard, when the Moon is in Libra,
  Sagittarius, Aquarius or Pisces.[3]

Readers demanded that the anatomy be included in every almanac. When some publishers tried to omit it as "superstitious," the outcry was so great and sales so slow that they were forced to include it in the next edition. Authors included poems commenting on the demand of readers for the man of signs:

The Anatomy must still be in
Else the Almanack's not worth a pin
For Country-men regard the Sign
As though 'Twere Oracle Divine
But do not mind that altogether
Have some respect to Wind and Weather.[4]

The anatomy was not the only health information in an almanac. Many almanacs, especially in the late eighteenth century, included extensive advice on preventing disease and staying healthy. Most of the health advice was salted with a heavy dose of moral judgment. This was not uncommon in the Colonial period and beyond. The health of the soul was intimately connected with the health of the body. Almanac readers were thus warned against drunkenness, sexual indulgence, gluttony, and idleness for the sake of their health. Sin was the shortest path to the grave, as this verse about the dangers of alcohol points out:

I've seen men, from health, wealth and ease
Untimely descend to the tomb,
I need not describe their disease,
Because they were lovers of Rum.[5]

Gluttony was almost as deadly as drunkenness: "Like an ox, the fatter he grows, the sooner he goes to slaughter, and shortens his journey to the land of worms."[6] Such sentiments would have appealed to the almanacs' audience for several reasons. It gave them simple advice for staying healthy, it confirmed the moral beliefs that they already heard from the pulpit, and it was often presented in clever verse. For those who already followed the tenets of moderation and self-restraint, this advice would have confirmed their worldview and satisfied them that they were doing the right thing.

For those who did fall ill, the almanacs provided comfort and more advice. Diseases could follow the seasons, and almanacs often included seasonal health recommendations. For instance, one almanac noted that the cold, wet summer it predicted could be dangerous. If the body's pores stood open as they would in damp weather, environmental toxins could creep in. The almanac's author therefore advised avoiding certain herbal medicines that could open the pores.

If all else failed, almanacs included recipes for home remedies. The diseases the almanacs purported to cure ranged from the mundane warts and headaches to the life threatening tuberculosis and dysentery. Most of the remedies prescribed in the almanacs followed principles that would have been familiar to their readers: the idea of humoral balance, which could be restored through bleeding, purging, and vomits. The medicines were not so much different from those a patient would have received from a physician. For instance, medicines for dysentery that appear in eighteenth-century almanacs distinguish between a "flux" and a "flux with fever," which contemporary physicians considered to be separate diseases requiring different cures. Almanacs thus served not just as entertainment and moral guides but disseminated professional medical knowledge to a popular audience.

HOME HEALTH GUIDES

Almanacs were not the only guides to health published in the Colonial period. Home health guides proliferated in the eighteenth century. Of these, the most popular was William Buchan's *Domestic Medicine*. Buchan was an English physician educated at the prestigious medical school at the University of Edinburgh. After serving as medical officer at a foundling hospital in Yorkshire, Buchan returned to Edinburgh where he wrote his most famous work. Buchan essentially invented the genre of the home medical manual. While there had been a previous guide written in French, Buchan's was the first published in English. *Domestic Medicine* was the best selling home health guide from its publication in 1769 until the twentieth century. It went through more than one hundred editions in both Great Britain and the United States.

Health guides such as Buchan's followed many of the same themes as almanacs but expanded upon them. They included advice on the functions of the body, staying healthy, and treating illness. As did the almanacs, they included recipes for medicines and instructions on caring for the sick. For instance, in a section of the book dealing with nursing mothers, Buchan recommends the following treatment for infected breasts and sore nipples:

> When an inflammation happens in the breast, attended with redness, hardness, and other symptoms of suppuration, the safest application is a poultice of bread and milk, softened with oil or fresh butter . . . When the nipples are fretted or chapt, they may be anointed with a mixture of oil and bees-wax, or a little powdered gum-arabic may be sprinkled on them. I have seen Hungary water applied to the nipples have a very good effect.[7]

Like the almanacs, Buchan livened his medical advice with verse. In a section lauding the benefits of breastfeeding for infants, Buchan wrote: "By arts like these/Laconia [Sparta] nurs'd of old her hardy sons;/And Rome's unconquer'd legions urg'd their way,/Unhurt thro' every toil in every clime."[8]

Many Americans owned copies of Buchan's book. The audience for the advice they contained, however, was much wider than even their strong sales would indicate. For instance, the Philadelphia diarist Elizabeth Drinker owned a copy of Buchan that she consulted for her own family; but she also lent the book to friends and suggested remedies from its pages to her servants and acquaintances.[9]

COTTON MATHER'S *ANGEL OF BETHESDA*

Another genre of health literature combined theology and medicine, much as the almanacs did. One example of this genre was the Reverend Cotton Mather's health treatise, *The Angel of Bethesda*. *Angel* was one of Mather's last major works probably completed in 1724, but he did not manage to find a publisher before his death in 1728.

In his proposal for the book, Mather made it clear that it was intended to be a popular work with a broad audience. He described his book as "A Family-physician" designed for "every Family of any Capacity." In this he was addressing the same audience as the almanacs. Also like the almanacs, Mather made a clear connection between moral virtue and health. However, unlike the almanacs, Mather did not offer bland guidelines to healthy living; instead he made his own harsh Calvinist God the center of the book.[10]

The Angel of Bethesda is thus a strange concoction of fire and brimstone sermons and practical medical tips. Mather made the theology the primary purpose of his book. In his proposal, "The Sentiments of Piety whereto Invalids are to be awakened," is the first on his list of selling points for the manuscript. He also opens the manuscript with a chapter on "The Grand Cause of Sickness," which was, of course, humankind's sinful nature: "Our first parents criminally applied themselves to the forbidden Tree of Knowledge . . . Sicknesses are among the Punishments of that . . . Crime." Each subsequent chapter, in which Mather addresses specific illnesses, opens with similar sentiments. Every sin brought with it its own specific illness.[11]

The book is nevertheless an immensely useful medical guide. After Mather admonishes the reader to repent, he offers several pages of treatments and medicines. Mather clearly meant his treatise to be comprehensive; the chapters dealing with specific diseases begin with a chapter entitled "Cephalica, or Cure for the Head-ache" and continue through "Asdodes or the Piles [hemorrhoids]." Mather also includes chapters on childbirth and children's diseases, and gives instructions on planting a "physick garden" of medicinal plants.

The Angel of Bethesda is a snapshot of one kind of early American medical thinking. As the editor of the printed edition points out, within only a few years of Mather's death, the heavy handed theology and sermonizing that characterizes the book would have seemed dated to readers. However, it gives us insight of the ways in which people of the early Colonial period thought about the relationship between body and soul.

THE POETRY OF ANNE BRADSTREET

Anne Bradstreet is widely known as America's first published poet. She was born in England in 1612 and immigrated to Massachusetts with her family at the age of 18. Her father, Thomas Dudley, became the second governor of the colony, and her husband Simon Bradstreet served in many Colonial offices and eventually became governor himself. Bradstreet wrote poems on an array of subjects, ranging from English history to the deaths of her grandchildren. Her first collection, *The Tenth Muse*, was published in 1650 at the instigation of her brother-in-law, John Woodbridge. Since then, there have been multiple editions of her poems and her autobiographical writings. While some critics have complained of the didactic and formulaic nature of some of her work, there is no doubt that many of her poems offer a unique window onto the inner life of a pious New England woman.

To historians of medicine, however, what is most notable about Bradstreet's poetry is the multitude of medical and health metaphors that permeate her work. It seems clear that Bradstreet was fascinated by medicine, perhaps because of her own chronic illness. While we cannot know what afflicted her, Bradstreet was often exhausted and in pain, and this experience informed much of her writing. In addition to her personal experience, Bradstreet's father provided her with an unusually extensive education for a girl of the time. Thomas Bradstreet's library included several medical treatises, and Anne was clearly familiar with them.[12]

One of Bradstreet's early poems takes on a medical subject directly: "Of the Four Humours in Man's Constitution." In this poem, the four humors (personified as sisters) each make a case for being "predominant." As each humor presents her argument, it is clear that Bradstreet had a working knowledge of the humoral theory of her day. Choler yellow bile asserts her physiological supremacy by laying claim that the "heat" she provides is crucial to both bodily strength and reproduction: "It's not your muscles, nerves, nor this, nor that/ Does ought without my lively heat, that's flat." And: "and one thing more to close up my narration:/Of all that lives, I cause the propagation." Blood, Melancholy, and Phlegm all make similar claims. In the end, however, the poet concludes that no one of the humors can be effective without the others: "Nor jars or scoffs, let none hereafter see,/But all admire our perfect amity," which makes for a complete, balanced body.[13]

Even in poems that do not explicitly discuss physiological theory, Bradstreet uses the imagery of physical experience. Many literary scholars have pointed out that many of her poems discuss the experience of living in a female body. This is most obvious in her poems that deal directly with childbirth, such as "Before the Birth of One of Her Children," in which the poet contemplates the possibility of her own death and bids her husband a pre-emptive farewell: "How soon, my Dear, death may my steps attend/How soon't may be thy lot to lose thy friend."[14] Most women of the Colonial period looked at childbirth with dread; this poem personalizes that fear. See Chapter 4, Women's Health, for more on childbirth and women's fears.

However, Bradstreet also used childbirth, pregnancy, and miscarriage as metaphors for the human condition more generally. In writing of the sinful nature of human beings, Bradstreet presents the reader with a vivid image of Eve and her first-born son: "Here sits our granddame [grandmother] in retired place,/And in her lap her bloody Cain new-born ... His mother sighs to think of Paradise/And how she lost her bliss to be more wise."[15] In another stanza of the same poem, Bradstreet uses language that echoes that used by physicians to describe miscarriages to elaborate on the same theme. She describes the human soul as "This lump of wretchedness, of sin and sorrow," much as miscarried pregnancies were described as "lumps" and "without form."[16] In the same stanza, Bradstreet describes the human body as "This weatherbeaten vessel wracked with pain."[17] Bradstreet, who gave birth to eight children and who lived with chronic pain, drew on her own physical experience to inform her poetry.

Her poetry has remained popular and widely read, hundreds of years after its initial publication. Part of this ongoing resonance can be attributed to her use of these metaphors and images of the body. In her own lifetime, many readers would have identified with Bradstreet and her physical experience.

HEALTH AND MEDICINE IN COLONIAL ERA DIARIES

The primacy of the topics of health, disease, and physical experience was not limited to published writing. Colonial era diarists wrote often of their own illnesses, those of the their families, and of local epidemics. Even if the diaries neglect other personal issues and feelings, health was clearly both an important personal concern and one which diarists felt the need to record.

The diary kept by Boston shopkeeper Benjamin Walker from 1726 until 1749 is one example. Walker was an unusual man in some ways—he never married and he was an Anglican in a strongly Congregationalist colony. However, his diary is an important record of life in Boston. Walker's shop was in the busiest part of the city, and he thus was privy to much of the political and social life of Boston. He recorded much of the news and gossip brought to him by his customers, as well as events he watched from his window, ranging from funeral processions to official government receptions.[18]

What Walker's diary does not include is as interesting as what it does record. Unlike diaries from later periods, Walker's journal includes little personal information. We know little of his family life other than the names of the people in his household which included himself, his brother, and four enslaved Africans and nothing at all of his inner life or emotions. Walker clearly thought of his diary as a place to record public events rather than private thoughts and experiences. The one exception to this rule was his discussions of health and medicine.

When it came to health, Walker was a meticulous record keeper. One historian who has worked extensively with the diary made a list of all the ailments Walker mentioned in his diary: "rheumatism, St. Anthony's fire, fever, fluxes, bloody fluxes, fits, breast cancer, sore breast or ulcer between the breasts, consumption, strangury, 'apoplectick fits,' ague, gout, sore throats, throat distemper, smallpox, coughs, and colds."[19]

Walker noted his own illnesses as well as those of his brother, his slaves, his customers, and his neighbors.

In addition to recording illnesses, Walker described practitioners and treatments. Midwives, physicians, and nurses all turn up in the diary, as do the efforts of informal practitioners, including Walker's slave Mary and his unmarried sister, Elizabeth. Walker recorded remedies prescribed by all of these varied health workers, as well as those he invented himself or found in a book or almanac.

Walker also took careful note of epidemics that affected Boston, including smallpox outbreaks in 1729 and 1730. In April of 1730, he wrote: "This month past has bin Verey sickley Many Visitd in Gods way with ye small pox." Walker's slave Cuffe died during this epidemic. Walker, like many of his contemporaries, was virulently opposed to the practice of inoculation. He condemned Zabdiel Boylston an inoculation proponent for "malepractice" and blamed inoculation for the 1730 out-break, calling it a "Vile practice."[20]

Occurrences such as smallpox epidemics and the debate over inoculation were public events, and thus in keeping with the rest of the diary. But why did Walker discuss private health matters so extensively? One scholar has suggested that Walker was influenced by the common religious belief that God punished the sinful with illness and rewarded the virtuous with health; thus, one's bodily state also revealed the state of one's soul.[21] This is one likely reason. It is also important to remember that in the Colonial period, any illness might prove mortal, making health a matter of deep concern. In addition, minor illness, nagging pain, and toothaches were an inescapable part of daily life. Perhaps Walker recorded so much health information simply because it was always on his mind.

The diary of Elizabeth Drinker, a woman who lived in a different city at a different time, reflects many of the same themes as the diary of Benjamin Walker. Drinker was a wealthy Quaker woman who lived in Philadelphia. She kept her diary for much of her life, from 1758 until shortly before her death in 1807. Historians treasure her diary for its vivid discussions of topics ranging from the American Revolution to family life. While Drinker was much more expressive in her diary than Benjamin Walker, she shared with him a deep concern with medical matters.

Like Walker, Drinker kept track of epidemics. In 1762, she copied out newspaper articles describing a local outbreak of smallpox, as well as a list of those who had died. Unlike Walker, Drinker was an advocate of inoculation. As a young unmarried woman, she was interested enough in the process to observe the procedure when it was performed on the son of a friend. When she had children of her own, she had them all inoculated at a young age.[22]

Drinker shared the fears of her city during the great yellow fever epidemic of 1793. As a wealthy woman, Drinker was able to flee Philadelphia for her country estate shortly after the first cases were reported, and much of her description of the outbreak is taken from newspapers and news reported by friends. As she did during the earlier smallpox epidemic, Drinker copied newspaper accounts and kept track of the mounting mortality figures from the city.

In Drinker's diary, personal experiences outweigh public events. Daily entries usually include a notation on her own health for that date, as well as any medicine she had taken. Drinker thought of herself as a sickly woman and often confined herself to the house on account of her health. It is hard to tell if her perception was accurate or reflected a touch of hypochondria; either way, Drinker lived to the ripe age of 72.

Drinker also recorded extensive details about the health of her own family. Each year of the diary ends with a summary of the events of the past year, including comments on everyone's health: her own, her husband's, her children's and her grandchildren's. When there was a medical crisis in the family, she wrote lengthy entries describing every symptom and every treatment. The childbirth experiences of her daughters are described in particular detail. Drinker was especially concerned with childbirth because she believed that she and her daughters were especially susceptible to complications. Drinker's detailed diary entries describe the state of the art obstetrics of their time, and are some of the earliest documentation of physician-attended birth and the use of forceps.

Childbirth was not Drinker's only concern. Some of the most moving passages in the diary describe the long illness and death of her eldest daughter Sally. Sally suffered from what was probably lymphatic cancer and died in 1807, only a few months before her mother. Drinker described the many treatments Sally underwent for her condition, including hemlock pills and oak gall blisters. Sally's death was a deep emotional blow for Drinker; both her contemporaries and historians have speculated that her own death was hastened by the profound grief and depression she suffered after Sally passed on.

Drinker's diary records the names and methods of some of Philadelphia's most prominent physicians. In addition to the obstetrician William Shippen, the diary discusses Benjamin Rush who cared for Drinker's husband and surgeon Philip Syng Physick. Drinker herself maintained a lifelong friendship as well as a professional relationship with Dr. John Redman, who inoculated her children against smallpox.

Clearly health, disease, and physicians were such important parts of everyday life that Drinker and Walker felt compelled to discuss them in great detail in their diaries. The descriptions they have left provide historians with important sources for understanding the history of medicine. But the diaries are also forms of literature—carefully crafted documents that tell important and compelling stories.

THE ARTS IN NATIVE AMERICAN AND AFRICAN AMERICAN MEDICINE

Most of the portrayals of medicine and healing in Anglo-American art and popular culture depend on the written word. In African American and Native American cultures, music, dance, recited poetry, and visual art play a larger role. In both African American and Native American medicine, healing practices are closely related to religious ritual. Because of these ties, there is more scope for the use of the arts in medicine.

Native American healing practices are particularly good examples of the ties between healing and the arts. In many though not all Native American cultures, physical ministrations to the patient such as herbal drugs, baths, or surgery are accompanied by singing, poetry, or dance. Music and singing seem to be the most common elements. As one scholar put it, "The use of rattles or drums seems to be universal." In some cultures, the music imbued the physical treatment with the power to heal, as in this Illinois/Miami ritual described by a French observer in the seventeenth century. The shaman began by shaking his rattle and chanting over the herbs. Twice a day, until the patient was cured, the shaman returned and sang over the patient. When the sick person recovered, the practitioner sang a song of gratitude to his personal spirit guide for its help in curing the patient.[23]

Perhaps the culture that incorporates the most forms of art into its healing rituals is the Navajo or Dine people of what is now the southwestern United States. Dine rituals, which are still practiced, include singing, dance, poetry, drama, and visual art. While most of the descriptions of Dine "chants" or "sings" were collected in the twentieth century, each chanter learns from an older medicine man, who learned his skill from someone of the previous generation. The oral tradition is of great age, and it seems likely that these rituals were practiced in the seventeenth and eighteenth centuries in forms similar to those practiced today.

There are many different healing rituals in Dine culture. Each addresses different deities or spirits, and each is prescribed for different kinds of illness, including mental illness and spiritual distress. For instance, the Flint Way is used to heal injuries, including broken bones and burns; the Blessing Way can be used to invoke good health and good luck, and is also used for initiating young girls into womanhood; and the Night Way addresses "diseases of the head" including blindness and mental illness. Another category of ritual focuses on banishing evil spirits or counteracting witchcraft.[24]

All the rituals have a common structure. The first step is a ritual purification of both the chanter and the patient. Both participants bathe, purge their bodies with emetics, and dress in special ritual clothing. The house where the ceremony is performed is also purified, and the chanter creates the sand paintings necessary to the ceremony. The ritual itself begins with an evocation of the proper spirits with a variety of artistic media.

Perhaps the most striking form of art used in Dine ritual is sand painting. Sand paintings are just that—paintings made on the floor of the ritual space using colored sand. The paintings are elaborate and beautiful. The paintings are symbolic evocations of healing powers and deities, and sometimes depict scenes from Dine religious stories.

The paintings are not the only art form used in the rituals. Dine healing procedures are called "sings" or "chants," and music and poetry is the core of the process. The medicine man sings lengthy songs that honor the spirits and tell their stories. The stories are told with rich and imagery with repetition and rhythmic devices that add to their power. This is a translated excerpt from the Night Chant, one of the most elaborate Dine healing rituals. The chanter addresses the deities after placing incense sticks in the patient's hands:

I have made your sacrifice
I have prepared a smoke for you
My feet restore for me
My legs restore for me
My body restore for me
My voice restore for me.[25]

When the ritual is ending, the chanter sings:

From the pond in the white valley
The young man doubts it,
The god takes up his sacrifices,
With that he now heals.
From the pools in the green meadow,

The young woman doubts it,
He takes up the sacrifice,
With that he now heals.
With that your kindred thanks you.[26]

The songs and paintings are supplemented with other appeals to the senses. The medicine man's assistants portray the gods with masks and dancing. They touch the patient with ritual objects to channel healing power into the patient's body. A Dine healing ritual thus is both a medical procedure and an elaborate artistic performance, which includes song, dance, drama, and visual art.

African American healing practices were less elaborate and less well documented, but they too contained artistic elements. The simplest form of art used in medicine was the amulet or charm that a patient wore on the body to cure or prevent illness. Some were as straightforward as a piece of braided leather worn around the wrist to prevent rheumatism. Others resembled jewelry, combining many objects together in elaborate bracelets or necklaces. Coins were common elements, as were buttons, pebbles, "Indian beads," spices such as a piece of nutmeg, or animal parts or skins such as a rabbit's or mole's foot. Sometimes these objects were wrapped in cloth and worn on the body, with the ingredients a mystery to the patient.[27]

"Conjures," "hoodoos," or "witches" were often cited as the cause of illness. Malicious magic could be warded off with countermeasures, which included amulets such as those described previously, as well as poems or rhymes:

Keep 'way from me, hoodoo and witch,
Lead my path from de poorhouse gate
I pines for golden harps and sich,
Lawd I'll just set down and wait.[28]

Conjure could be used for both healing and harming. In both cases, the spell required a ritual involving drums, dancing, and song. One exslave, interviewed during the 1930s, described a ritual she had heard about as a child: "Voodoo docter hol' up his han's and dey commence to dance while de drums beat. Dey dance faster an' still faster; dey chant and pray 'til dey falls down in er heap."[29]

Like Native American rituals, African American healing rituals appealed to spirituality and magical belief as well as physical cure. Dance, music, and visual art played their part in these rituals, and they used artistic expression to invoke healing deities.

Medicine, health, and disease are important parts of the human condition in any historical era or culture. Artists of all kinds use the power of art to express this experience, and they use the power of art to heal. The Colonial period of American history was no exception.

NOTES

1. Thomas A. Horrocks, *Popular Print and Popular Medicine: Almanacs and Health Advice in Early America*. Amherst, MA: University of Massachusetts Press, 2008, p. 18.

2. Ibid., p. 28.

3. Ibid., p. 23.

4. Ibid., p. 30.

5. Ibid., p. 74.

6. Ibid., p. 79.

7. William Buchan, *Domestic Medicine, or, A Treatise on the Prevention and Cure of Diseases by Regimen and Simple Medicines, with an Appendix, Containing a Dispensatory for the Use of Private Practitioners to Which are Added, Observations on the Diet of Common People*. Halifax, NC: Abraham Hodge, 1801, p. 313.

8. Buchan, *Domestic Medicine*, p. 22.

9. Sarah Blank Dine, "Diaries and Doctors: Elizabeth Drinker and Philadelphia Medical Practice: 1760–1810," *Pennsylvania History: A Journal of Mid-Atlantic Studies*, 68, no. 4 (Autumn 2001), pp. 413–434.

10. Cotton Mather, *The Angel of Bethesda*, edited with an introduction and notes by Gordon W. Jones. Barre, MA: Barre Publishers, 1972, p. 1.

11. Ibid., pp. 1, 6.

12. Jean Marie Lutes, "Negotiating Theology and Gynecology: Anne Bradstreet's Representations of the Female Body," *Signs: Journal of Women in Culture and Society*, 22, no. 2 (1997), pp. 309–340.

13. Anne Bradstreet, *The Works of Anne Bradstreet*, Edited by Jeannine Hensley. Cambridge, MA: Harvard University Press, 1967, pp. 37, 50.

14. Ibid., p. 224.

15. Ibid., p. 208.

16. Lutes, "Negotiating Theology and Gynecology," p. 328.

17. Bradstreet, *Works*, p. 213.

18. Barbara McClean Ward, "Medicine and Disease in the Diary of Benjamin Walker, Shopkeeper of Boston." In Peter Benes (Ed.), *Medicine and Healing: The Dublin Seminar for New England Folklife Annual Proceedings, Vol. 15*. Boston: Boston University Press, 1990, pp. 45–46.

19. Ibid., p. 46.

20. Ibid., pp. 47, 51.

21. Ibid., p. 46.

22. Dine, "Diaries and Doctors," pp. 416, 420.

23. Virgil J. Vogel, *American Indian Medicine*. Norman: University of Oklahoma Press, 1970, p. 30, 32.

24. Donald Sandner, *Navaho Symbols of Healing*. New York: Harcourt Brace Jovanovich, 1979, pp. 44–46.

25. Ibid., p. 81.

26. Ibid., p. 92.

27. Herbert C. Covey, *African American Slave Medicine: Herbal and Non-Herbal Treatments*. New York: Rowman and Littlefield, 2007, pp. 56, 132–138.

28. Ibid., p. 55.

29. Ibid., p. 55.

Glossary

Abortifacient—a drug that terminates a pregnancy.

Almshouse—a shelter for the poor funded by local taxes. Colonial era alms-houses offered medical care to the indigent as well as shelter.

Apoplexy—the Colonial era term for stroke.

Apothecary—a person trained in the uses and compounding of medicines.

Astringent—a drug that causes inflamed tissues to shrink. Astringents are applied externally.

Cathartic—a laxative drug.

Diaphoretic—a drug that induces sweating.

Doctoress—a woman who practiced medicine but who was not a midwife.

Emetic—a drug that induces vomiting.

Febrifuge—a drug that reduces fever.

Flux—a Colonial era term for diarrhea.

Galenic medicine—a medical theory named for the ancient Roman physician Galen (130 C.E. to 200 C.E.), based on the theory of the balance of bodily fluids or "humors."

Gastroenteritis—any disease that causes disturbances of the digestive system. Symptoms usually include vomiting and/or diarrhea.

Humors—the four bodily fluids that determine health and temperament in Galenic medicine. The four humors were blood, phlegm, black bile, and yellow bile.

Indentured servant—a servant bound by contract to serve a master for a set term, usually five to seven years. Many English immigrants to the American colonies paid for their passage by becoming indentured servants.

Inoculation (also called variolation)—a procedure in which patients were deliberately infected with a mild case of smallpox to ensure later immunity to the disease. Inoculation differs from vaccination in that full strength virus is used, rather than a weakened version.

Lancet—a tool used to open veins for therapeutic bleeding.

Miasma—"bad air" that causes disease.

Midwife—a female medical practitioner who specialized in childbirth and other women's health issues as well as the care of newborn infants.

Palsy—a Colonial era term for paralysis.

Physick—a Colonial era term for the practice modern people would call "internal medicine" as opposed to surgery. "Physick" was also a generic term for medicines.

Purge—a laxative drug.

Scurvy—a disease caused by lack of vitamin C. Symptoms include bleeding from the gums, nosebleeds, swollen joints, easy bruising, fatigue, and slow healing.

Seasoning—the attack of illness that many immigrants experienced shortly after they reached America. People of the time believed that the illness was caused by bodies adjusting to their new environment.

Shaman—a religious leader who communicates directly with spirits or deities. Shamans or shamanistic religious practices were common in both Native American and African American cultures. Many shamans in these cultures were also healers.

Tonic—a drug that strengthens the body.

Trephination—a surgical procedure that removes pieces of bone from the skull.

Vermifuge—a drug that killed or expelled intestinal parasites.

Suggestions for
Further Reading

Benes, Peter (Ed.), *Medicine and Healing* (Boston: Boston University Press, 1990).

Boster, Dea H., "An 'Epilectick' Bondswoman: Fits, Slavery, and Power in the Antebellum South," *Bulletin of the History of Medicine* 83 (2009): 271–301.

Bullough, Vern L., "An Early American Sex Manual, or, Aristotle Who?" *Early American Literature* 7 (1973): 236–246.

Byrd, W. Michael and Linda Clayton, *An American Health Dilemma*. Vol. 1, *A Medical History of African Americans and the Problem of Race: Beginnings to 1900* (New York: Routledge, 2000–2002).

Calloway, Colin G., *New Worlds for All: Indians, Europeans, and the Remaking of Early America* (Baltimore: Johns Hopkins University Press, 1997).

Calvert, Karin, *Children in the House: The Material Culture of Early Childhood: 1600–1900* (Boston: Northeastern University Press, 1992).

Campell, Gwyn, "Children and Slavery in the New World: A Review," *Slavery and Abolition* 27 (2006): 261–285.

Cash, Philip, *Medical Men at the Siege of Boston: April 1775–April 1776: Problems of the Massachusetts and Continental Armies* (Philadelphia: American Philosophical Society, 1973).

Covey, Herbert C., *African American Slave Medicine: Herbal and Non-Herbal Treatments* (Lanham: Lexington Books, 2007).

Crawford, Patricia, "Attitudes Toward Menstruation in Seventeenth Century England," *Past and Present* 91 (1981): 47–73.

Crosby, Alfred, *The Columbian Exchange: Biological and Cultural Consequences of 1492* (Westport, CT: Greenwood Publishing, 1973).

Dary, David, *Frontier Medicine: From the Atlantic to the Pacific: 1492–1941* (New York: Knopf, 2008).

Demos, John Putnam, *Entertaining Satan: Witchcraft and the Culture of Early New England* (New York: Oxford University Press, 1981).

Dine, Sarah Blank, "Diaries and Doctors: Elizabeth Drinker and Philadelphia Medical Practice: 1760–1810," *Pennsylvania History: A Journal of Mid-Atlantic Studies* 68 (4, Autumn 2001), 413–434.

Duffy, John, *Epidemics in Colonial America* (Baton Rouge: Louisiana State University Press, 1953).

Earle, A. Scott (Ed.), *Surgery in America: From the Colonial Era to the Twentieth Century* (New York: Praeger, 1983).

Ellis, Harold, *The Cambridge Illustrated History of Surgery* (Cambridge, UK: Cambridge University Press, 2008).

Estes, J. Worth and Billy G. Smith (Eds.), *A Melancholy Scene of Devastation: The Public Response to the 1793 Philadelphia Yellow Fever Epidemic* (Canton, MA: Published for the College of Physicians of Philadelphia and the Library Company of Philadelphia by Science History Publications, 1997).

Fenn, Elizabeth A., "Biological Warfare in Eighteenth Century North America: Beyond Jeffery Amherst," *Journal of American History* 86 (2000): 1552–1580.

Fenn, Elizabeth A., *Pox Americana: The Great Smallpox Epidemic of 1775–1783* (New York: Hill and Wang, 2001).

Fett, Sharla M., *Working Cures: Healing, Health and Power on Southern Slave Plantations* (Chapel Hill: University of North Carolina Press, 2002).

Gamwell, Lynn and Nancy Tomes, *Madness in America: Cultural and Medical Perceptions of Mental Illness Before 1914* (Ithaca, NY: Cornell University Press, 1995).

Gevitz, Norman, " 'Pray Let the Medicines Be Good': The New England Apothecary in the Seventeenth and Early Eighteenth Centuries," *Pharmacy in History* 41 (1999): 87–101.

Gill, Harold B., *The Apothecary in Colonial Virginia* (Charlottesville: University of Virginia Press, 1972).

Gillett, Mary C., *The Army Medical Department: 1775–1818* (Washington, DC: Center of Military History, U.S. Army, 1981).

Godbeer, Richard, *The Devil's Dominion: Magic and Religion in Early New England* (New York: Cambridge University Press, 1992).

Gould, Drusilla and Marie Glowacka, "Nagotooh (Gahni): The Bonding between Mother and Child in Shoshoni Tradition," *Ethnology* 43 (2004): 185–191.

Grob, Gerald, *The Mad Among Us: A History of the Care of America's Mentally Ill* (New York: Free Press, 1994).

Hillam, Christine (Ed.), *The Roots of Dentistry* (London: British Dental Association, 1990).

Horrocks, Thomas A., *Popular Print and Popular Medicine: Almanacs and Health Advice in Early America* (Amherst: University of Massachusetts Press, 2008).

Jimenez, Mary Ann, *Changing Faces of Madness: Early American Attitudes and Treatment of the Insane* (Hanover, NH: University Press of New England, 1987).

Jones, David S., "Virgin Soils Revisited," *William and Mary Quarterly*, 3rd Series, 60 (2003): 703–742.

Kaufman, Martin, *American Medical Education: The Formative Years: 1765–1910* (Westport, CT: Greenwood Press, 1976).

Kupperman, Karen Ordahl, "Apathy and Death in Early Jamestown," *Journal of American History* 66 (1979): 24–40.

MacLeod, D. Peter, "Microbes and Muskets: Smallpox and the Participation of Amerindian Allies of New France in the Seven Years' War," *Ethnohistory* 49 (1992): 42–64.

Martensen, Robert L., *The Brain Takes Shape: An Early History* (New York: Oxford University Press, 2004).

Medicine in Colonial Massachusetts: A Conference Held 25 and 26 May 1978 by the Colonial Society of Massachusetts (Boston: The Society, 1980).

Mustakeem, Sowande, "'I Never Have Such a Sickly Ship Before: Diet, Disease and Mortality in Eighteenth Century Atlantic Slaving Voyages," *Journal of African American History* 93 (2008): 474–496.

Nash, Gary, *Red, White and Black: The Peoples of Early America* (Upper Saddle River, NJ: Prentice-Hall, 1992).

Powell, J. H., *Bring Out Your Dead: The Great Plague of Yellow Fever in Philadelphia in 1793* (Philadelphia: University of Pennsylvania Press, 1949).

Reiss, Oscar, *Medicine and the American Revolution: How Diseases and Their Treatments Affected the American Army* (Jefferson, NC: McFarland, 1998).

Reiss, Oscar, *Medicine in Colonial America* (Lanham, MD: University Press of America, 2000).

Rosenberg, Charles E., *The Care of Strangers: The Rise of America's Hospital System* (New York: Basic Books, 2000).

Rountree, Helen C., "Powhatan Indian Women: The People Captain John Smith Barely Saw," *Ethnohistory* 45 (1998): 1–29.

Rutman, Darrett B. and Anita H. Rutman, "Of Agues and Fevers: Malaria in the Early Chesapeake," *William and Mary Quarterly*, 3rd Series, 33 (1976): 31–60.

Sandner, Donald, *Navaho Symbols of Healing* (New York: Harcourt Brace Jovanovich, 1979).

Siraisi, Nancy G., *Medieval and Early Renaissance Medicine: An Introduction to Knowledge and Practice* (Chicago: University of Chicago Press, 1990).

Smith, Billy G. (Ed.), *Down and Out in Early America* (University Park: Pennsylvania State University Press, 2004).

Smith, Billy G. (Ed.) *"The Lower Sort": Philadelphia's Laboring People: 1750–1800* (Ithaca, NY: Cornell University Press, 1990).

Starr, Paul, *The Social Transformation of American Medicine* (New York: Basic Books, 1982).

Stevenson, Brenda, *Life in Black and White: Family and Community in the Slave South* (New York: Oxford University Press, 1996).

Tannenbaum, Rebecca J. *The Healer's Calling: Women and Medicine in Early New England* (Ithaca, NY: Cornell University Press, 2002).

Ulrich, Laurel Thatcher, *A Midwife's Tale: The Life of Martha Ballard Based on Her Diary: 1785–1812* (New York: Knopf, 1990).

Voeks, Robert, "African Medicine and Magic in the Americas," *Geographical Review* 83 (1993): 66–78.

Vogel, Virgil, *American Indian Medicine* (Norman: University of Oklahoma Press, 1970).

Watson, Patricia A., *The Angelical Conjunction: The Preacher-Physicians of Colonial New England* (Knoxville: University of Tennessee Press, 1991).

Weinberger, Bernhard, *The History of Dentistry* (2 volumes) (Birmingham, AL: Classics of Dentistry Library, 1981).

Williams, William H., *America's First Hospital: The Pennsylvania Hospital: 1751–1841* (Wayne, PA: Haverford House Publishers, 1976).

Wynes, Charles E., "Dr. James Durham, Mysterious Eighteenth-Century Black Physician: Man or Myth?" *Pennsylvania Magazine of History and Biography* 103, (3, July 1979): 325–333.

Index

About the Author

REBECCA TANNENBAUM teaches at Yale University, where she offers courses on early America, women's history, and the history of medicine. She has published many articles on the history of women in medicine as well as a book, *The Healer's Calling: Women and Medicine in Early New England*, which focuses on women medical practitioners in early New England. Her current research project looks at the roles of women and medical professionals in creating modern motherhood.